HITLER

HITLER

AN ILLUSTRATED LIFE

ROBIN CROSS

Quercus

CONTENTS

FOREWORD

On 20 April 1939 the German chancellor, Adolf Hitler celebrated his fiftieth birthday. It was no ordinary celebration. Orchestrated with painstaking attention to detail by his propaganda minister, Josef Goebbels, the festivities had begun on the evening of the 19th when Hitler was driven from the Reich Chancellery, at the head of a column of fifty limousines, along Berlin's newly built east-west axis. The completion of this road marked the start of a massive building programme, planned to transform Berlin into Germania, the new capital of the world.

The limousines swept past cheering crowds, billowing banners and blazing torches to a brief opening ceremony conducted by Albert Speer, Hitler's court architect. Speer had been charged with the planning of Germania, a megalomaniac fantasy of colossal but lifeless classical buildings, dominated by a four-hundred-foot-high Victory Arch, and a People's Hall seventeen times bigger than the dome of St Peter's which would hold a million people.

Hitler then returned to the new Reich Chancellery, also designed by Speer and completed early in 1939, where from the balcony he watched a parade of Nazi Party officials representing each of Germany's *Gaue* (units of regional administration). At midnight the leading members of the Führer's court lined up to shower him with birthday gifts. Speer presented Hitler with a model of Germania's Victory Arch. Heinrich Himmler, the feared head of the SS, gave him an equestrian portrait of Frederick the Great by Adolf von Menzel. Captain Hans Baur, Hitler's personal pilot, gave him another model, that of the four-engined Focke-Wulf FW200 Condor which would become Hitler's personal aircraft later that summer.

The climax of the chancellor's birthday came the next day with a massive military parade of fifty thousand troops and the cream of Germany's military hardware. The ambassadors of Britain, France and the United States, who had been recalled in March 1939 after Germany's annexation of Czechoslovakia, were notably absent. The outbreak of World War II was just over four months away.

Six years later, in a Reich Chancellery now pounded and pockmarked by bomb blasts, Hitler – attended by his Nazi paladins Speer, Martin Bormann, Josef Goebbels, Hermann Göring and Joachim von Ribbentrop – celebrated his fifty-sixth birthday in markedly different circumstances. The fall of the Third Reich was imminent, its Führer disintegrating, as Captain Peter Hartmann, a witness to the melancholy afternoon birthday gathering, observed:

Near the very end, on the day he celebrated his last birthday, he seemed closer to seventy than fifty-six. He looked what I would call physically senile. The man was living on nerves, dubious medicaments, and driving willpower. Sometimes even the willpower seemed to slacken. Then suddenly it would flash again with the old drive and fury.

These pages follow the grim career of Adolf Hitler from his modest origins to the pinnacle of power, and trace the downward curve of the descent to his death and that of the Nazi Party, recording the havoc and destruction that was heaped on Russia and Europe by the Führer's armies – and on Germany itself as a result of his rule.

However, the principal task which confronts any attempt to explain Hitler's early life and thought is that of disentangling the would-be politician of the early 1920s from the penniless dilletante ranting to his cronies in pre-war Vienna. In 1912 Hitler was a nobody, whose fantasies of fame had been rudely shattered. Twelve years later he was a rising politician, a man with a following, whose world view reached many more than his audience of idlers killing time in the reading room of a Men's Home to which his poverty had driven him. Adolf Hitler had a story to tell, and few would emerge in later years to challenge him on the facts.

The pre-1914 Hitler was, seemingly, a man with no political ambitions but with a mind nevertheless attuned to the turbulent cross-currents threatening to swamp the ailing Austro-Hungarian ship of state: Pan-Germanism and its antagonism towards the empire's Slav population; anti-Semitism, sometimes casual, often deep-dyed, which was part and parcel of nationalist politics; and a deep suspicion of both the Catholic Church and of Social Democracy.

The post-1918 Hitler, however, nationalist, xenophobe and zealot, was possessed by high ambition and greed for absolute power. With absolute determination and a gift for oratory, he watered the seeds of hatred that would result in catastrophe for millions.

Adolf Hitler, contradictory and mercurial, was in the end a destroyer who left only chaos and misery behind him.

In the early twenty-first century we are still living with his toxic legacy.

Robin Cross, Kent 2009

THE THIRD REICH, APRIL 1943

1940 RK
OF
NORWAY

Oslo

Rjukan

NORTH
SEA

Gothenborg

SWED

DENMARK

Arisaig

Edinburgh

Belfast

Dublin

Ringway

UNITED
KINGDOM

London

Beaulieu

Tangmere

1940 RK OF
NETHERLANDS

The
Hague

Rotterdam

Peenemünde

Berlin

Oder

ATLANTIC

CHANNEL
ISLANDS

Dieppe

Lille

Brussels

Venlo

Elbe

Görlitz

OCEAN

BELGIUM

GERMANY

Luxembourg

FRANCE

Paris

Seine

Lidice

Prag

PROT.

St Nazaire

Nantes

Loire

Rhine

BOHE

Vienr

Vichy

SWITZERLAND

Bordeaux

Demarcation line

Lyons

Berne

Geneva

CARINTHIA

PORTUGAL

Montauban

Rhône

Milan

Venice

Zagreb

Toulouse

CRO

Marseilles

Ravenna

Madrid

ANDORRA

Perpignan

Florence

VIS

ITALY

Lisbon

Barcelona

Vatican City

SPAIN

Rome

Naples

Tangier

Gibraltar

MEDITERRANEAN SEA

SPANISH
MOROCCO

Algiers

SICILY

Casablanca

MOROCCO

ALGERIA

Tunis

MALTA

TUNISIA

1

ANOTHER COUNTRY

FAMILY LIFE

On 20 April 1889, an unseasonably overcast and chilly spring day, Adolf Hitler was born at the Gasthof zum Pommer at Braunau am Inn, a charming town of pastel-coloured historic houses, on the south bank of the River Inn which separates Austria and Germany. Today the house is unmarked except for a large stone of Mauthausen granite, standing by the front façade, which was erected in 1989 and bears the legend, 'For peace, freedom and democracy, never again Fascism, millions of dead admonish'.

Adolf was the fourth child of six. His father, Alois Hitler, was a self-made man with little or no formal education who, by dint of hard work and diligence, had become a customs officer in the Austro-Hungarian civil service. He was well respected in Braunau but bore the marks of his caste. He was pompous, intensely jealous of his hard-won status, stingy, short-tempered and totally devoid of humour. His passion was bee-keeping, and it appears that the stuffy customs officer was more fond of the inhabitants of his apiary than of the members of his household.

Opposite: Adolf Hitler (ringed) caught on the camera of Heinrich Hoffmann in the crowd in the Odeonsplatz on the declaration of war in August 1914, one of the defining moments in his early life. Hoffmann joined the nascent Nazi Party in 1920 and became Hitler's official photographer – he took over two million photos of the Führer – and friend. Eva Braun was working as Hoffmann's assistant when she first met Hitler. In the 1930s Hoffmann wrote a number of books about Hitler, including *The Hitler Nobody Knows* (1933). After World War II, he served a prison sentence for Nazi profiteering.

His third wife, and Hitler's mother, was Klara Polzl, who had originally been a maid at Alois's home during his first marriage to Anna Glassl, a woman fourteen years his senior, from whom he had been legally separated in 1880. Alois then set up house with his mistress, Franziska (Fanni) Matzelberger, who was only a year younger than Klara and saw the maid as a potential rival. At her insistence, Klara was discharged. Fanni then bore Alois a son, before Anna's death in 1883 cleared the way for their marriage. A daughter arrived two months after the wedding, but in August 1884 Fanni, aged only twenty-three, died of tuberculosis

Fanni had sought a temporary reprieve from her illness in the countryside outside Braunau, which enabled Alois – whose love life at least was more lively than the sedate routines of the customs house – to re-engage Klara, the previously sacked maid, to look after the children. While Fanni was on her deathbed, Klara bore Alois a son. On 7 January 1885, Alois and Klara, who was now four months pregnant, were married at the church of St Stephan in Braunau. Klara was twenty-four and her husband forty-eight. The marriage ceremony, an understandably low-key affair, took place at 6 a.m., and shortly afterwards Alois was back at work in the customs house.

Opposite: Hitler (top row, extreme right) in a school photograph at Leonding. The pupil in the row below him, third from the right, is Ludwig Wittgenstein, who later became a distinguished philosopher at Cambridge University and the author of *Tractatus Logico-Philosophicus*. The economist John Maynard Keynes referred to Wittgenstein as 'God'. It is matter of some controversy whether Hitler and Wittgenstein ever knew each other.

None of Klara's first three children by Alois survived infancy. Otto died a few days after his birth, and Gustav and Ida both succumbed to diphtheria. Their fourth child was Adolf, his name meaning 'noble wolf'. In 1892 Alois was promoted to Higher Collector of Customs – the topmost rank he could achieve because of his lack of educational qualifications – and was transferred to Passau, another border town on the southern outskirts of the Bavarian Forest and at the confluence of the Danube and the Rivers Inn and Itz. It was the first move in Adolf Hitler's peripatetic childhood.

When Alois was moved to Linz in April 1894 Klara remained with her children and stepchildren in Passau. Here, in the prolonged absences of his domineering, testy father, Adolf Hitler was lapped in the unqualified, uncritical love of his young mother. To the end of his life, even in his last days in the Berlin bunker, he kept her photograph in his pocket. Later in life he would confess that, while he respected his father, he loved his mother. Perhaps Klara was the only human being to whom Hitler could extend anything approaching deep affection. In any event, she was powerless to prevent the dyspeptic Alois from thrashing his son while she listened, horrified and helpless, on the other side of the door.

It is possible that Alois's temper was also turned against his wife. There is a passage in Hitler's semi-autobiographical *Mein Kampf* (*My Struggle*) in which he provides a graphic description of a working-class mother's suffering at the hands of her abusive husband which might very well be drawn from his own personal experience. However, as with all deductions which may be drawn from the scant surviving evidence of Hitler's early years, this possibility must be treated with great caution. One thing, however, is certain: both his mother's love and his father's rages had a deep and lasting effect on the development of his personality.

Linz was Alois's final posting. He retired in the summer of 1895, and in November 1898 he purchased a small house with a plot of land in Michaelsbergstrasse in the village of Leonding on the outskirts of Linz. With a population of around fifty thousand, Linz had a distinctly German feel which won a permanent place in Adolf's heart. To the end of his days he would extol the small-town virtues of the town in contrast to the cosmopolitan decadence of Vienna. It was in Linz, imagined as rebuilt and transformed into the cultural capital of the Third Reich, that he planned to be buried. But, as with Germania, there was precious little rebuilding achieved, although after the swallowing of Czechoslovakia in 1939, a great deal of industrial plant was moved to the Linz area. One relic of the Third Reich which does survive is the former Hermann Göring-Werke, a steel plant which operates to this day.

In the absence of his father, the young Adolf Hitler seems to have enjoyed an idyllic childhood, devouring 'Wild West' books written by the German author Karl May and playing Cowboys and Indians in the garden and surrounding countryside. Once the Boer War broke out in 1899, the theme of Hitler's childhood games became the heroic struggle of the Boer settlers in South Africa against the dastardly British colonialists. Hitler recalled this period in his life as a 'happy time', when 'schoolwork was ridiculously easy, leaving me so much free time that the sun saw more of me than my room'.

Also seeing more of Adolf was his retired father with whom he remained frequently at odds. Although he had performed reasonably well at elementary school, Hitler's reports from the Linz Realschule, where he commenced his secondary education in September 1900, were generally critical of him. In a letter to Hitler's defence counsel in December 1923, written in the wake of the failed Munich putsch, Hitler's former class teacher, Dr Eduard Huemer, described his pupil as a thin, pale youth, lacking in application and self-discipline. There were also other family strains. Hitler's younger brother Edmund had died in February 1900 and his half-brother Alois Jnr had already left home. Alois Snr's principal hopes for his offspring now rested on Adolf's frail shoulders.

Understandably, perhaps, Alois was determined that his son should follow him into the civil service. When Adolf was thirteen, his father took him to the Linz customs house to introduce him to the dutiful but somewhat less than thrilling world of minor civil servants in the Austro-Hungarian Empire. The excursion had precisely the opposite effect to that which was intended. In *Mein Kampf*, Hitler wrote: 'I yawned and grew sick to my stomach at the thought of sitting in an office, deprived of my liberty; ceasing to be master of my own time.'

However, the battle of wills was to be shortlived. On 3 January 1903, Alois collapsed and died while drinking his regular morning glass of wine at a local hostelry. He left his family relatively well off and his son Adolf, now the man of the house, was not going to be pressured by his adoring mother into becoming a pen-pusher in Linz. His progress at the Realschule nevertheless remained unsatisfactory, and he was removed to another academy in Steyr, which was some fifty miles away and forced him to take lodgings in the town.

By the end of September 1905, Hitler had passed all the exams necessary to apply for a place at the higher Realschule, or technical school, but he had no relish for further formal education and found little difficulty in persuading his mother that he needed time to consider his options.

FLIGHTS OF FANCY

For the next two years, Hitler lived a life of cosseted idleness in his mother's comfortable new apartment in Linz's Humboldtstrasse, to which the family had moved in June 1905. There, all his needs were met by the women of the household, his mother, his sister Paula and his aunt, Johanna. Klara even bought him a grand piano, and he took music lessons in the winter of 1906–07. His routine was one of studied idleness, staying up to the small hours and rising late in the morning – a pattern which, once established, he maintained for the rest of his life. The future Führer's days were given over to grandiose fantasies of artistic fame, which he later remembered as having the quality of a 'beautiful dream'.

During this period of his life Hitler acquired a Boswell in August 'Gustl' Kubizek. The son of an upholsterer, Kubizek also harboured extravagant dreams of artistic fame and fortune, in his case in the world of music. His memoirs of the time, originally commissioned in 1938 by the Nazi Party and later embellished by the author, throw a remarkable, albeit unreliable, light on the character of the young Adolf Hitler.

In the working-class Kubizek, Hitler found a submissive and willing audience. The two young men – Gustl was nine months older than Adolf – were a perfect double act: Hitler was the dominant partner, always forcing the pace with a ready opinion on every subject; Kubizek was the devoted listener, hanging on every word. Most evenings they would set off for the theatre or the opera, Hitler sporting a straggly moustache and cutting a dandyish figure in black coat, dark hat, and a black cane topped with an ivory handle. A pattern was set which, many years later, would become familiar to those in Hitler's entourage who were obliged to endure uncomplainingly the Führer's interminable monologues lasting all night and well into the small hours.

One of Hitler's favourite topics was Wagner, whose opera *Lohengrin* is a vast repository of the windy Teutonic mysticism – castles, knights errant, falsely accused maidens – which entranced Hitler throughout his life. Although a practised musician, and far better qualified than Hitler to expatiate on grand opera, Gustl always took the back seat in these so-called discussions drenched by his friend's cataracts of words. Another of Hitler's favourite topics was architecture. The two young men would make regular tours of Linz by night – in contrast to Hitler, Kubizek laboured in his father's workshop by day – while Hitler outlined his plans to remodel Linz and eagerly showed him sheaves of sketches and plans.

Hitler's passion for grandiloquent architecture was further fuelled by a trip he made to Vienna in the spring of 1906, ostensibly to study the paintings in the Court Museum. At night he feasted on productions of Wagner which made the offerings of the Linz opera house seem like amateur night. He returned to his mother's new home in Urfahr, a suburb of Linz, seized with the idea of attending Vienna's Academy of Fine Arts, an ambition which his mother was happy to support.

Klara, however, was now stricken with cancer. In January 1907 she had undergone an operation and was placed under the care of the Jewish Dr Eduard Bloch. It was left to Bloch to inform Hitler that his mother was terminally ill, and he noted that Hitler wept on hearing the news. Nevertheless, the youth returned to Vienna at the beginning of September 1907 to sit the entrance exams for the Academy of Fine Art.

Here Adolf Hitler met with the first major setback in his life. He had assumed he would sail into the Academy and, indeed, succeeded in getting on to the list of candidates who were selected to sit a three-hour entrance exam in which they had to produce drawings on specified themes. The verdict on his work was 'Test drawing unsatisfactory. Few heads,' and he failed to make the final short list.

In *Mein Kampf*, Hitler described the rejection as a 'bolt from the blue'. When he asked for an explanation, he was told by his examiners that his talents clearly lay in the field of architecture, a profession for which he lacked the formal educational qualifications. He told neither his mother nor his friend Gustl about his failure and, by the end of October, he was back in Linz to attend to his mother, who was now on her deathbed. Both his sister and Dr Bloch later testified that the care he provided was unstinting. Klara died peacefully on 21 December 1907; she was forty-seven.

Adolf Hitler was racked with grief. He had lost the only person to whom he had ever been emotionally close.

—⁓—

Hitler's own account of what happened next is not to be trusted. He later claimed that poverty, and a desire to emulate his father by triumphing over adversity to qualify as an architect, compelled him to return to Vienna. In fact, there was enough left over from his mother's estate after the funeral to enable him to return to Vienna and avoid the unpleasant necessity of working for a living for at least a year. This, together with his orphan's pension and the remains of a loan made to him by Aunt Johanna in the summer of 1907 to fund his artistic studies, was sufficient to tide Hitler over in his new life in Vienna, to which he returned in February 1908 with his friend Gustl Kubizek. Hitler's other travelling companion was his persistent fantasy of becoming an artist. What lay ahead in reality was five years of aimless drifting, which were to fix many of the major co-ordinates of Adolf Hitler's personality.

INFLUENCES

Vienna was the capital of the Austro-Hungarian Empire, to which the working life of Adolf Hitler's late father had been dedicated. When Hitler returned to Vienna, that empire had become moribund, caught in the throes of a death rattle which had commenced well over half a century earlier.

The Austro-Hungarian Empire was an artificial creation consisting of many nationalities, among them Germans, Poles, Czechs, Slovaks, Ruthenians, Slovenes, Serbs, Romanians, Hungarians and Croats. No natural frontiers or common language united the peoples of the empire, but hundreds of years of war, treaties and dynastic marriages had shaped the creaking dominion on the Danube. Now it was breaking up, but the collapse was played out in slow motion.

The Italians had already broken away in the nineteenth century, and in 1867 the Hungarians had secured an equality which was reflected in the empire's name. By 1900 Vienna itself was the focus of the many tensions – social, political, cultural – which would sound the death knell of the nineteenth-century world. In the second half of the century the city had grown four times faster than Paris or London, and the majority of its inhabitants had been born elsewhere. On the surface, Vienna's magnificent public buildings radiated imperial grandeur and its artistic and intellectual life boasted many of the great minds and creative artists of the age – among them Schnitzler, Mahler, Schoenberg, Otto Wagner, Klimt and Freud.

The benign, bewhiskered Hapsburg emperor, Franz Josef, who had reigned since 1848, presented a façade of stability behind which fierce currents of nationalism, vicious ethnic conflicts, fear of modern mass production, the rise of organized labour, and mass politics created a cockpit in which Vienna's liberal bourgeoisie, its small traders and craftsmen, feared for their future. Decay and disintegration were in the air.

———⟋⟍⟋———

In Vienna, Adolf Hitler was exposed to and absorbed three seminal influences on his personal credo which, much later, formed the unchanging bedrock of his political career. The first was the philosophy of Georg Ritter von Schönerer. By the time Hitler arrived in Vienna, early in 1908, Schönerer's career was on the wane. Seven years earlier, however, his Pan-German Party had gained twenty-one seats in the Austrian parliament, the Reichsrat. Schönerer's programme contained embryonic elements of the Nazi philosophy, notably German nationalism with its belief in the overriding importance of all things German, and its infatuation with Kaiser Wilhelm I and the German Reich. Also high on the programme's agenda was social reform, coupled with a mix of fiercely anti-liberal populism and violent anti-Semitism, the last the binding agent of Schönerer's anti-Socialist, anti-Catholic and anti-Hapsburg agenda. Significantly, his followers adopted the 'Heil' greeting and referred to the Party boss as 'Führer'.

Hitler later noted that Schönerer's career had been sidetracked by sterile parliamentary debate and the failure to build a mass movement. Schönerer himself had nothing but contempt for the masses, a weakness which could never be levelled against Hitler's second political hero, Karl Lueger, the self-styled 'tribune of the people' and the leader of the Christian Social Party, who became Mayor of Vienna in 1897. An inspired platform speaker and rabble-rouser, Lueger played expertly on the fears of the German-speaking lower middle class, among whose bogeymen were international capitalists, Slav nationalists and Marxist social democrats. Again, the philosophical binding agent was anti-Semitism – in the 1880s Lueger had supported Schönerer's bill to block Jewish immigration into Vienna. However, in contrast to Schönerer, Lueger's style was deceptively *gemütlich*. Challenged to explain why many of his friends were Jewish, Lueger famously replied, 'I decide who is a Jew.' Nevertheless, his speeches dripped with anti-Semitism. In one such he declared that wolves, leopards and tigers were more human than the Jews, who were 'beasts of prey in human form'. On another occasion, when challenged for having said that it was a matter of indifference to him whether Jews were hanged or shot, Lueger snapped back with the correction, 'Beheaded!'

Hitler was among the thousands who lined the streets of Vienna to watch Lueger's funeral in March 1910. Later he would dismiss Lueger's anti-Semitism as merely a cynical device to garner votes. Nor did he have any time for Lueger's emphasis on Catholic piety or his support for the Hapsburg monarchy. What impressed him, however, was Lueger's genius for painting policy on the broadest possible political canvas and his shrewd use of propaganda to articulate the prejudices of the many and channel them into a mass movement. Above all, he learnt from Lueger the political gains to be made from popularizing the widespread hatred of the Jews.

There was another mass movement gaining ground in turn-of-the-century Vienna which both impressed and alarmed the young Adolf Hitler. The Social Democratic Worker's Party had been formed in 1888. At first it made little headway but, by 1907, in the first election held under universal male suffrage, it won eighty-seven of the five hundred and sixteen seats in the Reichsrat on a fundamentally Marxist programme which was anathema to Hitler. What made an indelible impression on him, however, was the movement's ability to mobilize tens of thousands to achieve its aims. Watching a Social Democratic demonstration in Vienna, Hitler stood for two hours gazing at a 'gigantic human dragon slowly winding by'. It left him feeling oppressed and anxious, but it also planted a seed in his mind which would later have a monstrous flowering at Nuremberg: politics as spectacle.

There is much that is contradictory and opaque about Hitler's years in Vienna and their impact on his world view in the early 1920s. His own account in *Mein Kampf*, as well as the memoirs of the few people he knew at the time, are often fanciful, self-serving or entirely fictitious. Having resisted family pleas to find work in Linz, Hitler arrived in the city in mid-February 1908 and moved into dingy lodgings in Stumpergasse 31, near the Westbahnhof, which he had rented the previous October, probably in anticipation of studying at the Academy of Fine Arts. Shortly afterwards he was joined in his lodgings by Gustl Kubizek, who had won a place at the Vienna Conservatoire.

In Vienna, the two young men resumed the routines which had characterized their friendship in Linz. Kubizek worked hard at the Conservatoire while Hitler slept till late morning and idled away his days. He did not tell Kubizek that he had failed his entrance exam, and when the truth finally emerged it prompted Hitler to throw a tantrum in which he railed and raged at the unfairness of the world. When the dust settled, he slid back into his idler's existence, animated intermittently by harebrained schemes – to write an opera, to invent a soft drink, to compile a report on Vienna's housing problems – all of which fizzled out after an initial burst of manic energy. Kubizek concluded that his friend was becoming mentally unbalanced, not least because Hitler's natural prudishness masked a revulsion at sexuality. He was repelled by homosexuality; he shuddered at the thought of contracting venereal disease from a prostitute; he physically shrank from women and talked for hours with Kubizek about preserving his virginity, 'the flame of life'.

It is almost certain that during this period Hitler began to read a racist periodical, *Ostara,* edited by Adolf Lanz, a former Cistercian monk and follower of Schönerer, who styled himself Jorg Lanz von Liebenfels. In *Ostara*, Lanz created a fevered fantasy world in which blond, blue-eyed heroes battled with dark sub-humans who preyed on Aryan heroines. Lanz's answer to the ills of the modern world was simple: the enslavement and enforced sterilization of inferior races and the restoration of the Aryan race to its true position as the evolutionary pinnacle. The newspaper Hitler read regularly was the *Deutsches Volksblatt*, which enjoyed a daily circulation of some fifty-five thousand and was virulently anti-Semitic, linking Jews to all manner of sexual and financial corruption with little or no regard to journalistic integrity.

At the beginning of July, Kubizek passed his exams at the Conservatoire and returned to Linz for the summer. Without telling his friend, Hitler moved out of their lodgings, possibly because he had failed in a second attempt to gain a place at the Academy and could not bear the thought of being branded a double failure. It would be many years before they met again.[1]

THE LOWER DEPTHS

In the autumn of 1909, Hitler drifted downwards until he hit rock bottom. His money ran out, and by Christmas of that year we find him, in sodden lice-ridden clothes, seeking shelter in a hostel for the homeless in Meidling. The petit-bourgeois idler with artistic pretensions had joined the dregs of Viennese society – the alcoholic, the destitute and the down-and-out.

But here Hitler had a lucky break. He met Reinhold Hanisch, a petty crook and con-man, who suggested that they earn a pittance shovelling snow, a task that rapidly proved beyond the famished Hitler, shivering in his shabby suit and with no overcoat. Then Hanisch had a better idea. In all probability, Hitler had spun him a vainglorious tale about studying at the Academy and had also mentioned the kindness of his Aunt Johanna. Doubtless Hanisch suggested that they touch her for another hand-out, ostensibly to help Hitler with his imaginary studies. The money duly arrived, enabling Hitler to buy an overcoat and the materials to set up as a jobbing artist, painting genre scenes of Vienna which Hanisch would then sell.

At about the same time, Hitler and Hanisch moved to slightly more salubrious surroundings, the Men's Home in the north-east of Vienna, which housed some five hundred residents who were clinging to a rung or two higher on the seedy pecking order of Vienna's lower depths. They were mostly tradesmen and minor civil servants down on their luck, the respectable poor. The Men's Home had a dining room, laundry, and other basic facilities, and afforded a degree of privacy to its inhabitants. Hitler was coming up for air.

Thanks to the slippery salesman Hanisch,[2] Hitler was able to scratch a living with his watercolours of street scenes. They were meticulous but inert studies, unenlivened by the human form. Hanisch placed many of them with Jewish dealers, whom, ironically, Hitler considered to be more straightforward and reliable conduits

---

1 Hitler and Kubizek were reunited in April 1938 in Linz. They met for the last time in July 1940. Shortly after the end of World War II, Kubizek was briefly incarcerated by the Americans. He died in October 1956.

2 Hanisch swindled Hitler over the sale of two paintings and, subsequently, was jailed for a short time by the police on an unrelated charge. Hitler never got the money nor did he see Hanisch again. Reinhold Hanisch is not to be confused with Karl Hönisch.

for his modest output than their Gentile equivalents. Another Jewish business associate was Joseph Neumann, who was on friendly terms with Hitler and valued his company. Other residents of the Men's Home at this time later testified that Hitler considered the Jews 'a clever people'. Indeed, his acquaintances at the Men's Home recalled that the main subjects of his frequent tirades were Socialists and Jesuits.

In contrast, we have Augustus Kubizek's testimony that Hitler was already a convinced anti-Semite when he was living in Linz. And there is the celebrated passage in *Mein Kampf*, the first volume of which was published in July 1925, in which Hitler wrote: 'Once, as I was strolling through [Vienna's] Inner City, I suddenly encountered an apparition in black caftan and black hair locks. Is this a Jew? was my first thought. For, to be sure, they had not looked like that in Linz. I observed the man furtively and cautiously, but the longer I stared at this foreign face, scrutinising feature for feature, the more my first question assumed a new form: Is this a German?'

Hitler, who had a morbid obsession with cleanliness, then moves on to link dirt and disease with Jews, whose malign influence lies behind all the elements which conspire to undermine and corrupt society, among them the liberal press, modern art, trades unions, and parliamentary deputies. Behind this phalanx of enemies lurks the spectre of a political force which by 1912 Hitler had indeed come to hate, Social Democracy. This, too, he asserts, had fallen under the control of the 'Jewish doctrine of Marxism'.

Just as different acquaintances later offered differing spins on Hitler's beliefs at this time of his life, as often as not to suit their own agendas, so physical descriptions of him around 1912–13 vary widely. One of the most convincing is that of Karl Hönisch, whose account was written in the 1930s for the National Socialist Party's archives. While couched in terms which paint Hitler in the best possible light, it nevertheless has a plausible ring to it. Hönisch describes Hitler, at the conclusion of his time at the Men's Home, as an unimpressive, weedy figure, shabbily dressed, undernourished and hollow-cheeked, with lank dark hair falling from his brow. Most of his days were spent in the writing room, catching the light from the window while he sketched or painted at a long oak table that the inmates acknowledged as his place – woe betide any newcomer who attempted, however, innocently, to usurp it.

THE 'GERMAN' NATIONALIST

In Vienna Hitler was merely a pallid face in the crowd, yet he had not been entirely overlooked by the Austro-Hungarian bureaucrats responsible for the conscription of young men to the empire's armed services. In the autumn of 1909, he had failed to register for military service, which he would have been obliged to serve in the following spring after he turned twenty-one. Had he been found unfit in 1910, the process would nevertheless have been repeated in 1911 and 1912. The pen-pushers in Linz were on his trail at a suitably leisurely pace.

The knowledge of his failure to register was, in part, the reason for Hitler's move to Munich in 1913. However, his departure had been delayed so that he could collect his share of his father's legacy on attaining the age of twenty-four. A month later Adolf Hitler, wearing a smarter suit than that described by Hönisch and accompanied by a friend from the Men's Home, twenty-year-old Rudolf Hausler, an unemployed shop assistant, set off for Munich. It was the beginning of a new and crucial phase in his life.

He was leaving a crumbling empire for one that was virtually brand new. It was now forty-two years since the jigsaw collection of German states had coalesced into the German Empire under Kaiser Wilhelm I. In that time Germany's power had increased enormously, overtaking Britain in the production of coal and steel – the sinews of war. In August 1914, Germany would be capable of putting 1.75 million men, regulars and reservists, in the field. Since the beginning of the century it had been locked in a spiralling and immensely costly battleship-building race with the Royal Navy.

Britain had only a small regular army but still boasted the world's most powerful navy, which guaranteed the security of its worldwide empire. Germany's colonies had been acquired late in the nineteenth century and consisted of tracts of Africa and possessions in the Pacific which were of little interest to the British and the French, the other major colonial powers.

Inasmuch as Hitler had no desire to fight for the Austro-Hungarian Empire, his subsequently stated reason that he went to Munich for 'political reasons' is true, although highly disingenuous. It had more to do with his failure to register for military service. Nonetheless, it was as a fanatical German nationalist that Adolf Hitler arrived, on 25 May 1913, in Munich – a truly 'German' city in comparison to the polyglot 'Babylon of races' that was Vienna.

Hitler was to remain deeply attached to Munich for the rest of his life. In the days before 1914 Munich was one of the pre-eminent cultural jewels of Europe, a forcing ground for modernist literature, painting and architecture. Hitler had no interest whatosever in any of these. Just as in Vienna, his mind was locked in a mid-nineteenth-century time warp in which neoclassical façades and galleries stuffed with the work of old masters spoke to him of grandeur and power.

In Munich he picked up the threads of his latter days in Vienna. He and Hausler rented a room in a run-down area in the north of the city, not far from the military barracks. Hausler moved out in February 1914, doubtless driven to distraction by the drumbeat of Hitler's obsessions, but returned a few days later to rent a separate room. Hitler, meanwhile, had resumed his career as a jobbing artist, copying scenes from postcards and making a modest living. As he neither smoked nor drank, he was able to save money.

He had no social life. His landlady, Frau Popp, recalled that he never had visitors. He painted by day and read by night. Frau Popp remembered him making frequent trips to the nearby Bayerische Staatsbibliothek. Hitler later claimed that during the evenings he immersed himself in the great political events of the day and devoured works on Marxism in an attempt to develop a theory which linked the political theory of Karl Marx to the Jews ('Jewish-Marxism'). This was at best a half-

truth. Hitler was not exploring new ground; he was simply going over old ground in order to confirm his prejudices. In *Mein Kampf*, he revealingly explained his reading regime from his days in Vienna:

A man who possesses the art of correct reading will, in studying any book, magazine or pamphlet, instinctively and immediately perceive everything which in his opinion is worth permanently remembering either because it is suited to his purpose or generally worth knowing. Once the knowledge he has achieved in this fashion is correctly co-ordinated within the somehow existing picture of this or that subject created by the imagination, it will function either as a corrective or a complement, thus enhancing either the correctness or the clarity of the picture … Only this kind of reading has meaning and purpose … Since my earliest youth I have endeavoured to read in the correct way, and in this endeavour I have been most happily supported by my memory and intelligence.

Those hapless German generals of World War II who were summoned to Hitler's headquarters, and who flinched under the bombardment of facts and figures delivered by the Führer – a *rage de nombre* all too often utterly meaningless to his interlocutors – could doubtless have ruefully attested to his memory if not his intelligence. But it was nothing more than the eternal chant of the autodidact, the deadly drone of the saloon bar bore down the ages.

In Munich, Hitler lived a solitary life. His acquaintances were, like him, the self-opinionated improvers of the world, the cranks and know-it-alls who haunted fly-blown beer halls and small cafés and had a ready answer for everything. This was the nearest he got to politics at this stage in his life, although in *Mein Kampf* he gave it a familiar spin: 'In the years 1913 and 1914, I, for the first time in various circles which today in part faithfully support the National Socialist movement, expressed the conviction that the question of the future of the German nation was the destruction of Marxism.'

While Hitler pondered the destruction of Marxism, the Linz police had finally caught up with him. The evasion of military service was considered a serious offence, punishable with a hefty fine. The Austrian authorities had tracked Hitler to Munich via the Men's Home, and on Sunday, 18 January 1914, a policeman turned up at Frau Popp's door to deliver a summons. Hitler was to appear in Linz within two days to register for military service and was, for the moment, under arrest.

He was saved from further humiliation by a chapter of accidents. There had been a delay in delivering the summons and the Austrian consulate in Munich, confronted with a sheepish, bedraggled Hitler, took pity on him. While telegrams pinged back and forth between Linz and Munich, and another weekend intervened, Hitler wrote a long letter, full of apologies, which attempted to explain his failure to register for military service. The authorities relented, and he was given permission to appear in Salzburg at the beginning of February. The consulate even gave him his travel expenses to get there, but on his arrival he was deemed too physically weak for military service.

THE SHOT AT SARAJEVO

Hitler resumed his aimless life in Munich, but it was soon to change for ever, along with those of millions of young men across Europe. On 28 June 1914, the Archduke Franz Ferdinand of Austria-Hungary, heir to the Hapsburg throne, and his wife, the Czech Countess Sophie, made an official visit to open a museum in the city of Sarajevo, the capital of Bosnia. Bosnia, and its sister province Herzegovina, were former Turkish possessions which had been administered by Austria-Hungary since 1879 and annexed by the dual monarchy in 1908. Many of Sarajevo's Serb inhabitants were bitterly resentful at not being allowed to become citizens of Serbia, their homeland, which had achieved formal independence in 1878. Some of them planned to give the Archduke a less than friendly welcome in Sarajevo, with the help of fellow Serbs infiltrated from the Serbian capital, Belgrade. They were members of Young Bosnia,

Opposite: One of Hitler's watercolours, painstaking but inert. There has always been a lively trade in the relics of Hitler's ambitions to be an artist, many of them of doubtful provenance. In April 2009, thirteen paintings, allegedly by Hitler and found by a British soldier at the end of World War II, were sold at auction for £95,859 at Ludlow, in the English county of Shropshire.

a secret society backed by Serbian military intelligence, which was pledged to liberating Slav lands from Hapsburg rule. They had drawn up plans to assassinate the Archduke.

The man who fired the fatal shots that day was Gavrilo Princip, a consumptive nineteen-year-old terrorist and nihilist straight from the pages of a Conrad novel. Two bullets from Princip's Belgian semi-automatic pistol, thoughtfully provided by Serbian military intelligence, mortally wounded the Archduke and his wife. Sitting bolt upright in their open-top limousine, they were already dying as they were driven to the residence of Bosnia's governor-general, where they were both dead within fifteen minutes.

Hitler recalled that on hearing the news he realized 'a stone had been set rolling whose course could no longer be arrested'. It took a month from the assassination for Austria-Hungary to declare war on Serbia, a diplomatic rather than a military ploy, since it would take several weeks for the Austrians to mobilize. Then the Russians stepped in. They were not prepared to countenance the humiliation of Serbia, nor permit the Austrians and their German allies to dominate the Balkans and thus, by extension, threaten Russia's access to the Mediterranean through the Dardanelles straits. Russian mobilization began on 29 July 1914.

On 1 August Germany declared war on Russia and mobilized, with the aim of having millions of men ready for action within a week. Russia's ally France also mobilized on the same day. On 3 August, at 6.45 p.m., Germany declared war on France, and invaded Belgium the following day. Belgium was a neutral country and the German invasion drew the British into the conflict. Britain despatched an ultimatum to Germany demanding an immediate withdrawal from Belgium. There was no reply, and by midnight (Berlin time) on 4 August 1914 Britain and Germany were at war. As the British foreign secretary, Sir Edward Grey, waited for the deadline, he observed, 'The lamps are going out all over Europe. We shall not see them lit again in our time.'

THE UNKNOWN SOLDIER

At the beginning of August, Munich was gripped by war fever. Hitler later wrote, 'I fell down on my knees and thanked Heaven from an overflowing heart for granting me the good fortune of being permitted to live at this time.' On 2 August, the day after Germany's declaration of war on Russia, he joined a huge crowd in a massive display of patriotism in Munich's Odeonsplatz. Years later, his court photographer Heinrich Hoffmann examined a photograph he had taken of the event and, in the process, identified the remarkable image of the young Hitler, his eyes ablaze, bellowing patriotic songs.

On 3 August Hitler submitted a personal petition to Ludwig III of Bavaria to serve as an Austrian in the Bavarian army.[3] In Hitler's account, his request was granted the next day. This seems most unlikely. He probably volunteered on

5 August, as he later attested, and was turned away in the chaotic rush to join the colours. However, on 16 August he was summoned to report to the recruiting depot, where he was kitted out, and by the beginning of September had been assigned to the Bavarian Reserve Infantry Regiment 16 (known as the List regiment after its commander) which was principally composed of raw recruits. At the end of October, following a period of basic training, the regiment left for the Flanders front. At the age of twenty-five Hitler found in his regiment a home and a purpose.

> ‘The lamps are going out all over Europe. We shall not see them lit again in our time.’
>
> SIR EDWARD GREY

The war was, in his own words, 'the greatest and most unforgettable time of my earthly existence'. It provided him with a fund of memories to which he would constantly return during World War II, the conflict which he instigated and drove. At the end of June 1940, in triumph after the humbled French had signed an armistice, Hitler, with two of his old comrades from the List Regiment, toured the battlefields on which he had served as a regimental despatch runner.

In *Mein Kampf*, Hitler omits to mention that he was a runner, possibly because he wanted to encourage the view that he was a front-line fighter. In fact his war service was honourable and his work as a despatch runner, carrying messages from the regimental command post to the battalion and company commanders in the front line, exposed him to considerable danger. Within two weeks of the regiment's arrival in the Ypres sector, three of the eight runners attached to the regiment were killed in a fire-fight with French troops. Two days later, moments after Hitler had left the forward regimental command post, it was obliterated by a shell.

Hitler spent much of his wartime service in the Fromelles sector, ten miles from Lille and fifty miles north of the Somme, where on 1 July 1916, the first day of the Battle of the Somme, the British Army suffered its heaviest losses in a single day of fighting – sixty thousand casualties, nineteen thousand of them fatal. Hitler was almost certainly involved in the Battle of Fromelles (19–20 July), a diversionary attack launched as the Battle of the Somme raged to the south.

At the regimental headquarters in Fromelles, Hitler had time to sketch, paint and adopt a small terrier, Foxl, which had strayed across no man's land into the German trenches. Foxl became a friend, always quick to obey, and Hitler was distraught when his unit moved and Foxl could not be found. Relations with his comrades were not so companionable. They found Hitler a queer fish, and noted that after 1915 he never received letters or parcels from home. In group photographs he invariably hovers on the edge, a painfully thin figure, sallow and self-absorbed, with a straggling moustache. He had none of the rough humour common to men at the front, and regularly exploded when anyone voiced even mild criticism of the conduct of the war. Hitler remained an implacable advocate

---

3 Technically, in 1914 Germany overall did not possess an army, but fielded the four separate armies of the kingdoms of Prussia, Bavaria, Saxony and Württemberg. There was no German Army until after the armistice of 1918.

of the ruthless prosecution of the war. He was appalled by the celebrated Christmas truce of 1914, when large numbers of British and German troops spontaneously met in no man's land, exchanged gifts and cigarettes, and played football.[4]

Max Amann, then a regimental staff sergeant and later Hitler's postwar crony and publisher, told his Allied interrogators in 1947 that Hitler often had political discussions with his comrades. At around the same time, however, several of his Great War comrades denied this; according to their testimony, Hitler almost never mentioned the Jews, and what remarks he did make on the subject passed unnoticed in the anti-Semitic atmosphere of the time. Nevertheless, one of Hitler's fellow soldiers, Balthasar Brandmayer, claimed in a 1932 memoir that in the latter stages of the war Hitler had called the Jews 'the wire-pullers behind our misfortune', an observation whose significance Brandmayer only grasped later.

Opposite: Hitler, remote and grimly unsmiling, with his fellow despatch runner Anton Bachmann and his dog Foxl, photographed at Fournes, their regimental headquarters on the Western Front, in the spring of 1915. Here Hitler found the time to paint and to read, according to his own account, the works of Schopenhauer, which he carried in his knapsack.

One experience which hardened Hitler's attitudes was the time he spent in a military hospital near Berlin in the late autumn of 1916, after being wounded by a shell fragment during the fighting in the Fromelles sector. He was appalled by the cynicism of many of his fellow patients and also by the low morale of the civilian population when he ventured into the city. Writing some eight years later, he ascribed these phenomena to the sinister influence of the Jews, who seemed to him to be occupying all the clerical positions in the army, clearly a rationalization of the position he took after the war. In the List Regiment there were Jews, but only in proportion to their numbers in the civilian population, and they were mostly good soldiers. It was a Jewish officer, Lieutenant-Colonel Philipp Engelhardt who, in December 1915, had recommended that Hitler be awarded the Iron Cross (Second Class).

Hitler returned to the front in March 1917. His battalion was moved to the Vimy sector, which saw heavy fighting in April during which the Canadian Fourth Division took the highest point of Vimy Ridge, a feature against which the Allies had been battering for two years. By the time the British opened a new offensive, popularly known as the Battle of Passchendaele, Hitler's battalion was back in the Ypres salient, where the opposing lines of trenches had been frozen since the winter of 1914. The Germans had ample warning of the offensive, and when it began on 31 July, there were nearly two million combatants crammed into the Ypres salient. The preliminary British bombardment destroyed the battlefield's fragile drainage system and thirteen British infantry divisions advanced into a glutinous morass.

---

4 The Allied high command shared Hitler's point of view and issued strict orders that the Christmas Truce was not to be repeated and that anyone attempting to fraternize with the enemy would be shot.

The attack ground on until the beginning of November, with progress being measured in hundreds of yards, before it was halted a mere five miles from the original start line. Each mile had been bought at the cost of fifty thousand casualties. The battle became synonymous with the seemingly futile carnage on the Western Front.

The poet Siegfried Sassoon wrote of the battle:

...I died in hell–
(They called it Passchendaele);
My wound was slight
And I was hobbling back, and then a shell
Burst slick upon the duckboards; so I fell
Into the bottomless mud, and lost the light.

Hitler's unit, which had been involved in the heavy fighting at the beginning of the British offensive, was pulled out of the line and transferred to Alsace. In September 1917, while the blood-and-mud bath of Passchendaele dragged on, Hitler took his first leave of the war. He went to Berlin where he stayed for eighteen days with the parents of one of his comrades and spent much of his time visiting museums.

He was on the move again when he returned to the front and witnessed the last great German offensive of the war, launched by First Quartermaster General Erich Ludendorff, effectively the German commander-in-chief in the West. It rolled within sixty miles of Paris before being halted by the French and Americans, the latter making their first decisive intervention of the war on the Western Front.

The Allies went on the offensive on 8 August. Within twenty-four hours they had driven ten miles into the German lines. Ludendorff called it 'the black day of the German army', and three days later tendered his resignation to the Kaiser, who refused it but nevertheless observed, 'I see that we must strike a balance. We have nearly reached the limits of our powers of resistance. The war must be ended.'

A week earlier, on 4 August, Adolf Hitler had been awarded his second Iron Cross, this time First Class, an exceptional achievement for a corporal, the rank he retained throughout the war.[5] He was nominated by a Jewish officer, Lieutenant Hugo Gutmann. Legend later had it that Hitler had won his Iron Cross after single-handedly capturing fifteen French soldiers, but the truth is that several weeks earlier he had got through with an important despatch, an effort which was worthy of praise if not an Iron Cross. The arguments which followed Gutmann's recommendation, and the delay in making the award, indicate that at least some of his superiors had their doubts.

---

5 Hitler might have been expected to rise higher and was nominated for promotion by his staff sergeant, Max Amann. He was also considered for promotion by the staff of the Linz regiment, who decided that he lacked leadership qualities. It was also clear that, throughout the war, Hitler was quite happy where he was.

At the end of the month Hitler was sent to Nuremberg for training in wireless telegraphy, and at the conclusion of his course took another spot of leave in Berlin. He then returned to the Ypres salient where he was wounded in a British mustard gas attack near Wervick on the night of 13–14 October. He and several comrades were temporarily blinded and stumbled out of harm's way, like so many thousands of others in the Great War, by clinging on to the man in front as they were shepherded to safety by another soldier who could still see. A week later Hitler was transferred to a military hospital outside Stettin in Pomerania.

The war was over for Adolf Hitler, and the end was fast approaching for the Kaiser's Germany.

BITTER FRUIT

In spite of the Kaiser's prophetic words to Ludendorff, the war still had a short time to run. The final Allied assault on the Hindenburg Line, a complex defensive system established in the autumn of 1916, began at the end of September, after the Americans had cleared the St Mihiel salient, which had threatened Allied movements in Champagne since 1914. The Hindenburg Line was then breached in the decisive Allied offensive of the war. French and American troops drove along the Meuse valley towards Mézières while the British advanced along the line of the Somme. By mid-October, shortly after Hitler was gassed, the German Army was on the point of disintegration.

By mid-October, the German Army was on the point of disintegration.

Germany's strategic position had been fatally undermined as, one by one, its allies had fallen by the wayside. Inside Germany, hunger and a growing influenza pandemic were taking a heavy toll. The Army, battered but still undefeated in the field, was losing more men to the pandemic than to the Allies. In the port of Kiel, forty thousand sailors mutinied. Events now followed each other with bewildering rapidity. On 27 October Austro-Hungary and Turkey, Germany's principal allies, signed ceasefire agreements, and Ludendorff was now dismissed by the Kaiser, who abdicated on 9 November when a Socialist government took power in Germany. Kaiser Wilhelm II, Germany's last emperor, took refuge in neutral Holland on 10 November. Since 7 November, a German delegation had been negotiating with the Allied commander-in-chief, General Foch, in his railway carriage headquarters at Compiègne. They had been instructed to agree whatever terms were offered. When they asked Foch what his terms for peace were, he replied, 'None.' The Germans admitted that they could not fight on. Foch replied, 'Then you have come to surrender.'

At dawn on 11 November 1918, a message went out to all the Allied armies. The opening words were: 'Hostilities will cease at eleven hours today, November 11th.' The guns were to fall silent. At first the men at the front were unable to come to terms with the sudden quiet which descended on their positions. After over four years of war it was eerie not to hear gunfire somewhere. Relief came later, then jubilation.

There were very different emotions in the Pomeranian hospital where Hitler was recovering from the effects of mustard gas. He had recovered enough of his sight to glean some alarming information from the newspapers; rumours of incipient revolution were circulating and he was told of the arrival at the hospital of a delegation from the sailor mutineers. On 10 November a pastor informed the patients of the abdication of the Kaiser, the new Socialist government, and the armistice talks. It was a bombshell for Hitler:

> I could stand it no longer. It became impossible for me to sit still one minute more. Again everything went black before my eyes; I tottered and groped my way back to the dormitory, threw myself on my bunk, and dug my burning head into my blanket and pillow. Since the day when I had stood at my mother's grave I had not wept … But now I could not help it … And so it had all been in vain … Did all this happen only so that a gang of wretched criminals could lay hands on the fatherland?

However one reads it, the shattering experience at the hospital represents a key staging post in Hitler's journey. Later, in the early 1920s, he would rearrange his account of the events of November 1918 into a neater narrative to dovetail with his burgeoning political career. But in November 1918 he did not have a political career, and nor did there seem to any likelihood that an unknown soldier, recovering from his wounds in 1918, would have the connections or contacts to launch himself on to the political stage. That lay in the future. However, the German surrender was a trauma which undoubtedly reinforced the still inchoate obsessions which formed the basis of Hitler's perception of the world – principally his hatred of Socialism and the Jews. It was only when he began to pick up the pieces and reassemble the broken model after the war, when he worked for the German Army as an intelligence agent infiltrating extremist groups, that anything like a fully formed philosophy emerged in his mind. World War I had provided Adolf Hitler with his first real home, in the Army. In the immediate aftermath of 1918 it would provide him with the building blocks for the creation of the Nazi Party in his own image.

Opposite: End of the line. German prisoners in a camp at Abbeville, October 1918.

2

THE FIREBRAND

VERSAILLES AND AFTER

In a Germany rocked by revolutionary unrest, ravaged by influenza and malnutrition, and dismayed by the abdication of the Kaiser, a feeling of numb bewilderment greeted the signing of the armistice. Ordinary German civilians had been unaware of the dramatic course of events, both military and diplomatic, since July 1918. They could not comprehend why the armistice had been signed while the German Army still occupied parts of France and Belgium. A feeling grew that they had been 'stabbed in the back', a sentiment held by all political classes. In November 1918, returning troops were greeted by the citizens of Berlin with flowers and laurel leaves, and a speech from the new chancellor, Friedrich Ebert, in which he declared, 'I salute you who return unvanquished from the field of battle.' But many of these men had new battles to fight in postwar Germany. Disconnected from civilian life, they soon joined paramilitary groups, the *Freikorps*, which the postwar Social Democratic government led by Ebert was to use against Communist revolutionaries.

Opposite: An actor prepares. In the 1920s, Hitler honed his speaking platform histrionics with obsessive attention to detail. His personal photographer Heinrich Hoffmann would capture each gesture and posture before Hitler studied the results to select the precise choreography required to deliver the maximum impact.

The feeling of betrayal felt by so many Germans grew when the victorious Allies met in Paris to redraw the map of Europe – and much of the world beyond – a task made all the more urgent by the collapse of the Russian, Austro-Hungarian and Ottoman empires. The principal treaty was signed by the Allies and Germany at the Palace of Versailles on 28 June 1919.

A famous painting by Sir William Orpen captures the moment of signature by the German delegates. In the centre of the frame are the Big Three – the US president, Woodrow Wilson, and prime ministers Lloyd George of the United Kingdom and Georges Clemenceau of France, all three of them serene and exquisitely suited, the victors of the Great War. Clemenceau later observed that Orpen had pictured him sitting between a would-be Napoleon (Lloyd George) and a would-be Christ (Woodrow Wilson).

On this occasion at least, Clemenceau got the better of Jesus Christ, although in the long run it did neither him nor France much good. Stalin had a famous saying, 'How many divisions has the Pope?' France, although grievously mauled by four years of war, still had the divisions. But if the war had continued into 1919 and beyond, which many believed it would until the sudden German collapse in the autumn of 1918, then the balance of power would have swung inexorably towards the Americans. However, just as many in the German military believed that they had been stabbed in the back by the armistice, so the French high command was convinced that the German collapse had denied them the crushing victory in the field that in 1918 was rightly theirs.

During the discussion of the peace terms, Lloyd George felt a premonition of the disaster which lay ahead. He observed then: 'If peace were made now, in twenty years' time the Germans would say what Carthage had said about the First Punic War, namely that they had made this mistake and that mistake, and by better preparation and organisation they would be able to bring about victory next time.'

Nearly all the peace terms imposed at Versailles had been anticipated at the time of the armistice. This was no conference between victors and vanquished. The Germans were merely required to turn up and sign on the dotted line – it was a matter of dotting the 'I's and crossing the 'T's. Control of coal mines in the Saar was given to the French for fifteen years as compensation for the German wrecking of the mines in north-east France; the east bank of the Rhine was demilitarized to a depth of thirty miles to be occupied by the Allies, also for fifteen years, with Germany paying for the cost of the occupation; conscription in Germany was to be abolished and the size of the German Army limited to one hundred thousand; Germany was stripped of her colonies and denied membership of the League of Nations. The League had been the last of Wilson's famous Fourteen Points which he outlined in January 1918, and was established to adjudicate international problems.

What really stuck in the craw of Germans of all political persuasions was the Allies' demand, led by the French, for massive reparations to pay for war damage and the cost of occupation. Germany was to be 'squeezed until the pips squeak', according to popular sentiment at the time. In December 1918, the French Minister of Finance, Louis-Lucien Klotz (according to Clemenceau, 'the only Jew who knows nothing about money') had made it clear that he expected France's budgetary deficits to be redeemed then, and in the future, by reparations. At Versailles, France claimed that its total war damages ran to 209,000 million gold francs, and the overall claims of the Allies amounted to approximately 400,000 million francs.

However, sceptical experts at the British Treasury thought that the most that could be squeezed from the Germans would be 75,000 million francs. Eventually the sum to be paid by Germany was left for future negotiations, and in 1932 it was written off. By then irreparable damage had been done. Reparations brought a lasting legacy of hatred in Germany, which was a crucial factor in the rise to power of Hitler and the Nazis – who repudiated Versailles, reparations and all.

After the armistice Hitler focused all his efforts on staying in the Army. In Germany anarchy reigned, and there seemed to be no future in civvy street. He returned to Munich in November 1918 and within a fortnight was one of some one hundred and fifty men assigned to guard duties at the Traunstein camp in Bavaria for Russian prisoners of war. At least there was some stability here as Bavaria drifted towards a civil war which the Social Democrat government in Berlin seemed powerless to prevent.

In Kiel, Berlin and Munich, Socialists assumed local authority, but in the chaotic conditions which prevailed in Germany they were unable to impose order. In Munich, an uneasy Socialist coalition, headed by Kurt Eisner, had been installed and the aged King Ludwig III had fled Bavaria. Over twenty years later Hitler would joke that at least he had the Social Democrats to thank for sparing him the trouble of removing these 'courtly interests'.

In Munich there had at first been little revolutionary fervour, only a feeling of exhaustion and war-weariness. While Eisner and his colleagues fretted about coaxing the overwhelmingly rural and deeply conservative population of Bavaria into supporting their gradualist experiment in Socialism, the revolutionaries, the so-called Spartacists (*Spartakusbund*), were ready to move. They seized their opportunity after Eisner was assassinated on 21 February 1919 by Graf Anton von Arco-Valley, a former officer who was studying at Munich University.

At the end of April, a full-blooded revolution proclaimed a 'Red Republic', promising 'a dictatorship of the proletariat' to be guaranteed by a twenty-thousand-strong 'Red Army' led by Rudolf Eglhofer, a twenty-three-year-old veteran of the Kiel mutiny. The declaration was followed by an orgy of murderous reprisals against prisoners of the 'Red Army' and brutal counter-reprisals by the so-called 'White Guards' *Freikorps* formations massing outside Munich. Civil war exploded as revolutionaries and reactionaries clashed in street battles which saw both sides employing flame-throwers, heavy artillery and armoured vehicles. Prominent in the fighting was the *Freikorps* Epp, a formation commanded by Franz Ritter von Epp, a regular officer who would rise to a position of some power in the Nazi Party. Serving under von Epp was another veteran of World War I who would play an even more significant part in Hitler's rise to power, Captain Ernst Röhm.

The battle for Munich, which lasted until 3 May, claimed some six hundred lives, over half of them civilian, and Eglhofer was murdered by the *Freikorps*. Sixty-five Spartacists were sentenced to hard labour and over two thousand were imprisoned. The Spartacist revolution had been put down but had left Chancellor Ebert's hands caked with blood. In Berlin, the Spartacist leaders Rosa Luxemburg and Karl Liebknecht were both murdered while being held by the *Freikorps* and their bodies dumped into a river.

In deeply conservative Bavaria the traumatic events between November 1918 and May 1919 provided a shot in the arm for the radical Right. They not only confirmed the Right's deep fear of the Bolshevism which had so recently been installed in Russia and was still fighting a bitter civil war against 'White' enemies of its own, but it also legitimized the use of extreme counter-revolutionary violence against the Bolshevik threat. Later, this provided Adolf Hitler with one of the principal planks in his political platform.

LEARNING THE ROPES

What was Hitler doing during these dramatic events? His duties at the prisoner-of-war camp, which had been cleared of its inmates by the beginning of February, had come to an end, and his military record shows that on 12 February he was assigned to a unit to await demobilization. Extremely keen to remain in the Army, he managed to do so until March 1920, by which time he had discovered the oratorical gifts which were to launch his political career. In *Mein Kampf*, however, he devotes only a few pages to the days of Munich's Red Republic, which were soon to offer so many lessons for the nascent Nazi Party. It seems that Hitler had good reason to be reticent about his weeks in Munich during the Bavarian Soviet's seizure of power and its brutal suppression.

Opposite: Spartacists are escorted into captivity in 1919. Many former soldiers, veterans of World War I, were among the recruits to the extreme right- and left-wing groups which clashed in pitched battles in the streets of post-war Germany. In Munich in March 1920, right-wing monarchists and *Freikorps* units briefly seized power in the so-called Kapp putsch (see p. 45). Hitler drew many lessons from this period of turmoil.

On 20 February 1919, Hitler's demobilization company was assigned to guard duty at Munich's Hauptbahnhof. The soldiers also earned a little extra cash by testing gas masks. Hitler, however, avoided his imminent demobilization. A routine order issued at the beginning of April identifies him as his company's representative (*Vertrauensmann*), and it is likely that he had held this post from February. The precise functions of the company representative were determined by the propaganda department of Bavaria's Socialist government and included providing 'educational material' to the troops. It would seem that Adolf Hitler's first hands-on involvement in politics was as a low-level stooge of the men he would later stigmatize as the 'November criminals'. Small wonder that this was a career move over which he was subsequently eager to draw a veil.

On 14 April, the day after the declaration of the Red Republic, the Munich Soldiers' Councils sanctioned a round of elections of barracks representatives to ensure that the Army toed the party line. Hitler was elected as the deputy battalion representative and soon afterwards became the battalion representative. During the turbulent days of the Red Republic, the Army stood squarely behind the Spartacists, and it is inconceivable that Hitler could have carried out his duties as a representative without falling into line. However, whether he was acting sincerely or merely ensuring that he retained his relatively cosy billet in the Army is a question which cannot be answered definitively. Although his subsequent career shows that Hitler was an opportunist *par excellence*, his opportunism in Munich in the spring of 1919 was not an episode to which he could easily apply a favourable gloss. He made no attempt to join the *Freikorps*, and in all probability marched in mass demonstrations wearing the red armband of the Marxists.

More significant was the fact that, only days after the fall of the Red Republic, Hitler was appointed to serve on a committee which was charged with investigating whether any of his battalion had been active Spartacist supporters. The appointment ensured the deferral of Hitler's discharge and, crucially, brought him into contact for the first time with counter-revolutionary politics within the army.

The end of the Red Republic effectively brought Munich under military rule, and the units which had been involved in putting down the uprising were organized into *Gruppenkommando* No. Four (*Gruko*). The *Gruko* moved swiftly to control the Education and Propaganda Department (*Nachrichtenabteilung, Abt.Ib/P*) which had been set up after the suppression of the Red Republic to instil in the troops the appropriate nationalist and anti-Bolshevist attitudes. Surveillance and propaganda were the orders of the day, and reliable speakers were recruited from the ranks to get the message across. This task would keep them in the Army for some time; it was the answer to Adolf Hitler's prayers.

Zu den Unruhen in München.
Abtransport gefangener Kommunisten.

A series of courses in anti-Bolshevism was initiated for the soldiers. The man in charge was Captain Karl Mayr, head of the Education and Propaganda Department and the first of Adolf Hitler's political patrons. Mayr was a man of influence beyond that merited by his rank. He was allocated considerable funds to establish a team of agents (effectively informants), devise a programme of education whereby officers and men would receive suitable indoctrination, and provide finance for nationalist and anti-Bolshevik political parties, organizations and publications.

Mayr first encountered Hitler in May 1919, in the aftermath of the battle of Munich, when Hitler was serving on the committee investigating the Communist affiliations of his comrades. Perhaps Mayr already knew of Hitler's previous incarnation as a small cog in the Red Republic's propaganda machine, but he seemed an ideal candidate for Mayr's purposes, a *tabula rasa* on which the messages of the Education and Propaganda Department could be transmitted. Years later Mayr wrote of Hitler, 'He was like a tired stray dog looking for a master … ready to throw in his lot with anyone who would show him kindness … He was totally unconcerned about the German people and their destinies.'

Early in June 1919, Hitler was taken on as a *Verbindungsmann* (a V-man or police spy). Within days he was attending his first anti-Bolshevik instruction course at Munich University, listening to lectures on German history, the theory and practice of Socialism, economics and the impact of the Treaty of Versailles, and the linkage between domestic and foreign policy. He soaked it up like a sponge. One lecturer who made an immediate impression on him was Gottfried Feder, a Pan-German nationalist, self-styled economics expert and critic of 'rapacious capital', which he associated with the Jews and contrasted with 'productive capital'. Hitler, who already had an ear for a striking turn of phrase, intuitively grasped that Feder's lecture on breaking 'interest slavery' had enormous propaganda potential. Feder would become an important figure in the early days of the Nazi Party.

Opposite: An early example of the Hitler myth. This membership card was exhibited during the Nazi era, claiming that Hitler was the fifth member of the German Workers' Party (DAP). In reality he was the fifty-fifth, and his membership number was later doctored to 555 so that the party would appear to have more members. Various versions of Hitler's DAP card have surfaced since, featuring numbers as diverse as 5, 555, and 7.

Mayr was impressed by Hitler and selected him as one of twenty-six instructors sent to attend a five-day course at Lechfeld, near Augsburg. The course was a response to complaints that many returned prisoners of war now awaiting discharge had been infected with Socialist ideas. It was the task of the instructors to wean them away from Bolshevism and re-introduce them to the 'correct' nationalist modes of thought. Hitler threw himself into the work. Faced with a crowd of cynical soldiers, he discovered that he could engage the attention of these listless men and sway them with his arguments. These were not the monologues to which he had subjected his friend Kubizek, the endlessly patient audience of one. Now his words had a bigger audience, and a measurable effect. He found a voice as he lectured his charges on the history of the Red Republic, the causes of World War I, and the political lessons to be learned from its aftermath. Later he was able to boast of his success: 'In the course of my lectures I led many hundreds, indeed thousands of comrades back to their people and fatherland. I "nationalised" the troops …'

Reports on the impact of his lectures at Lechfeld were uniformly enthusiastic. They characterized Hitler as a man born to be a public speaker and praised his 'fanaticism' and populist style. They also indicate that, now clearly heavily influenced by Gottfried Feder, at Lechfeld Hitler had ridden the anti-Semitic tide which prevailed at the time. Indeed, the commanding officer at Lechfeld, Oberleutnant Bendt, sought to restrain him in order to prevent charges of anti-Semitic agitation being levelled against the work being undertaken at the camp. Bendt's intervention had been prompted by Hitler's first public reference to the Jews during a lecture on capitalism.

Mayr was not so squeamish and was happy to refer queries on the 'Jewish Question' to Hitler, whom he evidently considered an authority on the subject. A response to a query from one Adolf Gremlich, on the Social Democratic government's position on the Jewish Question, provides us with the first written evidence of Hitler's developing attitude towards the Jews. He wrote that anti-Semitism should be determined by facts and not emotion. He considered that the application of 'reason' would lead to the conclusion that the Jews should be subjected to a systematic removal of their rights before they were removed themselves.

THE GERMAN WORKERS' PARTY

Adolf Hitler was about to enter the political arena. The setting was Munich's Sterneckerbräu, a beer cellar which was later to become a Nazi shrine. On the evening of 12 September 1919, still working as a V-Man, Hitler attended a meeting of the German Workers' Party (Deutsche Arbeiterpartei or DAP), one of over fifty small groupings flourishing in Munich's murky political undergrowth and covering the political spectrum from the extreme Left to the extreme Right. The Army kept all of them under close surveillance.

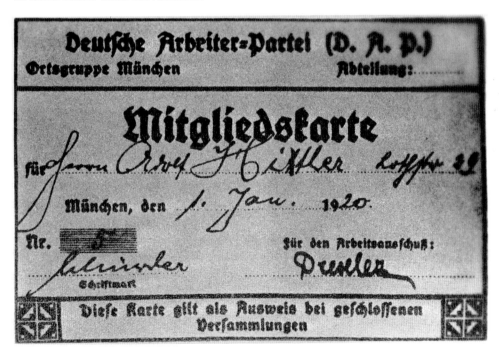

The DAP had been founded in January 1919 by the economics theoretician Gottfried Feder, already familiar to Hitler from his anti-Bolshevik course at Munich University; Anton Drexler, member of a Munich brewing dynasty and a *völkisch* agitator; and the journalist Karl Harrer. Feder, Drexler and Harrer were members of the Thule Society, a German occult group whose pseudo-scientific beliefs coalesced around the notion of the Volk, the repository of mystical nationalism and romantic racism and, in their eyes, a bulwark against the capitalist and consumerist excesses of the modern world. Into this seedy den of racist crackpots and fantasists stepped Adolf Hitler.

Due to speak that night was Dietrich Eckart, another Thule Society man, founding member of the DAP, and an anti-Semitic ideologue. He had developed a theory of the 'genius higher human' based on the writings of Jorg Lanz von Liebenfels, the publisher of the racist magazine *Ostara*, which Hitler read during his days in Vienna. However, Eckart was ill and cried off, to be replaced by Feder who treated the audience to a now familiar theme: interest slavery.

Hitler had heard it all before and spent some time observing the assembled company. They were an unpromising bunch, all forty-one of them, but it was in the smallness and shabbiness of the DAP that Hitler saw his chance. According to his own account, he was already thinking of founding his own political party but here was one already formed, albeit with only a handful of disorganized and down-at-heel adherents, which might nevertheless serve his purposes as a ready-made vehicle which would enable him to flex his nascent powers of oratory.

After Feder's address, comments were invited from the floor. A Professor Baumann, an advocate of Bavarian separatism, launched a fierce attack on Feder. This drew Hitler to his feet to deliver a stinging rebuke. Discomfited, the professor fled the tavern in disarray, prompting an impressed Anton Drexler to thrust a copy of his own pamphlet, *My Political Awakening*, into Hitler's hands.

Drexler was reported to have said of Hitler, 'Goodness, he's got a gob on him. We could use a man like him,' and invited him to another meeting.

Once again, Hitler's account of the aftermath of this second meeting has to be treated with caution. The details were subsequently tweaked to fit the 'Hitler myth'. He claimed that within a week of attending he had received a postcard which accepted him as a member and invited him to a committee meeting to further discuss the matter. In spite of his misgivings, he went along – he had at least been impressed by Drexler's pamphlet. The new venue, a seedy beer cellar in the Herrenstrasse, was singularly unimpressive, as were the four members of the DAP who were present. After a few days of indecision – a trait which Hitler displayed until the end of his days – he decided to throw in his lot with the DAP, an organization which, with a combination of false modesty and shrewd insight, he estimated was small enough to offer an 'opportunity for real personal activity'. In other words, he had decided to swap the Army for the DAP. Unlike the former, the DAP was small enough to provide the vehicle for Hitler's ambitions.

THE FIREBRAND · 41

Nevertheless, Hitler remained in the Army until 31 March 1920, when he was finally discharged, all the while drawing his army pay and with time available to devote to the DAP. Unlike other members of the DAP, who had regular jobs to go to, Hitler could now devote all his energies to his new-found career as a creator and disseminator of propaganda. Without the intervention of Captain Mayr, Hitler would in all probability have remained a face lost in the crowd, the archetypal 'little man' nursing unrealized fantasies of revenge on the world which ignored him. Hitler had not found politics; politics had found him, in the Munich barracks when he denounced his former comrades in the Red Republic and was talent-spotted by Mayr as a public speaker with a mesmerizing ability to connect with the gut instincts and basest prejudices of his audience. Karl Mayr had released Hitler's demon, not yet fully formed but, in hindsight, now recognizable. Indeed, Mayr had ordered Hitler to join the DAP while the latter was still in the Army, an infringement of the ban on soldiers participating in political activity, and had provided him with supplementary funds. Mayr's was an achievement of a baleful kind for which he, along with millions of others, would one day pay the ultimate price. His own political career followed a paradoxical trajectory from the far Right to the Left. He later became a Social Democrat, and when the Nazis came to power in 1933, he fled to France. However, after the outbreak of World War II, he fell into German hands and died in Buchenwald, the concentration camp near Weimar, in February 1945, two months before his protégé met his end amid the ruins of the Third Reich.

NATIONAL SOCIALISM

Initially, Hitler had nothing but contempt for the German Workers' Party. The movement, if such it could be called, lacked headquarters, headed notepaper, finance, inspiring leaders and, above all, membership. Drexler and Harrer, its leading lights, were both dull platform speakers with little or no talent for organization. Then and later, this last ability was a very long way from being Hitler's strongest suit but, in comparison with the DAP's founders, he was at this stage in his career an organizational dynamo.

Drexler and Harrer seemed quite content for the DAP to remain little more than a political discussion club. Hitler thought differently. He harried the leadership into placing newspaper advertisements in the *Münchener Beobachter* for a meeting on 16 October 1919 at the Hofbräukeller, a large drinking establishment east of Munich's city centre. Hitler was not the main speaker, but his speech, lasting some thirty minutes, brought the audience of one hundred and eleven people to its feet and raised three hundred marks for Party funds. Neither Drexler nor Harrer had served in the war, but Hitler, the Western Front veteran, had shrewdly enlivened the atmosphere by persuading some of his old army comrades to attend the meeting.

Buoyed by this initial success, Hitler insisted on bigger and more frequent meetings. Within a few weeks the audience was regularly reaching four hundred. At this point, according to *Mein Kampf*, Hitler insisted that the DAP stage a mass meeting, a demand which led to Karl Harrer's resignation. Once again, Hitler got his own way, and the meeting was set for 24 February 1920. The venue was the Festsaal of the Hofbräuhaus in the centre of Munich, which was often used for large political meetings.

When it was not being used for political meetings, the big hall was packed with beefy male patrons, many of them wearing *lederhosen*, drinking their fill from long tables stacked with stone beer mugs. Dirndl-clad waitresses bustled back and forth bearing foaming tankards of ale to their bellowing customers. The Festsaal provided Hitler with an ideal arena in which to stage political theatre, the designs for which had been forming in the back of his mind since he watched the Socialist 'human dragon' winding through Vienna in the days before World War I. The atmosphere was not notably different during political meetings, and the beer flowed just as freely. There were frequent interruptions from the floor, and brawling regularly erupted between rival claques. This was politics in the raw, and meat and drink to Adolf Hitler. He was not in the least worried about disruption – he had been present at a mass meeting on 7 January 1920, attended by some seven thousand people, which had descended into a giant brawl. He was more concerned that on 24 February only a handful would turn up.

His concerns proved groundless. He had prepared the ground carefully. Dramatic red posters and leaflets advertising the meeting had been distributed. The party's twenty-five-point programme, devised by Hitler and Drexler in the preceding weeks, was also printed and readied for distribution at the meeting. Significantly, however, there was no mention of Hitler in the advance publicity. On the night of 24 February, some two thousand people turned up, 20 per cent of them Socialist opponents spoiling for a scrap, to hear Dr Johannes Dingfelder, a well-known figure in Munich's *völkisch* circles, deliver the main speech. It was, considering the occasion, unexceptionable. Dingfelder made no mention of the Jews and preferred to place the blame for Germany's plight on the decline of religious faith and the rise of materialism. His answer? 'Order, work and dutiful sacrifice for the salvation of the Fatherland.'

The mood changed when Hitler stepped forward to address the hall. He spoke in short, punchy sentences, robustly phrased, with which his audience readily identified – they spoke like this every day of their lives, although with infinitely less fluency. Hitler laid into the November criminals and men like Isidor Bach, one of Munich's prominent Jewish capitalists, whom he attacked in tones both homely and deeply sinister: 'When it is necessary to take a bowl of eggs away from a little hamster, the government shows an astonishing energy. But it will not use it if the hamster's name is Isidor Bach.'

Explosions of frantic cheering greeted every slighting remark about Jews, and when Hitler turned his guns on war profiteers there were cries of 'Flog them! Hang them!' When he began to spell out the Party's twenty-five-point programme, applause greeted every one of them. The first point demanded the union of all Germans into a Greater Germany. Many Germans were now citizens of Austria, Czechoslovakia and Poland. To bring them back into Germany could only be achieved by force, and this, in all probability, would mean war. Thirteen of the points were aimed against the Jews, including the assertion that 'No Jew can be a citizen'. Jews were not to be allowed to hold public office or to publish newspapers. Those who had come to Germany after 1918 would be expelled.

There was spirited heckling from the Socialists in the audience, and the meeting constantly threatened to erupt into fisticuffs, but Hitler stuck to the last. At the climax of his speech he rebuked the government for providing food relief for Munich's Jewish community, a sally which produced a storm of catcalls. Many of the audience were prompted to leap on to tables and chairs and hurl insults at each other as Hitler moved towards the end of his speech with words which would become familiar over the years: 'Our motto is only struggle. We will go our way unshakeably to our goal.'

Hitler's words closing the meeting were drowned out by the uproar in the hall. Socialists and Communists spilled out into the streets bawling the International, raising three cheers for the Red Republic and hurling insults at the German war leaders Hindenburg and Ludendorff and at German nationalists. Hitler later wrote, mendaciously, of a 'hall full of people united by a new conviction, a new faith, a new will'. Nevertheless, the meeting had created controversy and had thus served its purpose very well. The fact that henceforth Nazi Party meetings were most decidedly not peaceful was a signal advantage which vividly set the DAP apart from its dull, bourgeois *völkisch* rivals. The opponents who packed DAP meetings before they began were themselves part of the spectacle. To deal with disruption, a 'hall protection' (*Saalschutz*) squad was formed – the seed from which the SA (*Sturmabteilung*) grew.

Dynamic design was also a vital ingredient in a mix which emphasized organisation, advance publicity, striking posters, and banners. The last was designed personally by Hitler and featured a black swastika (*Hakenkreuz*)[6] on a white circle, framed by a red square. The makeover was completed by a new name: the DAP became the National Socialist German Workers' Party (NSDAP) – the Nazi Party.

In Munich at least, the Nazis were now on the map, and Adolf Hitler had put them there. Only Hitler, a man who seemingly had sprung from nowhere, appeared able to generate this excitement. Word raced around Munich that anyone attending a meeting addressed by Hitler was guaranteed a lively time.

One young man who saw Hitler speaking early in 1920, and was captivated by him, was Hans Frank, a World War I veteran and an early member of the NSDAP who, in World War II, became governor-general of the German-occupied territories in Poland. Awaiting execution for war crimes at Nuremberg in 1946, he recalled the first time he saw Hitler:

---

6 The swastika is an ancient symbol dating from the Neolithic period and often carrying religious connotations. It is significant in the iconography of Eastern religions, among them Hinduism, Buddhism and Jainism. It occurs in many cultures of many different periods, including that of the North American Indians.

I was strongly impressed straight away. It was totally different from what was otherwise to be heard in meetings. His method was completely clear and simple. He took the overwhelmingly dominant topic of the day, the Versailles Diktat, and he posed all these questions: What now, German people? What's the true situation? What alone is now possible? He spoke for over two and a half hours, often interrupted by frenetic torrents of applause – and one could have listened to him for much longer. Everything came from the heart, and he struck a chord with all of us …

How did Hitler do it? The building blocks of his speeches were, in the main, commonplaces peddled by all the parties of Munich's nationalist Right: Germany laid low by the Allies, stabbed in the back, crippled by ruinous reparations and betrayed at home by corrupt politicians; the sinister figure of the Jew lurking behind all Germany's ills, and the expulsion of all Jews from the country; the invocation of social harmony through national unity and the restoration of national greatness; the safeguarding of the archetypal 'little man' from the depredations of international financiers. Hitler's list of enemies and his prescriptions for the future were, in themselves, unexceptional in the climate of the time. Where he differed was in the methods by which he ensured that his message got across, and the originality of his technique as an orator.

He spoke from rough notes, and at length, for two hours or more. In the Festsaal he cleverly addressed the audience from a beer table positioned on one of the side of the hall, thus placing himself in the middle of the crowd, the easier to gauge and orchestrate its mood. He quickly learned how to deal with shouted interruptions, foot-stamping, mocking laughter or even stony silence. He learned how to grab the attention of the audience, to read its collective mind – and individual minds – and to strike to the quick the listeners hanging on his every word.

Hitler's formula was simple and cynical: 'The receptive powers of the masses are very restricted and their understanding is feeble. On the other hand, they quickly forget. All effective propaganda must be confined to a few bare necessities and then expressed in a few simple phrases. Only by constantly repeating will you finally succeed in imprinting an idea on to the memory of the crowd … When you lie, tell big lies. This is what the Jews do. The big, cheeky lie always leaves traces behind it.'

Hitler's choice of words matched his method. His oratorical vocabulary was simple, direct and violent. It featured heavily what would now be called buzz words – 'smash', 'hatred', 'evil', 'power' – which pressed all the right buttons with his audience. It is also as well to note the topics which, at this stage in his career, he did not mention or to which he referred only infrequently. In only one speech did he call for the establishment of a dictatorship in Germany, but he did not single himself out for this role. Nor did he introduce what was later to become a crucial element in his philosophy, the notion of *Lebensraum* (living space) in Eastern Europe, which would be colonized by German settlers after the expulsion and elimination of their Slavic populations. For the moment, Britain and France remained the principal targets of his ire and, in August 1920, he admitted that he was no expert on Russia. Nevertheless, he was fast catching up, influenced by Alfred Rosenberg. An early recruit to the Party, Rosenberg was of ethnic German descent but had been born in Russia, and he had seen the Russian Revolution at first hand.

Crowd control was also an essential element in Hitler's method. The 'hall protection squad' was the first answer, burly ex-servicemen posted around the hall to silence troublesome hecklers. These roughnecks were later organized into strong-arm squads under the euphemistic name of the Gymnastic and Sports Division. In August 1921 the formation was strengthened by the addition of former members of the naval brigade led by Captain Hermann Ehrhardt, a seasoned campaigner in paramilitary activity and one of the leaders of the Kapp Putsch. In September 1921, the thugs from the Gymnastic and Sports Division played a prominent part in disrupting a meeting of the separatist Bayerbund, addressed by its leader Otto Ballerstedt. Ballerstedt brought charges against Hitler, and in January 1922 he was sentenced to three months' imprisonment, with two months suspended against future good behaviour. Hitler served his month-long imprisonment in Munich's Stadelheim prison between 24 June and 27 July 1922. After his release, he remained unrepentant. Savage clashes with opponents were the lifeblood of the Nazi Party and fed its hungry publicity machine.

By the summer of 1922, the ad hoc squads had been reorganized into the *Sturmabteilung* (stormtroops), a formation whose name was swiftly abbreviated to the SA. They were supplied with brown uniforms, jackboots and swastika armbands. The Brownshirts, as they became known, quickly acquired an ugly reputation. Not content with merely maintaining order at Party meetings, they moved on to breaking up those of their opponents. Nevertheless, they represented only one small element in the bear-pit of Munich politics, in which they were, for the moment, dwarfed by other private armies.

In August 1922, the SA numbered some eight hundred men. They made their

KAPP PUTSCH

In 1919 there were an estimated two hundred and fifty thousand men in Germany's Freikorps, bands of armed veterans of World War I. In March 1920, under the troop reductions required by the Treaty of Versailles, orders were issued for the disbandment of *Freikorps* units, one of which was the *Marinebrigade Erhardt*. The President of the Weimar Republic turned down an appeal from General von Luttwitz, commander of the Berlin Reichswehr, to resist the programme of troop reductions. Luttwitz then ordered the *Marinebrigade* to march on Berlin and occupy it under the nominal leadership of an East Prussian civil servant and extreme nationalist, Wolfgang Kapp. When the Reichswehr refused to intervene, the Weimar government was forced to flee to Dresden and then Stuttgart, where it issued a call to Germany's workers to resist the putsch with a general strike. The strike paralysed Germany, the putsch collapsed when other *Freikorps* leaders declined to support it, and Kapp and Luttwitz fled to Sweden.

first appearance as a paramilitary organization at a huge nationalist rally in Munich for the United Patriotic Associations of Bavaria, whose slogan proclaimed, with regionalist fervour, 'For Germany – against Berlin'. But, however menacing they might have seemed, the SA was dwarfed by the thirty thousand armed men of the Bund Bayern und Reich, a coalition of a number of right-wing factions which combined strong monarchist and Christian principles with anti-Semitism and hatred of Bolshevism. The Bund's watchword had a familiar ring: 'First the Home-land, then the World!'

The United Patriotic Associations of Bavaria soon collapsed in a welter of factional fighting. Hitler and the SA endured.

—∿—

The SA made its name in mid-October 1922 when it followed Hitler to Coburg, in Upper Franconia, to participate in the so-called German Day (*Deutscher Tag*). This was new territory for the Nazis, whose power base remained in Munich. Hitler had been asked to attend with a small delegation but, with his usual flair for a propaganda coup, arrived accompanied by his eight hundred stormtroopers. The police had issued orders banning a march, which Hitler pointedly ignored. The SA marched from the railway station into the town, banners unfurled and swastikas held high. Along the route, they clashed with workers and supporters of the Socialists, who lined the streets abusing them. The SA responded with clubs and rubber truncheons, and a pitched battle ensued. One of Hitler's men was Kurt Ludecke, a playboy 'man of the world' and recent recruit to the *Sturmabteilung*, who was at Hitler's side on the march into Coburg:

> The gates were opened against the protests of the now thoroughly alarmed police, and we faced the menacing thousands. With no music but only drums beating, we marched in the direction of the Schuetzenhalle. We who were in the forefront with Hitler were exposed to the very real danger for cobblestones were fairly raining upon us. Sometimes, a man's muscles do his thinking. I sprang from the ranks towards a fellow who was lunging at me with his club uplifted. From behind me, my good Ludwig followed. But at the same moment our entire column had turned on our assailants.

The police initially held back, but now they pitched into the fray on the side of the SA. Ludecke recalled, 'But soon, probably because they shared our dislike of the street rabble, most of them took our side, and before long we were masters of the field.' After a vicious battle lasting some ten minutes, the SA claimed the streets of Coburg and won another propaganda victory for Hitler. The NSDAP had left its mark; Coburg became a Nazi 'battle honour', and a special medal was struck for those who had taken part in the affray.

THE LEADER

Long before the SA began to crack heads in Coburg, Hitler was heading on a collision course with the leadership of the NSDAP. He was fast becoming central to the Party's success but his increasing eminence was not universally popular. Several of the Party's committee, including Gottfried Feder, were dismayed by what they considered to be his crude propaganda methods. The personal traits which were to characterize Hitler's later political career were becoming evident to his colleagues. He was tetchily sensitive to any criticism, by turns impatient, irrational and hesitant, sometimes endlessly delaying decisions, at others charging into them precipitately. He was also violently opposed to plans hatched by Drexler to merge the NSDAP with another far-right party, the German Socialist Party (DSP).

Hitler's truculent, unpredictable behaviour indicates that in 1921 he had not developed a rational, long-term plan to take control of the NSDAP. He had not anticipated a power struggle but nevertheless found himself in one, and prevailed by using all-or-nothing tactics – a desperate gamble which succeeded in unnerving his indecisive enemies, who failed to present a united front. It was a pattern he would repeat over the years and which, ultimately, proved the ruin of the Third Reich.

When the crisis broke, Hitler was in Berlin, raising funds. The malcontents in the NSDAP had been casting around for a counterbalance to their troublesome pre-eminence, someone to clip his wings, and lit upon Dr Otto Dickel. Dickel headed another recently formed *völkisch* organization, the *Deutsche Werkgemeinschaft*, who had recently scored a publishing success with *The Resurrection of the Western World*. Dickel's windy *völkisch* philosophizing was not to Hitler's taste, but his violent anti-Semitism and plans to build a classless community through national renewal dovetailed with Hitler's ideas. And, like Hitler, Dickel was a fiery orator. While Hitler was in Berlin, Dickel gave a well-received speech in one of Hitler's stamping grounds, the Festsaal of the Hofbräuhaus. More speeches were planned. Dickel seemed to be the answer to the prayers of those who were unhappy with the prima donna Hitler. Above all, he was controllable.

Hitler returned from Berlin to discover that talks about a new merger, this time with Dickel's party, were imminent. Like a spoilt child, he responded with a tantrum followed by moody sulking. And, like a child, he had failed to get his own way. On 11 July, he resigned from the Party. Now, it seemed, Hitler was back where he began. He would have to establish his own party. Then Drexler blinked. He realized, belatedly, that the loss of Hitler might prove catastrophic. Perhaps, after all, Dickel was not the man to replace him. Within days Hitler was asked to rejoin the Party. Hitler seized his chance. He would rejoin, but only on his own terms: he would assume the post of party chairman with dictatorial power;[7] the party headquarters must be in Munich;

---

7 On several occasions Drexler had offered Hitler the Party chairmanship but had been turned down. In the spring of 1921, Drexler had written to Feder:' ... each revolutionary movement must have a dictatorial head, and therefore I also think our Hitler is the most suitable for our movement, without wanting to be pushed into the background myself.' Hitler, however, recognized his own limitations as an organizer and administrator, tasks he would later leave to others.

the twenty-five-point programme was inviolate; and there would be no more attempts to merge with other parties. Within twenty-four hours the Party committee had caved in and acceded to Hitler's demands. On 26 July, six days after a triumphant rabble-rousing appearance before a packed house at the Circus Krone, he was welcomed back as Party member number 3680. Game set and match to Adolf Hitler.

There was another outburst of snapping and snarling before the dust settled, the last death twitch of Hitler's opponents in the NSDAP. Placards denouncing him were prepared and an anonymous pamphlet appeared attacking him as the agent of sinister forces. He brushed his opponents aside and, in an extraordinary meeting at the Festsaal, so recently the scene of Dickel's transient triumph, members voted five hundred and fifty-three to one to accept the new dictatorial powers sought by their leader. A constitution, hurriedly drafted by Hitler, confirmed his supremacy not once but three times. The Nazi Party was about to undergo a transformation. It was to become a 'Führer party', in which the Führer's word was law, subject to rubber stamp approval by the membership.

THE COURTIERS

In less than two years Adolf Hitler had travelled from being an anonymous police spy to assuming the leadership of the NSDAP. During these early years, he began to gather round him a circle of intimates, many of whom would, from 1933, occupy positions of untrammelled power in Germany, and later in Occupied Europe.

An important figure in these years was Captain Ernst Röhm, a scarred veteran of the 'front generation', who rapidly replaced Karl Mayr as Hitler's link with the German Army, the Reichswehr. Early in 1920, at a time when Hitler himself was still in the Army, Mayr had taken him to meetings of the Iron Fist club, an association of radical nationalist serving officers which had been formed by Röhm in defiance of the rule that the Reichswehr should remain apolitical. In all probability, Hitler had already been introduced to Röhm by Mayr in the autumn of 1919. Röhm had joined the DAP in October 1919, shortly after the meeting at which Hitler had first found his political voice.

In the winter of 1919, however, Röhm was more interested in the Citizens' Defence Force (*Einwohnerwehr*) than in the tiny DAP. This heavily armed paramilitary organization, numbering some four hundred thousand men, had been formed after the crushing of the Red Republic and presented the traditional face of Bavarian reaction. Röhm, nevertheless, kept a finger in the pie of any number of *völkisch* movements in Bavaria and, from 1921, became a significant figure in the NSDAP and the development of the *Sturmabteilung*. By 1923, the SA was some fifteen thousand strong and, thanks to the 'machine-gun king' Röhm, was armed to the teeth. Röhm was a man with sensitive political antennae but, like his associate Hermann Ehrhardt, was nevertheless wedded to the application of exclusively paramilitary answers to political questions. For Hitler, however, the wholesale integration of the SA into the political framework of the NSDAP was a problem which was to become increasingly troublesome as the years went by. The resolution, when it came, was bloody. Ernst Röhm, who had always lived by the sword, was to die by the sword in 1934 in the Night of the Long Knives.

Another significant early figure in Hitler's rise to prominence in the politics of Bavaria was Dietrich Eckart, an alcoholic who was to die in 1923. If the brutal, homosexual Röhm provided the brawn of the NSDAP, then Eckart was the brain. Twenty years older than Hitler, he was an unsuccessful poet and critic who had entered politics in December 1918 with the publication of a violently anti-semitic weekly magazine, *In Plain German* (*Auf gut deutsch*), whose regular contributors included Gottfried Feder and Alfred Rosenberg. Eckart had spoken at DAP meetings before Hitler had joined and later took the new recruit under his wing. He helped Hitler to widen his reading, gave him a little social polish and introduced him to significant financial backers. One of them was the Augsburg industrialist Dr Gottfried Grandel, who had funded *In Plain German* and also acted as guarantor for the funds that the NSDAP used to purchase the bankrupt newspaper the *Völkischer Beobachter* (*People's Observer*) in December 1920. Its first publisher was Dietrich Eckart.

Above: (left to right) Alfred Rosenberg, Hitler and Friedrich Weber, head of the *Bund Oberland*, during a parade of the SA and other paramilitaries marking the laying of the war memorial foundation stone in Munich, 4 November 1923.

One of Hitler's earliest and most slavish disciples was Rudolf Hess. Born in Egypt, the son of a successful wholesaler and exporter, Hess did not live in Germany until he was fourteen. He served in the List Regiment during World War I but had not met Hitler. After the war he joined the *Freikorps*, and while studying at Munich University came under the influence of the Thule Society and Professor Karl Haushofer, a former soldier. Haushofer's geopolitical theories of race and expansionism would play a part in the concept of *Lebensraum*, one of the last major elements in Hitler's *Weltanschauung* (world view). Hess joined the NSDAP on 1 July 1920, and after meeting Hitler, felt that he had been 'overcome by a vision'.

Among the earliest members of the NSDAP, Hermann Göring had the highest public profile. A World War I air ace with twenty-two victories under his belt, the fleshily handsome, flamboyant Göring had commanded JG1, the legendary Richthofen squadron, during the closing months of the conflict. In 1920 he married a wealthy Swedish countess, settled in Munich, and in 1921 had joined the NSDAP, making his aristocratic connections and wife's fortune available to the Party. In 1923 Göring was appointed head of the *Sturmabteilung.*

Undoubtedly one of the most unpleasant members of this unappealing bunch was Julius Streicher, a bald, burly bully and lecher, who thrashed his enemies with a rhino-hide whip. Another war hero – he was also awarded the Iron Cross (First Class) – Streicher was a virulent anti-Semite who, after the war, was one of the founding members of the German Socialist Party, or DSP (*Deutschsozialistische Partei*), whose basic philosophy differed little from Nazism. In 1923 Streicher established his own newspaper, *Der Stürmer* (*The Attacker*), which dripped with obscene caricatures of hook-nosed, bearded Jews ravishing innocent Aryan maidens and achieved the rare distinction of being banned in the Hitler Youth, and in all the departments of the Third Reich run by Hermann Göring. Vile though he was, Streicher proved an invaluable ally to Hitler in the development of the NSDAP in Protestant Franconia, in northern Bavaria, which was to provide the Nazi Party with a symbolic capital in the city of Nuremberg.

—⁓—

Although Hitler had now become a familiar player on Munich's political scene, his personal habits had in many ways changed little since his time in pre-war Vienna. The most significant difference was that he now had an audience hanging on his every word as he lounged around in his favourite haunts, among which was the Café Heck in Galerienstrasse, a popular watering hole of Munich's bourgeoisie, where Hitler would hold court for long hours. Among his inner circle were Max Erwin von Scheubner Richter, an engineer who had excellent contacts among Russian émigrés, Alfred Rosenberg and, from late 1922, Ernst 'Putzi' Hanfstaengl,[8] a tall, cultured half-American and a graduate of Harvard, who became Hitler's foreign press chief.

---

8 Hanfstaengl left Hitler's staff in 1933, fell out with the Führer, and was denounced by the British Fascist Unity Mitford. In 1937 he fled to Switzerland and then to England. In World War II he was interned by the British as an enemy alien but later became an intelligence asset for the Americans, compiling an exhaustive psychological dossier on Hitler for the Office of Strategic Services (OSS). He died in 1975.

Hanfstaengl, who came from a family of art dealers, was fascinated by Hitler, this awkward little man in a shabby blue suit, who was a mixture of NCO and railway clerk but nevertheless possessed the gift of swaying the masses. Hanfstaengl's fascination, however, was tempered by a snobbish attitude towards Hitler's clumsiness in clever and sophisticated company – he was awkward with a knife and fork, sprinkled sugar into vintage wines, knew little about art, about which Putzi knew a great deal, and frequently resorted to blustering monologues or long periods of brooding silence to cover his ignorance. In a small group, or one-to-one, Hitler often appeared an unimpressive, even sometimes ludicrous, figure. The fastidious Hanfstaengl could nevertheless overlook these social shortcomings because he considered Hitler 'a virtuoso on the keyboard of the human psyche'. Riding the irresistible emotional surge of a mass meeting, Hitler had no equal.

Just as Röhm ensured that Hitler enjoyed contacts at the highest level with representatives of the Reichswehr in Munich, so Hanfstaengl introduced him to the upper echelons of Munich society, whose dominant females vied with each other to present their newly found acquaintance with gifts of bulky dog whips and hefty donations to NSDAP funds. In this milieu Hitler cut a curious figure, prompting one *Freikorps* leader of the time, General Rossbach, to observe, with some accuracy, that he was 'a man mistrustful towards himself and what he was capable of, and so full of inferiority complex towards all who were anything or were on their way to outflank him …. He was never a gentleman, even later in evening dress.'

There were many in Hitler's inner circle who were also not gentlemen and who were happy to sit at his feet every Monday evening at the Café Neumaier. The company here was a world away from the decorous salons of upper-class Munich. Nazi philosophers like the anti-Semite Dietrich Eckart were joined by other more rough-hewn Party members: Christian Weber, a former bouncer and horse-dealer who, like Hitler, habitually affected a dog whip; Max Amann, Hitler's sergeant in the List Regiment; and Ulrich Graef, a butcher and amateur wrestler who was Hitler's personal bodyguard. At the end of the evening this band of cronies – the so-called '*chauffeureska*' – would act as bodyguard to their leader, theatrically dressed in a black trilby and long black overcoat, and escort him back to his modest lodgings in Munich's Thierschstrasse.

A NEW CRISIS

Between 1919 and 1923 Hitler's audiences grew steadily in size. In 1932 he recalled, 'I cast my eyes back to the time when with six other unknown men I founded [the Nazi Party], when I spoke before eleven, twelve, thirteen, fourteen, twenty, thirty, fifty persons. When I recall how after a year I had won sixty-four members of the movement, I must confess that that which has today been created, when a stream of millions is flowing into our movement, represents something unique in German history'.

By 1923, the stream of millions had not yet begun to flow. Hitler's followers were still numbered in thousands, but the events of that year provided a pretext for him to launch a military putsch in Munich. It ended in disaster, but its dramatic failure thrust Hitler for the first time on to the national stage.

The French had precipitated a crisis at the beginning of the year. In January 1923, in order to force the German government to sustain reparations payments which it had insisted it could not meet, the French government sent troops to occupy the Ruhr, Germany's industrial heartland, and extract payment at source. The French needed the income from reparations to balance their own budget and pay their debts to the United States, and imagined that the seizure of the factories and mines of the Ruhr would both solve the problem and exact the revenge denied by the German surrender in 1918.

The Ruhr was paralyzed, and the effect on the entire German economy was disastrous. The German mark collapsed and hyperinflation set in. In December 1922 the exchange rate stood at eight thousand marks to the US dollar. Ten months later it had soared to four million, two hundred thousand marks to the dollar. Money became worthless and barter took over as the normal method of trading. Workers were paid daily and spent the money as soon as they received it, lest its value plummet further. The government needed to print more and more money; eventually it had three hundred paper mills and two thousand printing plants working twenty-four-hour shifts to meet the demand.

Gustav Stresemann, who had become Germany's chancellor in August 1923, initially called for a campaign of passive resistance in the Ruhr. This did nothing to deter the French, but set an example of illegality which encouraged Communists in Saxony and Hamburg, separatists in the Rhineland, and former *Freikorps* men in Pomerania and Prussia, to threaten civil disobedience. In this situation most people were losers. In a matter of days a lifetime's savings could become valueless.

'Our misery will increase. The scoundrel will get by. The reason: because the state itself has become the biggest swindler and crook. A robber's state!'

Thus declared Adolf Hitler, to whom those hit hardest by the crisis – the German workers and middle classes – offered a fertile recruiting ground. A plan began to form in his mind, based not on a German but on an Italian example. The *Freikorps* phenomenon had not been confined to Germany. After 1918 the world was awash with weapons and with rootless men inured to violence. There was no shortage of freebooting officers eager to lead them on death or glory missions. Italy, with little to show for its six hundred thousand war dead, was an arena in which such desperate men flourished.

After the war there was an economic crisis which the traditional Italian parties, religious and political, were wholly incapable of solving. The only leader to promise salvation was Benito Mussolini, a former Socialist and founder, in 1919, of the Fascist Party (*Fascio di Combattimento*), the so-called Blackshirts (*Squadristi*). Like the *Freikorps*, the *Squadristi* were used by the government as strike breakers and as a stick with which to beat Socialists. Mussolini was the archetypal *Freikorps* type, a man of action who advocated military-style solutions to the country's difficulties. As with the *Freikorps*, the Fascist Party's activists were drawn from ex-servicemen, among whom the most effective were former *arditi* (stormtroops). Mussolini promised to establish strong government and restore national pride. Communism was identified as the principal threat, while Fascism offered the prospect of dynamic action and leadership in contrast to the inertia of the established parliamentary parties.

Mussolini's 'March on Rome' began on 27 October 1922. The Fascist leader was careful to be photographed striding out with his Blackshirts but did not walk all the way. He had made his aim clear in a speech delivered in Naples on 24 October: 'Our programme is simple. We want to rule Italy.' The Italian prime minister, Luigi Facta, fondly believed that Mussolini could be accommodated and, having been muzzled, given a role in government. But Mussolini now enjoyed the support not only of the Italian military, but also the business class, the political Right and King Victor Emmanuel III. Victor Emmanuel, assured by Mussolini that he would keep his throne, refused to sign an order declaring Rome to be in state of siege and, on 29 October, power was transferred to Mussolini, who became prime minister, within the framework of the Italian constitution.

The next day the new prime minister arrived in Rome, resplendent in a black shirt, black trousers and a black bowler hat. The March on Rome was never the heroic seizure of power later celebrated by Fascists. The Italian Army could have easily crushed the twenty thousand sodden, bedraggled marchers had it chosen to do so: the transition had been made possible by the surrender of public authorities in the face of Fascist intimidation. By the summer of 1924, Mussolini had become the dictator of Italy.

The March on Rome made a deep impression on the NSDAP. Mussolini was the kind of hero needed in Germany, striding to the rescue of the nation at the head of his own private army. At the beginning of November 1922, at a packed meeting at the Festsaal in the Hofbräuhaus, Hermann Esser, editor of the *Völkischer Beobachter*, declared, 'Germany's Mussolini is Adolf Hitler!' Just as the March on Rome launched Mussolini as Il Duce, the leader of Italy, so Hitler's followers were now to subscribe to the Führer cult which sprang up around their own leader.

In the Weimar Republic, tottering from one crisis to the next in a bullies' playground of warring private armies, the cult of a strong leader guiding his followers and the nation to salvation – a long German tradition – exercised an inexorable grip on the imagination of parties of the nationalist Right. After Mussolini's triumph, however bathetic, Hitler's role in the NSDAP was cast in a different light. In December 1922 the *Völkischer Beobachter* suggested that he was a special kind of leader, that indeed, like Mussolini, he was the leader for whom Germany was waiting. Rank and file Nazis had long thought this, and Hitler had done little to discourage them. But he had also done little actively to foster a personality cult around himself. In 1922 he disingenuously told the Hamburg neo-conservative intellectual

Arthur Moeller van den Bruck, 'I am nothing but a drummer and a rallier.'

Now a gradual process of change began. By the beginning of May 1923, in a speech lambasting the parliamentary system, Hitler invoked the image of two of Germany's greatest titans of the past, Frederick the Great and Bismarck. He affirmed that Germany could be saved only by a 'dictatorship of the national will and national determination'. But the task of the nation was to 'create the sword that this person will need when he is here. Our task is to give the dictator, when he comes, a people ready for him!'

MILITARY MANOEUVRES

The May meeting at which Hitler urged his audience to forge a sword for the future dictator of Germany came after six months of frantic political activity in Munich where, from December 1922, rumours were rife that a putsch was being planned by the NSDAP. When the French marched into the Ruhr in January 1923, Hitler turned his guns on the November criminals in a mass meeting at the Circus Krone. For him, the real enemy was within. It was a familiar roll call. Parliamentary democracy, Marxism, internationalism and the Jews had caused Germany to be held to ransom by the French. He expressly ordered Party members not to offer active resistance to the occupation.

At the end of the month the jittery Bavarian government declared a state of emergency in an attempt to prevent the NSDAP from holding its first 'Reich Rally'. Röhm saved the day, persuading the German Army to come out in support of Hitler, who assured the local commander, General Otto Hermann von Lossow, that the rally would be peaceful. The police and the government president of Upper Bavaria, Gustav Ritter von Kahr, were also brought on board, and Hitler was allowed to address twelve mass meetings on the same evening. In addition, he attended the dedication of SA standards at Munich's Marsfeld in the company of six thousand uniformed stormtroopers. It was a great propaganda triumph, which saw Hitler's first use of the Fascist outstretched-arm salute, borrowed from the Italian Fascists who had themselves filched it from the Romans.

A month later Ernst Röhm, the man who in January had enabled Hitler to defy the Bavarian government, cut across his leader's bows by establishing the Working Union of Patriotic Fighting Associations (*Arbeitsgemeinschaft der Vaterländischen Kampfverbände*). The Union combined the SA with a number of private armies of the nationalist Right as a force potentially to be used not against the French but against the government in Berlin. Hitler was furious at losing direct control of the SA, but Röhm had seen to it that he was now in the political fast lane, charged with drafting a statement of the Working Union's political aims and meeting, thanks again to Röhm's string-pulling, the commander-in-chief of the Reichswehr, Colonel-General Hans von Seeckt. Hitler, however, failed to impress the Colonel-General. The disdainful Seeckt nevertheless did his job well; by the time he was dismissed for harbouring monarchist sympathies in 1926, he had laid the foundations for the rapid expansion of the Reichswehr in the 1930s.

At the end of February, Hitler was brought into contact with his wartime com-
mander-in-chief, General Ludendorff, who had returned to Munich from exile in
Sweden early in 1919 and thrown his hat into the seething ring of Munich's politics.
Ludendorff urged the use of paramilitary formations in a strike against the French.
Hitler had already agreed to the military training of the SA by the Reichswehr in
January, and the stormtroops handed over their weapons to the army in anticipation
of a scrap with the French. Much of this manoeuvring was not to Hitler's liking, but
thanks to Röhm he had now been admitted to the political top table in Munich.

—m—

The price Hitler paid for these developments threatened to be a heavy one. He was
losing control of the very elements he needed to force the pace of political developments in Bavaria. He was being elbowed out of the action by more powerful figures whose agendas differed from his own. At the beginning of May, he was forced
into another confrontation with the government of Bavaria. On May Day, the
Socialists were to march through Munich, a demonstration for which they had
obtained police permission. In the feverish atmosphere of the time the nationalist
Right, for whom 1 May marked the anniversary of the downfall of the hated Red
Republic, saw this as an outright provocation. Violence was in the air; already, on 26
April, shots had been exchanged between armed Communists and members of the
NSDAP in which several of the combatants had been wounded. The armies of both
Right and Left were spoiling for a fight.

They were to be denied. First, the police withdrew permission for the Communists' march, restricting them to a limited demonstration in the centre of
Munich. Then the right-wing paramilitary groups' demand that the Reichswehr
return their weapons was denied. This time the jellied nerve of the state authorities
had remained firm. The paramilitary groups were given a sop – permission to gather
in a northern suburb of Munich near the barracks, but well away from the Communist demonstration. It was a low-key affair, attended by some two thousand men,
about half of them from the NSDAP, and ringed by a cordon of police. There was
some half-hearted drilling, with weapons supplied by the 'machine-gun king', but
this was no substitute for the anticipated pitched battle with the forces of the Left.

At a meeting that night in the Circus Krone, Hitler tried to make the best of a
bad job, railing against the Jews, whom he called a 'racial tuberculosis'. The police
observer reporting the meeting wrote of a 'pogrom mood'. As the summer wore on,
however, Hitler became acutely aware that the NSDAP, and more importantly the SA,
could not be kept on the leash indefinitely. Moreover, he was being outflanked by
the war hero Ludendorff, who since his return to Munich was rapidly becoming the
focal figure in Germany's 'national struggle'. It was Ludendorff who, at the beginning
of September, was the star attraction of the German Day held at Nuremberg and
attended by a crowd of over a hundred thousand. Scheduled to coincide with the
anniversary of the humbling of the French at Sedan in the Franco-Prussian War
(1870–71), it was a gathering of the nationalist Right which enabled Hitler to recover
much of the prestige he had lost after the May Day fiasco. He had a seat on the

saluting base for the climactic paramilitary march past, alongside Ludendorff and Prince Ludwig Ferdinand of Bavaria, and was judged to have given by far the best speech.

Reward of a kind came three weeks later when Hitler was given the 'political leadership' of the German Combat League (*Deutscher Kampfbund*) which amalgamated the paramilitary groupings, including the NSDAP, under the military leadership of Lieutenant-Colonel Hermann Kriebel, who had formerly headed the Union of Patriotic Fighting Associations. Once again, this realignment of the forces of the Right in another umbrella organization had been engineered by Röhm, who also ensured that the Bund's business manager was one of Hitler's cronies, Max Erwin von Scheubner-Richter. Again, this left Hitler in a no-man's-land, stranded between the military professionals – Röhm and Ludendorff – and the political activists. Röhm considered Hitler one of the latter, a born rabble-rouser but not the man to plan and lead a coup. Hitler, on the other hand, was determined to subordinate the role of the paramilitaries to the building of a revolutionary mass movement through the NSDAP. There was no effective meeting of minds on this thorny problem, but one thing on which Hitler, Röhm and Scheubner-Richter did agree was that any attempt to mount a coup in Bavaria in the teeth of opposition from the police and the military was doomed to failure.

THE BEER-HALL PUTSCH

On 26 September 1923 the government in Berlin called off the strike in the Ruhr and pledged to resume reparations payments. This threatened to take the wind out of the sails of the Communists and the nationalist Right. The longer the crisis lasted, the greater became the possibility of civil war from which those on each side of the political divide anticipated they would emerge victorious.

The Communist threat in Hamburg, Saxony and the Ruhr was swiftly snuffed out by the Army. It was all over by the end of October. The threat from the Left had been eliminated at the first whiff of grapeshot. The menace from the Right sprang from Bavaria, where extreme nationalists were using the 'Red threat' as an excuse to march on Berlin. Bavaria's immediate response to the ending of passive resistance was to proclaim a state of emergency which granted Gustav Ritter von Kahr, a monarchist of the old school, dictatorial powers as General State Commissar. One of his first acts was to ban a series of meetings to be held by the NSDAP. Kahr was to rule Bavaria at the head of a triumvirate whose other members were the state police chief, Colonel Hans Ritter von Seisser, and the local Reichswehr commander, General Otto Hermann von Lossow.

The triumvirate had its own agenda: envisaging a German version of Mussolini's March on Rome, they were aiming at the installation of a nationalist dictatorship in Berlin with the support of the Reichswehr. Hitler, Ludendorff, and the *Kampfbund* were excluded from the plan. In the fevered atmosphere of the time, the triumvirate was queasily aware that it could be outmanoeuvred by Hitler – if he made his move first. Seisser travelled to Berlin to square Seeckt but was sent away with a flea in his ear. The commander of the Reichswehr flatly refused to move against the legally constituted government. Seeckt followed up by sacking Lossow, a move which was simply ignored by the triumvirate, who made the troops in the state swear an oath of loyalty to the Bavarian government. Seeckt issued a stern warning that any move by the triumvirate would be crushed by force.

Hitler was now coming under intense pressure to act. Scheubner-Richter warned him, 'In order to keep the men together, one must finally undertake something. Otherwise the people will become Left radicals.' By 7 November, when the Combat League leaders met, a plan had emerged. In the principal cities and towns of Bavaria, communications hubs and police stations were to be seized. Communists, Socialists and trades union leaders were to be arrested. The Combat League leaders agreed to Hitler's demand that the strike should be launched the next day, 8 November, when all the prominent political figures in Munich would be gathered in the Burgerbräukeller to listen to a speech by Kahr denouncing Communism. Hitler had been forced to make a pre-emptive strike to launch his own Bavarian revolution before the triumvirate set its own plan in motion.

On the night of 8 November, three thousand people were packed into the Burgerbräukeller, one of the largest halls in Munich. It was a cavernous space with a high ceiling from which were suspended ornate chandeliers; a balcony ran down one side. The doors had been closed at 7.15 p.m. and a large crowd milled about outside in a light drizzle. Kahr had been speaking for about half an hour when Hitler began to push his way through the crowd accompanied by two stormtroopers brandishing pistols. He clambered on to a chair, drew a Browning pistol and fired a shot into the ceiling. When the tumult died down, he announced that the national revolution had begun and that the Burgerbräukeller was surrounded by six hundred armed men. He warned that if there was any trouble he would bring a machine gun into the gallery.

Hitler then invited the triumvirate to retire with him to an adjoining room. They had little choice in the matter. There, brandishing his pistol in a state of wild excitement, Hitler announced the formation of a new government with himself at its head, and promised ministerial posts to his captive audience if they agreed to co-operate. He warned them, in the tones of a ham actor, 'I have four shots in my pistol. Three for my collaborators if they abandon me. The last is for myself.' Then, putting the Browning to his temple, he declared, 'If I am not victorious, by tomorrow afternoon I shall be a dead man'.

Having laid his cards on the table, Hitler returned to the hall to reassure the restive crowd that his actions were not directed at the police or the Army, but 'solely at the Berlin Jew government and the November criminals of 1918'. He outlined his proposals for the new governments in Berlin and Munich and added that Ludendorff was to be made army commander-in-chief, with dictatorial powers. The crowd roared its approval when he declared that he would inform the triumvirate that it had the full support of the audience.

Shortly afterwards, Hitler, accompanied by the triumvirate and Ludendorff, who had arrived wearing the full uniform of the Imperial Army, returned to the podium.

Blood brothers: *Stosstruppe* Adolf Hitler (Adolf Hitler Assault Squad), which was Hitler's original personal bodyguard. Formed in May 1923, the *Stosstruppe* was a group of roughnecks led by Julius Schreck. They wore distinctive death's head badges, a link with the Imperial past which was later to be adopted by the SS. Schreck subsequently became the first *Reichsführer* SS (a post he never acknowledged) before becoming Hitler's driver. He died of meningitis in May 1936 and was given a state funeral at which Hitler delivered the eulogy.

After shaking hands with Hitler, they all made short speeches announcing their new roles and their willingness to co-operate. Spontaneously, the crowd burst into 'Deutschland über Alles'. Ominously, Rudolf Hess then began to call names from a list of those present who were to be detained for interrogation and trial. The remainder of the crowd was asked to leave as sympathizers from across Munich began to arrive. Hitler, it seemed, had carried the day.

Outside the hall, however, as well as taking over three large beer halls in the centre of Munich, Röhm and the SA had occupied the War Ministry, but had failed to commandeer its switchboard. This oversight allowed Lossow to order loyalist troops into the city. The cadets at the infantry school came out in support of the putschists, and paramilitaries loyal to Hitler had occupied the offices of the influential Münchener Post newspaper. But that was the extent of their success. Moreover, Ludendorff had made a fatal blunder. Left in charge of the Burgerbräukeller while Hitler went off on a vain mission to secure the engineers' barracks, he had allowed the triumvirate to leave, accepting their word as officers and gentlemen. They were now free to renege on the agreement they had made with Hitler at gunpoint.

In the centre of Munich high-spirited paramilitaries were parading with posters proclaiming Hitler as chancellor. But inside the Burgerbräukeller, amid the fug of cigarette smoke and piles of stale bread rolls, the moment of glory had passed.

Early the following morning a correspondent from *The Times* newspaper made his way to the Burgerbräukeller, where he found Hitler and Ludendorff in a small upstairs room. The quartermaster general and the corporal – the walrus and the carpenter – staring down the barrel of a gun. Hitler, the journalist wrote, was exhausted: '… this little man in an old waterproof coat with a revolver at his hip, unshaven and with disordered hair, and so hoarse he could barely speak'. Ludendorff, as well he might have, looked 'anxious and preoccupied'.

The putschists were glumly considering a rapidly dwindling list of options. Hitler suggested driving to Berchtesgaden to enlist the support of Crown Prince Rupprecht of Bavaria. Lieutenant-Colonel Kriebel urged a tactical withdrawal to Rosenheim, near the Austrian border, where an armed resistance could be mounted against the inevitable Reichswehr riposte. While they talked, the paramilitaries began to trickle away. Finally, Ludendorff came up with the idea of a demonstration march through the streets of Munich, a desperate gesture which just might pick up speed, like a snowball rolling downhill, to become an avalanche. Surely the presence of Ludendorff, the totemic nationalist hero, would prevent the police and troops waiting in the streets of Munich from opening fire.

Shortly after noon, a column of some two thousand men, many of them still armed, set off from the Burgerbräukeller into the centre of Munich. Their destination was the War Ministry. In the front rank, marching beneath the swastika and the flag of Imperial Germany, was Hitler, with Ludendorff and Scheubner-Richter on either side. Close by were the bull-necked Ulrich Graef, Gottfried Feder and Hermann Göring, resplendent in a full-length leather overcoat, his Pour le Mérite

THE FIREBRAND · 61

medal, the 'Blue Max',[9] at his neck. They were followed by SA men from the para-military Bund Oberland, marching four abreast in front of a car bristling with weapons. Bringing up the rear was a raggle-taggle army of students and fellow-travellers, some marching smartly in step and wearing their uniforms and medals from World War I. Many of them could not fail to notice that the posters proclaiming the revolution had already been torn down. To curious members of the public the march seemed like a funeral procession. And so it was.

The column broke through the first police cordon but encountered a second and more formidable barrier as it approached Odeonsplatz. Someone, possibly a bystander, cried out 'Heil Hitler' and then shots rang out, the preliminary to a fierce fire-fight which lasted only some thirty seconds but left fourteen putschists and four policemen dead. One of the dead was Scheubner-Richter, who pulled Hitler down with him as he fell, dislocating his leader's left shoulder. Hitler struggled to his feet and escaped in a car. Göring was shot in the leg and badly wounded. The lone figure of Ludendorff marched on through the carnage and the police cordon but no one followed. Behind him, the column broke and fled.

Two days later Hitler was arrested at Putzi Hanfstaengl's house in Uffing (Putzi had fled to Austria). While at Uffing Hitler had drafted a statement – the first of his co-called 'testaments' – placing the leadership of the Party in the hands of Alfred Rosenberg with Max Amann as his deputy. He was cast down but calm. When the police arrived to arrest him, he was incongruously dressed in a white nightgown, with his injured arm in a sling. He was taken to Landsberg prison and incarcerated in Cell No. Seven, whose previous occupant, Graf Anton von Arco-Valley, the assassin of Kurt Eisner, the Bavarian premier who had been murdered in February 1919, had been moved to make way for the new prisoner.

The putsch had collapsed like a pricked balloon and so, it seemed, had the political ambitions of Adolf Hitler. The writer Stefan Zweig later observed: 'In the year 1923 the swastikas and stormtroopers disappeared, and the name of Adolf Hitler fell back almost into oblivion. Nobody thought of him any longer as a possible threat in terms of power.'

LANDSBERG

The fever which had gripped Germany in the autumn of 1923, and had reached crisis point during the Munich putsch, then subsided. The road to economic recovery, a salve for many of the most savage wounds the nation had suffered, opened up. Gustav Stresemann, who had been German chancellor since August 1923, stabilized the currency with the introduction of the Rentenmark[10] and, with the aid of the

---

9 The Pour le Mérite was Prussia's highest military decoration until November 1918. In World War I its most famous recipients were fighter aces like Max Immelmann, after whom the term 'Blue Max' was coined, and Baron Manfred von Richthofen. Holders of the decoration were required to wear it when in uniform. Recipients included Hindenburg and Ludendorff, Ferdinand Schörner and Robert Ritter von Greim.

10 A currency, pegged to the US dollar, which was issued in Germany in 1922–23 to combat hyperinflation. The last Rentenmark notes remained valid until 1948.

Dawes Plan (named after its progenitor, the American banker Charles Dawes), adopted the phased repayment of reparations. Foreign loans were now made available to Germany, and the country entered a period of rehabilitation lasting until the arrival in the later 1920s of another economic tsunami.

After the Munich putsch, the NSDAP was banned. The *völkisch* vote, while initially holding up in local and national elections in the spring of 1924, swiftly fell away. The paramilitaries' bluff had been called. Without the support of the Army they had no chance of seizing power, a lesson that was not lost on Adolf Hitler as he awaited trial in Munich. In the aftermath of the putsch, the Combat League was dissolved, the paramilitaries had their weapons confiscated and restrictions were placed on their activities. The triumvirate of Kahr, Lossow and Seisser were relieved of their responsibilities. In Bavaria, power passed to a cabinet under a new prime minister, Dr Heinrich Held, a leading figure of the Catholic establishment.

Below: The accused at the trial of the Munich putschists strike a defiantly unrepentant pose for the camera. Seventh from the left is Friedrich Weber, and next to him are Wihelm Frick and Hermann Kriebel. Erich Ludendorff, staring straight ahead, clutching his gloves, is on the right of Hitler, who is gripping his soft hat as if for dear life. On Hitler's left, scarred and noticeably jaunty, is the 'Machine Gun King' Ernst Röhm.

Nevertheless, it was the Bavarian Right which ensured the survival of Hitler's career at the very time when he should have been shown the political door and firmly thrust into the outer darkness. His fingerprints were all over the failed putsch – from the its slapdash planning and all-or-nothing

execution to the lack of any fall-back position if, as duly occurred, the enterprise fell apart in his hands. However, Hitler had not acted alone. There were many who had colluded in the crisis, from the triumvirate, with its own plans for a 'March on Berlin', to the Reichswehr which, in the months leading up to the beer-hall putsch, had trained and armed the paramilitaries who carried it out. Ludendorff, no less, had lent his name to the ill-starred enterprise. Embarrassing revelations threatened to reveal the complicity of many in the Munich putsch unless, of course, Adolf Hitler could be shown as solely responsible. And this was a responsibility he was only too happy to shoulder.

The trial of the putsch leaders was held at the People's Court in Munich between 26 February and 27 March 1924. Hitler was reportedly depressed and suicidal after his arrest, but by the time the trial opened he had regained his composure. He was well aware of the hand he held and also of the fact that the judge was far from impartial. Sitting on the bench was the nationalist George Neithardt, the very man who had passed the sentence for breach of the peace on Hitler in January 1922. Hitler was technically still within his probation period for good behaviour, but Judge Neithardt conveniently forgot this, and much else. He tampered with Ludendorff's initial statement to make it appear as if the quartermaster general was ignorant of Hitler's plans; and before the trial he predicted that the veteran soldier

would be acquitted. Ludendorff arrived every day in a luxury limousine; Hitler wore a smart blue suit and his Iron Cross, and was permitted by Neithardt to talk at length. Afterwards, the judge lamely explained that he could find no way of interrupting the torrent of words. Hitler was also allowed to interrogate witnesses – he subjected the triumvirate to a particularly gruelling session from which only Lossow emerged still clutching some shreds of credibility – all the while giving a relentless political 'spin' to his questions.

Opposite: Hitler in brooding mood at Landsberg, contemplating his future. He later confessed that the prison provided him with the nearest thing he ever knew to a university, 'paid for by the state', as he ironically observed. By his own account he read an impressively wide range of literature during his relatively comfortable incarceration, although his reading regime was designed solely to confirm and reinforce his own prejudices.

In his closing speech to the court, a speech which was reported throughout Germany and which made him, for the first time in his career as a demagogue, a national figure, Hitler expressed his relief that it was the police and not the army which had fired on him and the Combat League. He declared:

> The Reichswehr stands as untarnished as before. One day the hour will come when the Reichswehr will stand at our side, officers and men … The army we have formed is growing from day to day … I nourish the proud hope that one day the hour will come when these rough companies will grow to battalions, the battalions to regiments, the regiments to divisions, that the old cockade will be taken from the mud, that the old flags will wave again, that there will be a reconciliation at the last great divine judgement which we are prepared to face.

The verdicts were read out on April Fool's Day, 1924. Ludendorff was acquitted, a verdict which the old soldier took as a personal insult. Dr Friedrich Weber, head of the *Bund Oberland*, Kriebel, and Ernst Pöhner, a former Munich chief of police and NSDAP sympathizer, received five years for high treason. Others indicted received a range of lighter sentences, among them Röhm, who got fifteen months. Adolf Hitler received a sentence of five years, also for high treason, less the four months and two weeks he had been in custody. The court also decided not to deport him under the terms of the Protection of the Republic Act, because he 'considers himself a German' and because of his admirable war record in the German Army.

Even in Munich's right-wing circles, the leniency of the sentences caused a stir. The shooting of policemen, the taking of hostages, the wanton destruction of the offices of an SPD newspaper, the looting of large sums of money during the putsch, were all brushed under the carpet. Hitler, who had been allowed to dominate the courtroom throughout the trial, returned to Landsberg prison, fifty miles west of Munich, in triumph.

The relatively short time Hitler spent in Landsberg enabled him to complete the journey from 'drummer' for the *völkisch* movement to fully fledged national leader of the NSDAP, the man who would be Germany's Führer. In this, his incarceration proved singularly fortuitous. Before he returned to prison, he had placed the Party in the hands of Alfred Rosenberg, a man whose incompetence and lack of the slightest vestige of leadership strongly recommended themselves to Hitler. In the

wake of the putsch, the NSDAP had been banned, so Rosenberg reconstituted it as the *Grossdeutsche Volksgemeinschaft* (GVG, the Greater German National Community). As things fell apart, and the squabbling *völkisch* movement drifted into factional feuding, the attractions of the 'lost leader', in studiedly romantic exile in Landsberg, would appeal ever more strongly to his former followers. Rosenberg was highly unpopular in the Party, and other leading members of the GVG hierarchy, notably Julius Streicher and Hermann Esser, who combined to oust Rosenberg in the summer of 1924, could be relied on to excite even more loathing.

There was, though, a downside to this tactic, and it came in the burly form of Ernst Röhm. While he remained in Landsberg, Hitler could exercise only very limited control of day-to-day events, and the battle-scarred front fighter was up to his old tricks. Röhm remained determined to establish a nationwide paramilitary organization, the Frontbann, and there was little that Hitler could do to deter him. Röhm had been released on probation after serving a short term in prison and was now seeking the patronage of Ludendorff.

MEIN KAMPF

Hitler had a comfortable time in Landsberg and celebrated his thirty-fifth birthday there. He received parcels and gifts of flowers which filled several rooms. He had a constant stream of visitors and was allowed to receive as many books, newspapers and letters as he wished. Most of the warders were sympathetic. On 15 September the prison governor, Otto Leybold, wrote a glowing report on his model prisoner:

> Hitler shows himself to be a man of order, of discipline, not only with regard to his own person, but also towards his fellow internees. He is contented, modest, and accommodating. He makes no demands, is quiet and reasonable, serious and without any abusiveness, scrupulously concerned to obey the confinements of the sentence … He occupies himself every day for many hours with the draft of his book, which should appear in the next weeks and will contain his autobiography, thoughts on the bourgeoisie, Jewry and Marxism, German revolution and Bolshevism, on the National Socialist Movement and the prehistory of the 8th of November 1923 … During the ten months of his remand and sentence he has without doubt become more mature and quiet than he had been …. He will be no agitator against the government …

Doubtless, Hitler's spotless record was inspired as much by his keen desire to win parole as by any fundamental change in his moral make-up. It failed, however, to impress the Munich police, who warned against granting him the parole he craved and who commented acutely that, in their opinion, he would reconstitute the NSDAP immediately on his release and renew his campaign of 'meetings, demonstrations, and public outrages'. The outcome would be a 'ruthless struggle with the government'.

The book to which Leybold referred in his glowing tribute to Hitler was, of course, *Mein Kampf* (*My Struggle*), on which Hitler had been working during his last five months in prison. Hitler had much time for reading in Landsberg, and he later told Hans Frank that the prison was his 'university paid for by the state'. He claimed that during his time at Landsberg he had devoured everything he could get hold of, from Nietzsche to Marx, stacks of military memoirs, and the writings of the Englishman Houston Stewart Chamberlain.[11] As we have seen, however, Hitler's reading habits were not those of the earnest seeker after truth. He read merely to confirm his own prejudices. The result was *Mein Kampf*, which was dictated to his chauffeur Emil Maurice and the faithful Rudolf Hess, both of whom were also serving sentences for their part in the Munich putsch.

Originally, Hitler wanted to give the book the leaden title 'Four and a Half Years of Struggle against Lies, Stupidity, and Cowardice', but had been persuaded to go for the snappier *My Struggle* by his publisher Max Amann, whose idea it had probably been in the first place that Hitler might fill his hours, and make some money, from an account of the putsch. Perhaps Amann, and others in Hitler's inner circle, imagined that their roles in the putsch would be immortalized in Hitler's book. They were to be sorely disappointed. The author was a mesmerizing speaker but as a writer he was a clumsy amateur.

The original version was a rehash of what Hitler had said in countless speeches, interspersed with vainglorious accounts of episodes in his life. Otto Strasser, who worked on the draft, described it as 'a veritable chaos of banalities, schoolboy reminiscences, subjective judgements and personal hatred'. Putzi Hanfstaengl, Max Amann, Rudolf Hess, the music critic Stolzing-Cerny, and a former monk, Father Bernard Stempfle, were among the editors who undertook the thankless task of massaging *Mein Kampf* from an unreadable shambles into a state in which it was readable, if only barely so. Hitler himself had the good grace to concede that his draft was badly written.

The first volume, which appeared in the summer of 1925, was largely autobiographical and concluded with Hitler's announcement of the NSDAP programme at the Hofbräuhaus in July 1920. The second volume, written after his release from Landsberg and published in the winter of 1926, dealt principally with the philosophy of Nazism, propaganda and foreign policy. At first *Mein Kampf* was no bestseller, but sales picked up in the late 1920s. By 1934 it had sold nearly a quarter of a million copies. By the end of the war, about ten million copies had been sold or distributed free, largely to newly-weds and soldiers. Hitler never paid taxes on his royalties, and when he became chancellor in January 1933 the debt was waived.

For all its literary shortcomings, *Mein Kampf* is very revealing of Hitler's thinking at this stage in his career. Thereafter, he did not significantly change his world view, which was startling in its simplicity. The one new element he introduced was that of *Lebensraum* (living space), the concept he borrowed from the geopolitician Professor Karl Haushofer. *Lebensraum* posited that the German people were to find in Eastern Europe that living space which the Anglo-Saxon peoples had found in the New

---

11 A British-born author, long resident in Germany, whose book *Foundations of the Nineteenth Century* (1899) is a hymn to the Aryan race, of which the Teutonic peoples were the finest examples. It became a key text for followers of the Pan-German movement and for Nazi racial philosophers.

World. A German equivalent of the United States would appear in the Ukraine, enabling Germany to withstand blockade in a future war with Britain and France, although Hitler cynically professed that such a conflict was unthinkable. In effect, the notion of *Lebensraum* reflected Hitler's desire to rewrite the history of World War I. Germany had pursued a similar policy in European Russia in 1917, but without the geopolitical trimmings. Hitler wanted to restore those territorial gains.

The acquisition of living space was inextricably linked with the destruction of 'Jewish-Bolshevism'. Jews and Marxism were synonymous in Hitler's mind as, paradoxically, were Jews and capitalism. Of course, Hitler did not invent anti-Semitism – every fantasy in his philosophy had its forerunners and parallels. The only difference was that Hitler took his ideas literally, and anti-Semitism most literally of all. While other right-wing politicians talked of eliminating Jewish influence from political or cultural life, without any clear idea of what they meant, Hitler saw the answer in precise terms of physical destruction. Thus the acquisition of living space and the destruction of the Jews could be seen as two sides of the same coin:

> If we speak of soil in Europe today, we can primarily have in mind only Russia and her vassal border states … For centuries Russia has drawn nourishment from [the] Germanic nucleus of its upper leading strata. Today it can be regarded as almost totally exterminated and extinguished. It has been replaced by the Jew … He himself is no element of organisation, but a ferment of decomposition. The giant empire in the east is ripe for collapse. And the end of Jewish rule in Russia will also be the end of Russia as a state …

WEIMAR

The warnings of the Munich police were ignored when in December 1924 Adolf Hitler emerged from Landsberg, released as part of a general amnesty for political prisoners. Including time on remand, he had served little more than one year of his sentence.

When he left Landsberg, the political situation in Germany had calmed and the economy had improved. Progress was also being made on the diplomatic front. Chancellor Gustav Stresemann had established a close working relationship with the French foreign minister, Aristide Briand, the fruit of which was the Dawes Plan and the Locarno Pact, signed in December 1925 and confirming the inviolability of the Franco-German and Franco-Belgian borders, the demilitarizing of the Rhineland, and repudiating the use of force to revise Germany's western border. The measures – the so-called 'Spirit of Locarno' – did much to ease international tension and cleared the way for Germany's entry into the League of Nations in 1926. Two years later, in 1928, sixty-five nations signed the Kellogg-Briand Pact renouncing war, and in 1929 the Young Plan further reduced German reparations. Europe had set a course for a peaceful future. Or so it seemed.

The middle years of the Weimar Republic, from 1924 to 1929, saw a steady improvement in Germany. American loans enabled industry to modernize, and coal and steel production figures for 1928 showed an increase of 120 per cent on those for 1913. The building industry was revived and by the late 1920s some three hundred thousand houses and apartments were being built each year. Health insurance was extended to cover over twenty million people. Two new universities were built, at Hamburg and Cologne, and distinguished figures in Germany's cultural and intellectual life included Albert Einstein, Paul Klee, George Grosz, Arnold Schoenberg, Paul Hindemith, Bertolt Brecht, Thomas Mann and Fritz Lang. An American journalist, William L. Shirer, arrived in Berlin in 1925. In his monumental book, *Rise and Fall of the Third Reich*, Shirer recalled the atmosphere of the mid-1920s:

> I was stationed in Paris and occasionally London at that time, and fascinating as they were to a young American, they paled a little when one came to Berlin and Munich. A wonderful ferment was working in Germany. Life seemed more free, more modern, more exciting than any other place I had seen. Nowhere did the arts or intellectual life seem so lively. In contemporary writing, painting, architecture, in music and drama, there were new currents and new talents. And everywhere the accent was on youth. One sat up with young people all night in the pavement cafes, the plush bars, the summer camps, on a Rhineland steamer or in a smoke-filled artist's studio and talked endlessly about life. They were a healthy, carefree, sun-worshipping lot, and they were filled with an enormous zest for living to the full and in complete freedom. The old, oppressive Prussian spirit seemed dead and buried.

POLITICAL GAMES

On his release from prison, Hitler moved swiftly to re-establish his primacy on Bavaria's nationalist Right. At the end of February 1925, the *Völkischer Beobachter* appeared for the first time since the Munich putsch. In a leading article, Hitler outlined his plans for the future. Religious disputes were to be avoided, a necessary precaution in Catholic Bavaria and an implied criticism of the *völkisch* movement, which had accused him of making concessions to Catholicism. The Party's power base was to remain in Munich.

Hitler appealed to 'former members' of the NSDAP to rejoin the Party, which was waiting for the lifting of the ban imposed after the 1923 putsch. There would be no post-mortems over past behaviour. The simple requirements would be unity, loyalty and obedience, in effect a 'pax Hitleriana'. Unity was essential in the fight against Marxism and Jewry, and the SA was to be withdrawn from the Bavarian paramilitary scene, a measure which within weeks provoked the resignation of Ernst Röhm, who departed to Bolivia to act as a military adviser.

On the evening of 27 February 1925, Hitler made a dramatic return to the political arena at the Burgerbräukeller. Three thousand were crammed inside to hear him speak and another two thousand had been turned away. He spoke for two hours, telling his audience that the art of all great popular leaders consisted 'at all times in concentrating the attention of the masses on a single enemy' – a coded reference to the Jews. Moving towards the climax of his speech, he urged all members of the *völkisch* movement to bury their differences. In a pointed reference to Rosenberg, Streicher and Esser, Hitler reminded the audience that while he had been in Landsberg the Party had been 'looked after by others'. Amid tumultuous applause he said, 'Gentlemen, let the representation of the interest of the movement from now on be my concern!' Acceptance of his leadership must be unconditional, enabling him to assume total responsibility in the movement. In a year he would be held to account.

There was one more *coup de théâtre*. Hitler's opponents within the movement – men such as Hermann Esser, Julius Streicher, Gottfried Feder and Wilhelm Frick – mounted the stage to shake hands with Hitler and pledge their undying loyalty. No matter that for some such loyalty was little more than skin deep. Hitler was the only man who could engineer such a public demonstration. However, one figure retained, for the moment, sufficient popularity to destabilize Hitler's position – Quartermaster General Erich Ludendorff.

Events now came to Hitler's aid. On 28 February 1925, Friedrich Ebert, the first president of the Weimar Republic, died after an operation for appendicitis. Hitler insisted on adopting Ludendorff as the National Socialist candidate in the elections for Ebert's successor. Ludendorff accepted, and duly went like a lamb to the electoral slaughter in a contest in which Hitler correctly estimated that he had no chance of making the slightest impression. The new president was another World War I hero, Field Marshal Paul von Hindenburg, Ludendorff's fellow warlord in 1914–18. In the war, Ludendorff had been the dominant partner; now their roles were reversed. Ludendorff's fate was that of the old soldier – he slowly faded away on the lunatic fringes of the *völkisch* movement. The movement in Bavaria now had one leader: Adolf Hitler.

ENTER GOEBBELS

Shortly after his comeback address in the Burgerbräukeller, Hitler was banned from making public speeches in Bavaria, and in other German states including Prussia. This enabled him to step up his appearances at closed Party meetings, where he could reinforce in the most effective way the bonds which ensured the loyalty of individual members of the NSDAP. It was what today's politicians call 'face time', the establishment of eye contact with your supporters, a manly handshake and a pat on the shoulder – loyalty guaranteed.

This worked well in Bavaria, but the ban proved problematic further afield. Hitler sought the help in northern Germany of Gregor Strasser, a Bavarian apothecary from Landshut who had been elected to the Reichstag in 1924. A bluff, open-faced character who was equally at home in a beer hall mêlée or reading Homer in the original Greek, Strasser was perhaps the most attractive of the early Nazis.

Naturally, he was an anti-Semite but not an obsessive like Hitler and his Munich rat-pack. Strasser was also one of the few Nazis for whom the concept of Socialism meant something, and he nuanced his presentation of the Party's programme to appeal to the northern industrial working class.

In this he was joined by Joseph Goebbels, who in 1926 had been appointed *Gauleiter*[12] – regional party leader – of Berlin. A graduate of Heidelberg University, Goebbels had subsequently worked as a journalist, bank clerk and caller on the stock exchange. His deformed right foot and unfulfilled literary ambitions left him with chips on both shoulders and a strong streak of self-pity. He offset these traits with an exceptionally sharp mind and a biting tongue. His desire to succeed in a political movement in which physical infirmity was frequently derided fostered a driving ideological fanaticism. Moreover, he had an unbounded admiration for Hitler which, at times, resembled a schoolboy's crush. He wrote in his diary in October 1925: 'Who is this man? Half plebeian, half God! Actually Christ or only John [the Baptist] … This man has everything to be a king. The born tribune of the people. The coming dictator.'

Strasser and Goebbels were behind the creation of a loose organization of Party districts in northern Germany, the so-called Working Community (*Arbeitsgemeinschafte,* AG) of the North and West, which principally concerned itself with the exchange of speakers. The AG was loyal to Hitler but highly critical of his Munich entourage. Strasser also hoped to replace Hitler's 'immutable' programme of 1920 with a manifesto of his own which envisaged a racially integrated German nation sitting at the heart of a Central European customs union, a primitive early version of the European Community.

These stirrings posed a threat to Hitler. Pressed into action by Gottfried Feder, the original Party philosopher, he travelled to Bamberg, in Upper Franconia, on 14 February 1926 to address a meeting of Party leaders and bring the Working Community to heel. Clearly, the AG presented a threat to his authority. It was a bitter blow for Goebbels, who confided in his diary his estrangement from Hitler: 'Probably one of the greatest disappointments of my life. I no longer fully believe in Hitler. That's the terrible thing: my inner support had been taken away.'

After the crushing of the Working Community, the lovelorn Goebbels was nevertheless swiftly welcomed back into the fold. In April, he was invited by Hitler to speak in Munich, where he was given red-carpet treatment. During his stay, Hitler's powerful Mercedes-Benz limousine was placed at his disposal for sightseeing trips into the country. After Goebbels's speech in the Burgerbräukeller, in which he nimbly retreated from his Socialism, Hitler embraced him with tears in his eyes. The next day the Führer jerked the leash, inviting Goebbels and his north German colleagues to Party headquarters, where they were given a stern

---

12 *Gauleiter* were the Nazi leaders who from 1933 dominated local government. By 1938, Germany was divided into some thirty *Gaue*, or regions. The title was established in 1925 in the wake of the failed Munich putsch, and ceased to exist after the Third Reich. By the end of the 1920s the *Gauleiter* also had a paramilitary function, ranking second to that of *Reichleiter* (National leader).

dressing down over the Working Community before Hitler, all magnanimity, suddenly offered to wipe the slate clean. It was a classic example of a Mafia boss dealing with his moll, keeping her guessing over whether the next move will end with her swathed in mink or with a bruised and battered face. It was all too much for Goebbels, who wrote in the diary: 'Adolf Hitler, I love you because you are both great and simple at the same time. What one calls a genius.' The threat to Hitler's twenty-five-point programme of 1920 had been nipped in the bud. It would remain immutable. Hitler observed, with cynical relish, 'It stays as it is, the New Testament is also full of contradictions, but that hasn't stopped the spread of Christianity.'

The process which transformed the NSDAP into a 'Leader' party rolled on smoothly. Weimar was a town in which Hitler was permitted to speak in public, and in a rally held there on 3–4 July 1926 it provided the setting for a demonstration of the strength and unity of the movement. Discussion and debate were kept to a minimum, and all decisions on matters of substance were subject to Hitler's veto. Some eight thousand Party members participated in an orgy of speeches, ritual and marching. On display for the first time was the *Blutfahne*, or Blood Flag, of 1923, which had fluttered at the head of the march into Munich and had reputedly been soaked in the blood of three Nazi martyrs whose names were engraved on silver finials on the shaft. Every SA man at the rally – some three thousand six hundred of them – swore an oath of personal loyalty to Hitler. Also present for the first time were a hundred and sixteen men of the *Schutzstaffel* (Protection Squad or SS) which had been established in April 1925 and acted as Hitler's personal bodyguard.

THE ACTOR

By now, Hitler had established a routine which he would maintain for the rest of his life. He was a hard man to see; those who met him regularly – the *chauffeureska* cronies, his secretary Rudolf Hess and his factotum Julius Schaub – were members of a surrogate family who had been with him during the putsch and, in some cases, had served time at Landsberg. The few shielded Hitler from the many who came seeking decisions on Party matters. Hitler was content to conspire in this isolation; it suited the image of the remote, brooding leader and also enabled him to disguise the fact that he was quite incapable of applying himself to long hours of systematic work. When lieutenants and supplicants were finally granted an audience, it heightened the sense of awe which they felt in his presence.

Hitler was also a superb actor and manipulator. The 'tough love' methods he used to overawe the impressionable Goebbels provide a graphic example of the skill with which he played on the emotions of those around him. From time to time, though, he struck a false note. The sanguine Putzi Hanfstaengl noted that, while staying with him after his release from Landsberg, Hitler would frequently freeze in mid-conversation and cast a long, melodramatic look over his shoulder, explaining,

SCHUTZSTAFFEL: THE SS

From the earliest days of the Nazi Party, there had been SS (*Schutzstaffel*), or protection squads, formed as personal bodyguards of Adolf Hitler. From these unsavoury origins, the SS evolved into the most powerful arm of the Nazi state, and from 1928 was placed by Hitler under the personal control of Heinrich Himmler, the son of a Bavarian schoolmaster and himself a poultry farmer, who had taken part in the Munich putsch. Himmler immediately expanded the size and role of the SS, which came into its own after the emasculation of the SA in the Night of the Long Knives in June 1934. The SS consisted of two principal branches. The General Staff SS (*Allgemein*) staffed the concentration camps, supervised deportations, formed the *Einsatzgruppen* (task groups) which followed the Wehrmacht into Poland and Russia and were tasked with the execution of Jews, Communists and non-Aryan elements, and imposed the Nazi diktat throughout occupied Europe. The Waffen (armed) SS provided military formations dedicated to the Führer and the Party which fought alongside the German Army. From the winter of 1941–42, the Waffen SS benefited greatly from Hitler's growing disillusionment with the Army. In June 1941, at the start of Barbarossa, it numbered some hundred and sixty-five thousand men. By the end of the war, forty SS divisions had been raised, on paper at least, twenty-seven of which were composed of foreigners, and the number of men under the SS oath had risen to some seven hundred thousand, more than 10 per cent of the entire German Field Army. From October 1939, SS formations were subject to the provisions of the legal military code but could only be tried by special SS courts staffed by Himmler's nominees.

unconvincingly, that this unfortunate tic was a relic of his imprisonment. When confronted with an audience, however, Hitler was pitch perfect, deploying all the staples of oratory – a slow, quiet beginning, the dramatic use of the hands, savage wit directed at enemies, the inexorable build-up to a spine-tingling climax – to enormous effect. Nothing was left to chance, as is evidenced by the large number of photographs taken by Hitler's personal photographer, Heinrich Hoffmann, which reveal Hitler rehearsing the poses he intended to strike during a speech. Only after careful scrutiny were the most appropriate selected.

When it came to clothes, Hitler paid the same attention to detail. Different occasions demanded different outfits. For the Party faithful, it was the light-brown uniform of an SA man with Sam Browne-type strap over his right shoulder, knee-length boots and swastika armband. When addressing an audience of prosperous businessmen, as he did in Hamburg on 26 July 1926, both Hitler's sartorial and oratorical styles were radically different: sober dark suit, white shirt and tie, and no railing against the Jews. His method brings to mind Stanislavsky's great book on dramaturgy, *An Actor Prepares*. Hitler prepared, obsessively, leaving nothing to chance. Unlike Mussolini, who liked nothing better than to pose for photographers bare-chested while supposedly lending a hand with the harvest (not unlike a modern equivalent, Vladimir Putin), Hitler recoiled from such fraudulent spontaneity. He always appeared fully clothed and was paranoid about eliminating any possibility for embarrassment.

The central themes on which he relied when addressing the Party faithful remained the same. A Social-Darwinist interpretation of history in which 'politics is nothing more than the struggle of a people for its existence'. For Hitler, it was an 'iron principle' that in the struggle the weak would always go to the wall so that 'the strong gain life'. Three constants determined the fate of a race – blood, personality and self-preservation. These elements, possessed by the Aryan race, were threatened by three opposing vices – democracy, pacifism, and internationalism – the last the child of 'Jewish-Marxism'. The only way forward was under a strong leader, to whom his followers must be blindly loyal.

> **The only way forward was under a strong leader, to whom his followers must be blindly loyal.**

By the mid-1920s, Hitler did not have to labour this point. Propaganda, which did it for him, regulated every aspect of the Nazi Party's machinery and remained his abiding preoccupation. The nuts and bolts of Party administration held no appeal for Hitler.

Then and later he remained a broad brushstroke man, leaving the detailed work to others. Max Amann handled the Party's finances along with its treasurer Franz Xaver Schwarz; there was also an efficient secretariat in Munich, and propaganda during the latter half of the 1920s was in the hands of Gregor Strasser, who streamlined procedures on a nationwide scale. For the moment at least, Strasser was one of Hitler's most canny appointments.

Nevertheless, in the mid-1920s the NSDAP was yet to make a significant impact on national politics across Germany. Indeed, at the very moment that the Party's overall prospects began to improve, it suffered a series of potentially disabling setbacks. At the end of January 1927, Saxony became the first large German state to lift its speaking ban on Hitler. Five weeks later Bavaria followed suit, on the condition that his first public meeting should not be in Munich. He chose to hold a meeting on 5 March at Vilsbiburg in Lower Bavaria, but the hall was only two-thirds full. However, on 8 March it seemed as if it was business as usual at the Circus Krone in Munich, where a capacity crowd of seven thousand cheered Hitler to the echo. However, the police spy who filed a report on his speech observed that it was remarkably dull – Hitler was still careful not to court any trouble with the authorities – and wondered how he could have come this far if his speeches had been as feeble in 1923.

At subsequent meetings, attendance fell away sharply. In Munich, his power base, Hitler seemed to be losing his touch. The waning appeal of the NSDAP was duly noted by the police. The Party rally in August 1927, held for the first time at Nuremberg, was a damp squib in spite of determined efforts to orchestrate it for maximum propaganda effect. The authorities concluded that the threat posed by the Nazi Party was a passing phenomenon, and Prussia rescinded the ban on Hitler in the autumn of 1928. In the Reichstag elections in May of that year, NSDAP candidates secured just twelve seats. Party membership was becalmed on one hundred and seventy-eight thousand in a nation of some twenty million registered voters.

THE GREAT DEPRESSION

Another economic downturn, of the most savage kind, came to the rescue of the NSDAP. In 1929 the world's economic bubble burst. In Europe and the United States the Great Depression was the central event of the interwar years. Within three years it had propelled Hitler and the Nazis into power. Inasmuch as we are still living with many of the consequences of World War II, for which Hitler was wholly responsible, we are still feeling the backwash of the Great Depression today.

The onset of the Depression can be dated precisely. Since 1921 the American stock market had prospered as never before, and in the eighteen months before the crash in the autumn of 1929 had enjoyed a runaway boom. On 29 October 1929, the boom burst; share prices fell even faster than they had risen, and thousands of speculators faced ruin. The US financial collapse soon overwhelmed Europe. America's loans to Europe had already stopped; now American purchases from Europe ground to a halt. The European economy was teetering on a cliff-edge. Postwar recovery had boosted industry but had not brought a corresponding expansion of markets, and it was the flood of US dollars that had maintained prosperity. European factories were now forced to close their gates. World trade was more than

Above: (from left) Rudolf Hess, Hitler, Julius Streicher and Alfred Rosenberg in Nuremberg in August 1927. Hitler dedicated *Mein Kampf* to Hess, who had been a fellow-prisoner at Landsberg and was Deputy Führer until early September 1939. In 1935 Streicher was appointed *Gauleiter* of Franconia but was removed from public life, for gross corruption, in 1940.

halved within two years and unemployment soared, particularly in the most industrialized countries. In Germany it would reach six million. The hopes of the NSDAP rose with the rising tide of unemployment.

—⚜—

In the months preceding the Wall Street Crash, there were some significant indications that the fortunes of the NSDAP were describing an upward curve.

There were encouraging local and state election results, and in June, Coburg in northern Bavaria became the first town in Germany to elect a Nazi-run town council.

The vexed issue of reparations also gave the Party a shot in the arm. On 7 June agreement had been reached on the terms of the American-devised Young Plan to regulate the payment of reparations. The terms were lower than those prescribed by the Dawes Plan but the reparations would not be paid off until 1987. As a sweetener, the Allies offered to withdraw from the Rhineland by the end of June, five years earlier than had been stipulated in the Treaty of Versailles. The nationalist Right reacted with fury. A Reich Committee for the German People's Petition was formed to organize a plebiscite demanding that the government reject the Young Plan. The leading light in the Reich Committee, Alfred Hugenberg, a director of the industrial giant Krupp, press baron, movie magnate and leader of the German National People's Party (DNVP), persuaded Hitler to join. Hitler's association with captains of industry was not to the liking of the NSDAP left, represented by Gregor Strasser and his brother Otto, but Hitler could see the opportunities it presented. The plebiscite was a failure, but Hitler and the NSDAP benefited hugely from the exposure they were given by the Hugenberg press.

Association with the Reich Committee brought Hitler into contact with other industrial magnates, including Fritz Thyssen, president of the largest steel combine in Europe. Thus far, the Party's chief industrialist benefactor had been been the Ruhr magnate Emil Kirdorf, who had been introduced to Hitler by Winifred Wagner, the widow of the composer's son Siegfried, and doyenne of the Bayreuth Festival.[13] Kirdorf and Wagner were both guests at the Party Rally held at Nuremberg at the beginning of August 1929, which was attended by some forty thousand people. At the rally, Hitler's mastery over the movement he had created was total. The crisis which would bring him to power was about to unfold.

The *Völkischer Beobachter* did not run a story on the economic meltdown on the day after the Wall Street Crash, but the massive shock it administered to the fragile democracy established by the Weimar Republic acted as a recruiting sergeant for the NSDAP. Bitterness and betrayal did their work, as did the idealistic 'national community' offered by Hitler as the solution to the catastrophe. The dynamic alchemy of Nazi propaganda turned the base metal of prejudice into the gold of patriotism. Those who did not belong to the national community, notably the Jews, would be

---

13 From 1933 to 1939, Hitler attended the Bayreuth summer festival as a guest of the Wagner family. In *Mein Kampf* he wrote, 'At the age of twelve, I saw the first opera of my life, *Lohengrin*. In one instant I was addicted. My youthful enthusiasm for the Bayreuth Master knew no bounds.'

dealt with harshly. Within the community, the right of the individual would be subordinated to the common good. This was the only way to ensure that Germany was released from the straitjacket of Versailles. The essential preliminary to this process of national renewal was the liquidation of the democratic system itself.

The democracies in the United States, Britain and France were severely shaken by the Depression but were nevertheless able to survive it. But in Germany the democracy established after World War I was a sickly growth, in spite of the improvements wrought by Weimar from 1924 to 1929. The yearning for an authoritarian alternative ran deeper than the shallow roots of Weimar democracy. Significant sectors of society – landowners, civil servants, many intellectuals – had been prepared only to tolerate the Republic rather than actively throw their support behind it. Now Germany's political class conspired to ensure its destruction.

ELECTIONEERING

The drama was characterized by a series of critical miscalculations by Germany's politicians. On 27 March 1930 the chancellor, Hermann Müller, who headed an uneasy coalition government, resigned over the question of unemployment insurance. Müller's administration was replaced by a minority cabinet. The new chancellor, Heinrich Brüning of the Roman Catholic Centre Party (*Zentrum*), lacked a majority in parliament and proposed to implement measures through presidential decree, which was permitted by Article 48 of the Weimar constitution. However, Brüning rapidly found that he could not entirely dispense with the support of the Reichstag. When a bill which aimed drastically to reduce public spending was rejected by the German parliament, Brüning decided to dissolve the Reichstag rather than negotiate his way painfully towards a majority.

New elections were set for 14 September. The NSDAP's recently appointed propaganda chief, Josef Goebbels, threw himself into a summer of frantic agitation. In the climate of the time, the NSDAP benefited hugely from the combination in its name of the words 'National' and 'Socialist'. Nationalists could be counted among former officers, businessmen, landowners and members of the bourgeois professional classes. The Socialist appeal reached the working class alienated by the internationalist approach of the German Communist Party (KPD) and its adherence to orders from Moscow. The KPD's leaders were in no position to exploit Germany's bruised pride to their advantage.

This enabled Hitler to claim an interest in, and the attention of, a cross-section of classes within German society. To the military he promised expansion and rearmament; to businessmen he promised full order books and the crushing of the Communists who wanted the nationalization of industry; to the unemployed he promised work; to the middle classes, ruined by inflation and the effects of the Depression, he promised to extirpate the root cause of their misery – the Jews and the money barons; to nationalists he promised the revival of German greatness and an end to the Treaty of Versailles. Rather than being the representative of special interest groups, Hitler could claim to speak for the nation as a whole.

RALLIES

The first NSDAP rallies were held in 1923 in Munich and in 1926 in Weimar. From 1927 they were held at Nuremberg in Franconia, a German state whose *Gauleiter* was a Hitler favourite, Julius Streicher. From 1933 the rallies were held in the first half of September on a parade ground – the Zeppelin Field – the size of twelve football pitches which could accommodate some two hundred and fifty thousand spectators housed in stands designed by Albert Speer. By 1937, the original wooden stands had been replaced by stone structures dominated by a monumental grandstand, modelled on the ancient altar of Pergamon, the central feature of which was the Führer rostrum. From 1933 the rallies were themed. In 1937 the theme was 'The Rally of Labour', which celebrated the reduction in unemployment since 1933. This rally was also marked by Speer's 'cathedral of light', one hundred and fifty-two searchlights casting vertical beams into the night sky to symbolize the walls of a building. Much of the ceremonial at and around these rallies partook of a quasi-religious symbolism, an essential element of the Führer cult. This was evoked in the 1934 Leni Riefenstahl documentary *Triumph of the Will*, which opens with shots of steeply banked cloud formations underscored by the drone of Hitler's invisible aircraft. Here, the pagan myth of the universal father Odin and his host raging in the skies was fused with the mountain cult of Weimar cinema.

Alone in the crowd. Hitler and entourage at a rally at Bückeberg, January 1931.

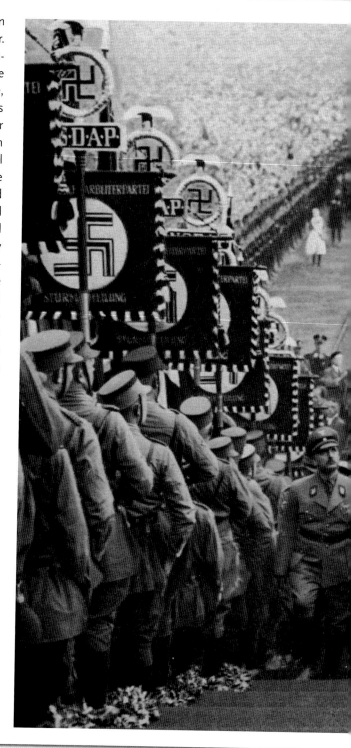

The drive and dynamism of the NSDAP campaign earned grudging praise from normally hostile papers like the *Dortmunder General-Anzeiger* which observed of the Party's campaign in the Ruhr during the summer of 1930: 'Here one can only accord the strongest recognition of the organization, activity and will to power which inspires the National Socialists ... For years the flag-bearers of the party have not avoided going into the most outlying villages and casting their slogans to the masses in at least a hundred meetings a day in Germany.'

———⁓———

In the run-up to polling day, Hitler gave twenty major speeches. On 12 September he addressed a crowd of twenty-five thousand in Breslau's Jahrhunderthalle while the six thousand who could not get in listened to him over loudspeakers. In his speeches he toned down his attacks on Jews and the demands for living space, instead emphasizing the abject failures of the Weimar system and promising a new Germany which would transcend class divisions. Only the 'high ideal' of National Socialism could provide the answer to Germany's ills and the liberation of its entire people. Hitler was not selling a political programme; he was promising national redemption. It was like the Salvation Army all over again, this time promising Heaven on Earth.

In reality, the National Socialist programme was a tired replay of Pan-Germanism's greatest hits, to which Hitler nevertheless imparted a furious energy which none of his opponents could begin to match. To many voters who were disillusioned with the predictable posturing of conventional politicians, the NSDAP seemed to be singing a fresh tune.

When the votes had been counted, the NSDAP had increased the number of seats they held from twelve to one hundred and seven. It was now the second largest party in Germany. New recruits rushed to join, and membership of the SA rose to half a million. Hitler was now a politician of national, even international significance. He was only too happy to give an interview to the British *Daily Mail*, whose right-wing proprietor, Lord Rothermere, had greeted the results of the election as 'the rebirth of Germany as a nation' and welcomed the National Socialists as a 'bulwark against Communism'. The journalist who conducted the interview, Rothay Reynolds, was utterly disarmed: 'Hitler spoke with great simplicity and with great earnestness. There was not a trace in his manner of those arts which political leaders are apt to employ when they wish to impress. I was conscious that I was talking to a man whose power lies not, as many will still think, in his eloquence and in his ability to hold the attention of the mob, but in his conviction.'

Hitler was triumphant but tired. The day before he gave that interview he had appeared as a major defence witness at the trial in Leipzig of three young army officers, whose enthusiasm for the Nazi Party had resulted in charges of high treason for involvement in a purported putsch by the National Socialists. (Reichswehr officers were banned from participating in activities which were aimed at changing the constitution.) Defence counsel for one of the officers was Hans Frank, who called Hitler as a witness.

Predictably, Hitler was allowed, once again, to use the courtroom as a bully pulpit, praising the Reichswehr as 'the basis for the German future'. He denied that the Party had any plans to launch a putsch. Indeed, he continued, the NSDAP intended to achieve power by constitutional means. Goebbels was later to assure one of the defendants, 'Now we are strictly legal', and Putzi Hanfstaengl ensured that there was wide coverage of the trial in the overseas press. Two of the officers were cashiered, but their fate was not the big story. Rather, it was Hitler's pledge not to stray from the constitutional path, and the widespread coverage it received – another skilfully handled publicity coup, which encouraged sceptical conservatives to reconsider their initial reluctance to work with the leader of the Nazi Party.

A notable exception was Chancellor Brüning, who met Hitler at the latter's request early in October. Brüning was hoping to brief Hitler on the current negotiations to obtain a substantial foreign loan and, by taking him into his confidence, coax him into leading a loyal opposition. The chancellor was trying to take the heat out of an already tricky situation, which had only been exacerbated by Hitler's intemperate attacks on the Young Plan. There was no meeting of minds. To Brüning's distaste, he was subjected to an hour-long monologue during which he fastidiously noted the frequency with which Hitler spat out the word 'annihilate', a fate to be meted out to a long list of enemies from the French to the KPD. Brüning intended the meeting to be kept secret but Hitler, who had started hesitantly, soon hit his stride as squads of SA men drilled noisily outside, a manoeuvre which Brüning realized had been pre-arranged. By the time Hitler finished his tirade, it was as if he were addressing a mass rally at the Circus Krone rather than an audience of four – Brüning, Reich Minister Treviranus, and Hitler's own colleagues Gregor Strasser and Wilhelm Frick.

Before the meeting, Hitler had given his word to Brüning that the discussion would remain confidential. But immediately afterwards he briefed Putzi Hanfstaengl, who leaked the information to the American ambassador. Although the two men parted on civil terms, Brüning developed a heartfelt antipathy towards Hitler, whom he characterized as an unsophisticated but highly dangerous demagogue. The feeling was mutual. On Hitler's part, however, it was prompted by a paranoid conviction that he had been patronized by the chancellor. And hate was the fuel which fired Hitler. Brüning was added to the long list of enemies to be annihilated.

—m—

Although Hitler appeared unsophisticated to the fastidious Brüning, his lifestyle had changed dramatically since the days when he lived in modest lodgings in the Thierchstrasse. He had now moved to a luxury apartment in Munich's fashionable Bogenhausen district. Here he was looked after by his half-sister Angela and his niece Geli Raubal. Hitler rarely entertained there, preferring the company of his shifting cast of cronies at the Café Heck, where he held interminable court. The remoteness he cultivated, and his personal dominance over those around him, enabled him to extend indefinitely the undisciplined, dilettante life he had lived during his early days in Vienna. Now, however, the settings in which he wove his spells were on a grander scale.

Hitler adored the cinema, and the environments he chose for himself had all the impact of a Hollywood or UFA epic but lacked the slightest trace of intimacy. Nowhere was this more evident than in his so-called *Arbeitzimmer*, or work room in Munich's Brown House, the headquarters of the NSDAP. The vast room was dominated by a colossal portrait of Frederick the Great and an outsize bust of Mussolini. The furniture was on a similar scale. The room was a cinema art director's dream, but not a space in which one can imagine anyone having a single original thought. Hitler was childishly proud of it but seldom there. Indeed, his lieutenants were hard put to it to know exactly where he was at any given moment. Meetings were there to be broken when Hitler was seized by a sudden whim. Pinned down, he often refused to address the matter in hand but embarked on another flight of fancy. The one place where he could be located with any degree of certainty by ruffled subordinates was in the Café Heck, surrounded by the *chauffeureska*.

Hitler's dominating personality ensured that those who worked for him had to adapt their own rhythms and routines to accommodate his singularities of behaviour. They learned to 'work towards the Führer', to anticipate when they could translate his often cloudy generalizations into detailed plans of action. This was effective enough in the early 1930s when the Party had a single, well-defined aim, that of gaining power. But it was a method ill-suited to the governance of a modern state, a peculiar style of working that poses problems for historians when they consider numerous aspects of the Third Reich, not least the Holocaust.

THE GADARENE SWINE

After the Reichstag election of September 1930, the Weimar Republic raced to destruction like a runaway train. Rational debate was replaced by street violence. All the leading parties had their own private armies. In addition to the SA, there were, most prominently, the Steel Helmets (*Stahlhelm*), a nationalist paramilitary grouping consisting of veterans which, in 1930, boasted half a million members. The Schufo was the paramilitary arm of the conservative Reichsbanner, a smaller party that supported the Republic. The aim of the Schufo was to prevent a putsch by the NSDAP or the Communists, but it was disabled by simply standing for the status quo. The Red Front Fighters' Association (*Rotfrontkampferbund*) was the paramilitary arm of the KPD, and its principal enemy was the SA, to which it often came a poor second in street battles.

At the time there was also fierce conflict within the Nazi Party over the autonomy of the SA, now some eighty thousand strong. Many of the stormtroopers baulked at control by a civilian Party leader and still hankered after the permanent revolution promised by Ernst Röhm before his departure to Bolivia. Men like Walter Stennes, the SA chief in eastern Germany, were determined to go their own way. At the end of August 1930, disaffected SA men ransacked the Party headquarters in

Berlin; a panicking Goebbels urged Hitler to assume overall control of the SA and SS. A combination of Hitler's impassioned oratory and a number of financial inducements defused the situation, but the respite was not to last long.

At the end of November 1930, Ernst Röhm, now returned from Bolivia, was appointed the SA's chief of staff. His lack of involvement in the recent dispute encouraged the case for his appointment, although he had many opponents in the SA who were less than happy with his flamboyant homosexuality. In any event, the crisis which had marked the summer was boiling up again. Stennes was calling for a putsch, forcing Hitler to block any such action. In speeches, and in the *Völkischer Beobachter*, he declared that this flew in the face of Nazi policy. He told SA men in Munich, 'We need the SA for more important things, namely for the construction of the Third Reich.'

On 28 March 1931 an emergency decree gave the Brüning government sweeping powers to combat 'political excesses'. Hitler, fearing a new ban on the NSDAP, ordered the SA to comply, but the SA's leadership in Berlin responded with a stinging personal attack on Hitler, accusing him of despotism and demagogy. However, Stennes had shot his bolt; when the SA membership was asked to choose between Hitler and the rebels, they quickly fell back into line.

Hermann Göring was parachuted in to deal with the aftermath – although Goebbels cannily remained in charge in Berlin – and about five hundred SA men in north and east Germany were purged. The SA was back on the leash, still snapping and snarling but for the moment held in check. Röhm was given the task of heading a new recruitment drive, trebling SA membership by the early winter of 1931, and charged with the formation's reorganization. In rural areas, far from the savage street fighting which scarred Germany's cities and towns, the SA now took on a more respectable image. Nevertheless, the old soldier Röhm was storing up trouble for the future. The SA remained first and last a popular militia. Many stormtroopers hoped that it would form the core of a renewed German Army. The Party and the SA were on a collision course.

GELI RAUBAL

In the autumn of 1931, Hitler faced another problem, which was personally traumatic and had the potential to damage him politically – the suicide of his niece Geli Raubal.

The precise nature of Hitler's relationships with women will always remain problematic. Gregor Strasser highlighted the essential coldness of Hitler's nature when he observed, 'He doesn't smoke, he doesn't drink, he eats almost nothing but green stuff, he doesn't touch any woman! How are we supposed to understand him to put him across to other people?'

Strasser was not quite right on the women. Hitler did, from time to time, enjoy the company of women, and would invariably make courtly, if laboured, attempts to put them at their ease. During World War II he was always very attentive to secretaries like Traudl Junge. Sometimes the actor took over and he would briefly abandon his formal manners. On one occasion, when he was alone with Putzi von Hanfstaengl's wife Helena, he fell to his knees and confessed his love for her. However, the worldly Putzi later dismissed this as mere role-playing, on a par with Hitler's deeply unconvincing traumatized prisoner routine.

Certainly Hitler never treated women as equals, and although they were not banned from the sessions at the Café Heck, they were never encouraged to join the conversation in the rare intervals between Hitler's monologues. For Hitler, whom Helena Hanfstaengl considered a sexual neuter, the nearest thing to emotional fulfilment came at the climax of his big speeches, delivered to what he always considered was the 'feminine mass' of his followers. His own stated preference was for women who were pretty, domestic airheads, a description which, until she bravely decided to spend her final days in the Berlin bunker, fitted Eva Braun for most of her life.

Geli Raubal fell into this category but she nevertheless struck a deep chord in Hitler's perverse psyche. Briefly, Uncle 'Alf' became the centre of Geli's world. He paid for her to have singing lessons, although she was never likely to become an operatic diva. She accompanied Hitler around Munich; wherever they went, he sang her praises. Then it all went sour. Geli developed a crush on Emil Maurice, Hitler's chauffeur. Hitler threw a tantrum spectacular even by his standards and packed Geli off to stay with one of the Party's benefactors. When she returned, Hitler became pathologically possessive. Raubal was now a virtual prisoner in his apartment, and she took to describing Uncle Alf as a 'monster'. She planned to return to Vienna.

Hitler never treated women as equals ... His own stated preference was for women who were pretty, domestic airheads, a description which fitted Eva Braun for most of her life.

On Friday 18 September, after a bitter argument, Hitler denied Geli permission to go to Vienna before himself leaving on a trip to Nuremberg. Early the next morning he was brought rushing back by the news that Geli had shot herself with his revolver. Hitler's enemies could hardly believe their luck. Stories of increasing improbability, laced with feverish sexual innuendo, raced around Munich.

The facts, however, were tragically simple – Geli had shot herself in the head. The NSDAP shot itself in the foot by issuing a lame explanation of her death – it had apparently happened entirely by accident when she was playing with Hitler's gun. Was Geli's death a tragic accident? Or was it a cry for help which somehow went wrong? The truth will never be known. Hitler turned her room in the Prinzregentenplatz apartment into a shrine. What is clear is that the death of Geli Raubal plunged Hitler into a deep depression, and for a few days he spoke about dropping out of politics altogether. Then the actor regained control. Hitler was due to speak in Hamburg and, although he looked pale and strained when he appeared on the platform, his speech was rapturously received. Politics had reclaimed him.

THE HARZBURG FRONT

Sensing that the Weimar Republic was mortally wounded, the forces of the extreme Right gathered for the kill. The autumn of 1931 saw the formation of the Harzburg Front, a grouping of parties of the Right with the aim of presenting a unified opposition to the Brüning government. Fritz Thyssen was involved, but representatives of big business and heavy industry were notably absent when the Front was established at the spa town of Bad Harzburg, in Brunswick, on 21 October. However, the usual suspects were there – Hugenberg's DNVP, the leadership of the Steel Helmets, and the NSDAP. Lurking on the fringes, there was an interesting supporting cast of characters: the Hohenzollern princes Eitel Friedrich and August Wilhelm (sons of the exiled Kaiser Wilhelm II), the former army chief of staff, General von Seeckt and, significantly, the former president of the Reichsbank, Hjalmar Schacht, who had resigned over the implementation of the Young Plan in December 1930 and was now leading an ostensibly pro-Republican party, the DDP.

On the face of it, Schacht was an unlikely fellow-traveller with the NSDAP, but he had been introduced to Hitler after a dinner with Göring in January 1931. Schacht, an immensely wily operator, was impressed by Hitler's 'absolute conviction of the rightness of his outlook and his determination to translate this outlook into action. Even at this first meeting it was obvious to me that Hitler's powers of propaganda would have a tremendous pull with the German population if we did not succeed in overcoming the economic crisis and weaning the masses from radicalism. Hitler was obsessed by his own words, a thorough fanatic with the most powerful effect on his audience, a born agitator in spite of a hoarse, sometimes broken and not infrequently croaking voice.'

Alfred Hugenberg had intended to use the Harzburg meeting to forge, under his leadership, a united opposition of the Right and to urge the choice of a single candidate to represent it in the forthcoming presidential election. However, his efforts foundered on the failure of those at Harzburg to agree on anything beyond their detestation of the Weimar Republic. Mutual suspicion was the order of the day. The NSDAP, in particular, viewed Hugenberg with the deepest distrust. Hitler thought the Front's manifesto, demanding new Reichstag elections and the suspension of emergency legislation, hardly worth the paper on which it was written. He had also delivered a very public snub to the Steel Helmets at the Harzburg Front's concluding rally, taking the salute from the SA before abruptly leaving the podium, having kept the Steel Helmets waiting for half an hour. Hitler now felt sufficiently confident that the NSDAP could go it alone. A week later he attended a rally in Braunschweig and took the salute at a march past of over a hundred thousand SA and SS men.

Reich President Hindenburg's seven-year term of office was due to end on 5 May 1932. In the prevailing climate of crisis, a move was made to confirm the aged war hero for a further term without the need to hold a divisive election. Approval

required a two-thirds majority in the Reichstag, but this could not be secured without the support of the NSDAP and the DNVP.

Hitler withheld the support of the NSDAP on 'constitutional, foreign-political, domestic and moral grounds'. After the customary delay, which drove Goebbels into a frenzy of impatience, Hitler agreed to his name being put forward as a candidate for the presidency. The corporal would stand against the field marshal; the fire-breathing political adventurer against the hero of Tannenberg and symbol of national values above party politics. When Goebbels announced Hitler's candidacy at a rally in the Sportpalast on 22 February, the crowd cheered itself hoarse for ten minutes.

A minor but nevertheless crucial technicality still stood in Hitler's way. He was not a German citizen and therefore could not run for public office. However, swift steps were taken to appoint him a government councillor in the Office of State Culture and Measurements in Braunschweig and as state representative in Berlin. Thus it was as a civil servant that Hitler acquired citizenship of a state he was shortly to destroy.

There were other candidates,[14] but the election boiled down to a straight contest between Hitler and Hindenburg. The Nazi programme presented Hitler as the candidate for change. At a massive rally in Berlin's Sportpalast on 27 February, he urged the old man to step aside. Germany was then engulfed in a delirium of electioneering – this was the first of five elections in 1932. Hitler polled 30 per cent of the thirty-eight million votes cast, while Hindenburg with over 49 per cent nonetheless failed to achieve an absolute majority. There had to be a second round.

This saw the adoption by the NSDAP of a new propaganda weapon. Hitler hired an aircraft for the short campaign, which was truncated by Easter, enabling him to make twenty speeches before a combined audience of nearly a million. While Hitler increased his share of the vote, at over thirteen million, to 37 per cent – over one-third of the German population – it was Hindenburg, with 53 per cent, who was re-elected.

April saw more state elections and more 'Germany Flights' by Hitler, crisscrossing the country from the biggest cities to the deepest countryside. It was a sensational progress. Crowds waited for hours in drenching rain to see him and hear him speak. When the sun shone the listeners dubbed it 'Führer weather'. One of them was a schoolteacher, Luise Solmitz,[15] who saw him near Hamburg on 23 April after waiting nearly three hours:

> The hours passed, the sun shone, the expectation mounted … It got to three o'clock. 'The Führer's coming!' A thrill goes through the masses. Around the platform, hands could be seen raised in the Hitler greeting … There stood Hitler in a simple black coat, looking expectantly over the crowd. A forest of swastika banners rustled upwards. The jubilation of the moment gave vent to a rousing cry of 'Heil'. Then Hitler spoke. Main idea: out of the parties a people will emerge, the German people. He castigated the system … For the rest, he refrained from personal attacks and also unspecific and specific promises. His voice was hoarse from speaking so much in previous days. When the speech was over, there were more roars of jubilation and applause. Hitler saluted, gave his thanks, the German Anthem sounded … Hitler was helped into his coat. Then he went. How many look to him in touching faith as the helper, a saviour, the redeemer from over-great distress. To him, who rescues the Prussian prince, the scholar, the clergyman, the peasant, the worker, the unemployed out of the party into the people.

Opposite: Hitler with the so-called 'Blood Banner', a swastika flag carried during the Munich putsch and a key element in Nazi iconography. It had reputedly been soaked in the blood of Nazi martyrs who had fallen in the November 1923 putsch, primarily Andreas Bauriendl, who had died underneath it. At Nuremberg rallies, in a pseudo-religious gesture, Hitler touched other Nazi banners with the 'Blood Flag'. It was last seen in public at a *Volkssturm* initiation ceremony on 18 October 1944, which was conducted by Heinrich Himmler and attended by many of the Nazi paladins.

---

14 The candidate of the bourgeois Right was Theodor Duesterberg, deputy leader of the Steel Helmets (*Stahlhelm*). On the Left, the Communist KPD nominated its leader, Ernst Thalmann. Thalmann was subsequently arrested by the Gestapo in 1933 and held in solitary confinement before being shot, on Hitler's orders, in Buchenwald in 1944.

15 Solmitz's husband was a World War I veteran and a Jewish convert to Protestantism who, along with his wife, welcomed Hitler's accession to power. However, his status as a citizen fell foul of the Nuremberg Laws and in 1938, during the Czech crisis, he was turned away when he tried to volunteer for military service. Racism had triumphed over nationalism, as it always did in Nazi Germany.

HITLER YOUTH
(HITLERJUGEND)

The Hitler Youth emerged as an arm of the Nazi Party in the summer of 1926. Its membership comprised youths aged between fourteen and eighteen, and by 1930 some twenty-five thousand members had enlisted. Boys aged between ten and fourteen could join a junior organization, the *Deutsches Jungvolk*; young women between the ages of ten and eighteen were given their own organization, the League of German Girls (*Bund Deutscher Mädchen*, or BDM).

In 1932 the Hitler Youth was banned by Chancellor Heinrich Brüning, but a significant expansion began after Hitler became Chancellor in 1933 and Baldur von Schirach was appointed the first Reich Youth Leader (*Reichsjugendführer*). The Hitler Youth were seen as the 'Aryan Supermen' of the future, and their training emphasized physical toughness, military schooling and anti-Semitic indoctrination. Their uniforms aped those of the SA, with similar ranks and insignia. Membership was organized into corps under adult leaders, and from 1936 it was compulsory for all young German men. It was seen as an important stepping stone to membership of the SS and, for a significant minority, a forcing ground for future officers of the Wehrmacht. Outstanding Hitler Youth members also attended special Adolf Hitler schools for grooming as the Party leaders of the future.

By 1938 there were eight million young men and women in the Third Reich's youth organizations, although some three million remained outside in spite of severe penalties for parents who refused to co-operate. During World War II, under the leadership of Artur Axmann, the Hitler Youth manned the air defences in Germany's cities and played a significant role in the air raid precautions programme and other auxiliary services. From 1943, the Hitler Youth provided a manpower reserve for the Third Reich's depleted armed forces. The Twelfth SS Panzer Division *Hitlerjugend*, composed principally of boys between the ages of sixteen and eighteen, earned a fearsome reputation during the Normandy campaign of 1944. By early 1945, as the Red Army advanced on Berlin, Hitler Youth members were swelling the ranks of the *Volkssturm*, the last-ditch defenders of the Third Reich.

Left: *Hitlerjugend* drummers at a Party rally. The movement stressed the importance of ultra-patriotism in German national life and used camps and rallies to inculcate the Nazi creed.

The elections confirmed that the NSDAP was Germany's largest political party, overhauling the SPD (*Sozialdemokratische Partei Deutschland*) which had been the dominant political player since 1919. In Anhalt, where the Nazis recorded just under 41 per cent, they were able to nominate the first Nazi Minister President of a German state. Goebbels noted jubilantly, 'It's a fantastic victory that we've attained. We must come to power in the foreseeable future. Otherwise we'll win ourselves to death in elections.'

—m—

The creaking wheels of German democracy were working loose as successive coalition governments went through a routine which was becoming ominously familiar: the formation of a coalition, an attempt to get to grips with Germany's difficulties, government by decree, the setting aside of the parliamentary system, collapse. By 1932, it was the Army which effectively kept governments afloat, or sank them, by granting or withholding its willingness to back any given combination of parties, all the while steadfastly denying that it was in the least interested in politics. The convention established by Seeckt, in which the Army was above politics, had completely broken down. However, once the Army had got its hands on the political tar baby it defiled everything else it touched.

On 30 May 1932, Chancellor Brüning resigned, brought down by the disastrous effects caused by his deflationary policies. Casting around for a new chancellor acceptable to them, the Army chose Franz von Papen,[16] an urbane and well-connected Catholic aristocrat. Papen's path to the chancellorship had been cleared by General Kurt von Schleicher, head of the ministerial office, the political office in the Reichswehr. Papen envisaged a form of government independent of party, and thus forced to depend wholly on emergency decrees. He was not overly impressed when he met Hitler a week after taking office, and his postwar recollection of their initial meeting drips with well-bred disdain:

> He was wearing a dark-blue suit and seemed the complete petit bourgeois. He had an unhealthy complexion, and with his little moustache and curious hairstyle had an indefinable bohemian quality … As he talked about his party's aims I was struck by the fanatical insistence with which he presented his arguments. I realised that the fate of my government would depend to a large extent on the willingness of this man and his followers to back me up, and that this would be the most difficult problem with which I should have to deal.

The Reichstag voted down the proposal to adopt Papen's non-party government, and another election was set for 31 July. Thanks to the intervention of Schleicher

---

16 Von Papen was later ambassador to Turkey from 1939 to 1944. His last meeting with Hitler was in 1944. At the end of the war he was captured by the Americans and tried for war crimes at Nuremberg. He was acquitted and died in 1969 at the age of eighty-nine.

WORKING TOWARDS THE FÜHRER

From 1933, the dynamic of the Nazi state was geared to 'working towards the Führer', meaning, essentially, tailoring policies to conform with the Führer's often cloudily expressed world view. Moreover, from 1938, Hitler curtailed all cabinet meetings. Thus, to the many cogs in the Nazi machine, power depended on access to Hitler, which few obtained on a regular basis. By the same token, the successful ability to interpret the will of the Führer and put it into effect was the path to gaining and retaining Hitler's favour. This involved competing arms of the Nazi state attempting to realize Hitler's vision. They vied with each other over action against the Jews, from the 1935 Nuremberg Laws to the rampage on *Kristallnacht*, and sometimes found themselves at odds with Hitler, invariably on tactical rather than substantive grounds. In contrast, initiatives such as the euthanasia programme of 1939, prosecuted by the Aktion T4 organization to kill mentally and physically handicapped children, was launched outside the framework of government but with the vital support of Hitler, in effect a few lines typed on Hitler's private headed notepaper. As a result, nearly a hundred thousand children were murdered by doctors using injections of luminal or carbon monoxide poisoning. Doctors then lied about the cause of death. Ambitious officials had attempted to secure the Führer's blessing by designing a policy which chimed with his world view. Hitler can thus be seen as the demonic but often distant enabler for the vilest excesses of the Third Reich.

the SA, which had been banned before the state election campaign, was allowed to re-form. As a result, the summer saw a savage escalation of political violence which brought Germany to the edge of civil war. In the last two weeks of June, after the lifting of the ban on the SA, there were seventeen politically motivated murders. In July there were eighty-six as the Nazis and the Communists fought it out on the streets. In the worst incident, at Altona on 17 July, four were killed and forty-six wounded as shooting broke out during an SA parade which was seen as a direct provocation to the Communists. The campaign also featured another Nazi propaganda innovation: a combination of films about Hitler and the distribution of fifty-thousand gramophone records of him making an Appeal to the Nation.

When the votes were counted at the end of July, the Nazis had secured just under fourteen million votes, giving them two hundred and thirty of the six hundred and eight Reichstag seats. The Social Democrats trailed far behind, with eight million votes and one hundred and thirty-three seats, and the Communists made small gains but still came a poor third.

Nevertheless, anxiety was setting in among the Nazi Party leadership. Goebbels recognized that the Party had reached a dangerous crossroads: 'We have won a tiny bit … Result: now we must come to power and exterminate Marxism. One way or another! Something must happen. The time for opposition is over. Now deeds! Hitler is of the same opinion. Now events have to sort themselves out and then decisions have to be taken. We won't get to an absolute majority this way'.

—ᨒ—

Hitler then opened secret negotiations with Reichswehr Minister Schleicher. His demands were straightforward: the chancellorship for himself; the Air Ministry for Göring; the Ministry for the People's Education for Goebbels; the Interior Ministry for Wilhelm Frick; and the Labour Ministry for Gregor Strasser. Schleicher agreed to present Hitler's terms to Hindenburg. He was confident that, as Germany's political *éminence grise*, and with the Army in his pocket, he could control Hitler. But he could not control Hindenburg, who summarily rejected the proposal. The old warlord was adamant that he was not going to treat with the Bohemian corporal.

On 13 August Hitler met Schleicher and Papen and was informed that Hindenburg was not prepared to appoint him chancellor. Later that day he was summoned to a meeting with Hindenburg himself, who extended an invitation to him to serve in Papen's government. Hitler told him that it was the chancellorship or nothing. The president refused to budge, and told Hitler that he had no intention of placing the reins of power in the hands of a party which was so intolerant of others. Nor could he predict the effect of such a decision at home and abroad. He urged Hitler to conduct the opposition in a 'gentlemanly fashion' and shook his hand as though they were 'old comrades'.

But Hitler was no gentleman. He had kept himself under control during the twenty-minute audience with Hindenburg but emerged from the meeting incandescent with rage, only too well aware that he had suffered a major setback, the most serious since the failure of the Munich putsch. He had succeeded in what he had always done best, mobilizing and manipulating the masses, but had driven the NSDAP up a political cul-de-sac. In spite of its huge electoral success, with over thirteen million members of the electorate voting for the NSDAP, he had been rejected in his bid for the chancellorship by the one man whose assent, under the Weimar constitution, was indispensable.

The irony was that Hitler was nobody's first choice, but most people's second or third. The men who called the shots in Germany – the big businessmen, the established politicians, and the soldiers – devoted much of their time to making deals to shut him out. His followers urged him to launch a *coup d'état*, but he insisted on waiting.

THE DEATH OF WEIMAR

In the autumn of 1932, the Weimar Republic entered its death throes. Political power was now concentrated in very few hands, but the elite groups who exercised it did not form a united front. Politically and economically they were divided. It was the Harzburg Front all over again. They all wanted an end to democracy, the destruction of Marxism, which included the destruction of the SDP, and the introduction of an authoritarian government. There agreement ended.

From this process, the great mass of the German electorate was utterly excluded. However, the power elites had no control over the masses. Those whose sympathies lay on the Right were controlled by Hitler, whom the elites were determined to exclude, hence the political impasse of the autumn of 1932. Hitler could block any move designed to keep him out of power but, acting alone, was not sufficiently well-placed to gain that power. Once again, it was the lack of unity among his enemies that enabled Hitler finally to become chancellor. Effectively, his enemies conspired to hand him the prize.

After a vote of no confidence in the Papen government, supported by over 80 per cent of the deputies, the Reichstag was dissolved and new elections were called for November. Hitler was exhausted but the electioneering, in the fifth campaign of 1932, galvanized him. Beginning on 11 October, he launched another series of Germany Flights, giving fifty speeches in just over three weeks (on one occasion four in one day), all of them lambasting Papen and the 'Reaction', who lacked the smallest shred of popular support. He emphasized his own lack of ambition for office, instead claiming his preference as being the leader of the NSDAP. Papen, he said, was a rich aristocrat who still drew his chancellor's salary; he, on the other hand, was working for the people and would make no compromises on the way to power. 'My opponents deceive themselves above all about my enormous determination. I've chosen my path and will follow it to its end'.

> **'My opponents deceive themselves above all about my enormous determination. I've chosen my path and will follow it to its end.'**
>
> **ADOLF HITLER**

By now, the German people were as exhausted with elections as Hitler was energized by them, and turnout was at its lowest since before the onset of the Depression. When the results were announced, the Nazis had lost thirty-four seats and the Communists had gained eleven. A crisis of confidence ensued within the NSDAP, in part caused by Hitler's refusal to enter the cabinet in August. The scathing attacks on Papen had driven off many middle-class and rural voters. The Hamburg schoolteacher Luise Solmitz reluctantly cast her vote for the DNVP.

The NSDAP, however, remained the largest party in the Reichstag and Papen proposed to dissolve parliament again, along with an indefinite postponement of elections. At first Hindenburg backed this move, but Schleicher and the Army withdrew their support. They argued a worst-case scenario, a military move against Germany by Poland, and a simultaneous uprising by the Communists and the NSDAP. If this happened, the Army could not maintain order. Faced with this alarming but highly unlikely prospect, Hindenburg changed his mind. On 2 December 1932, General Kurt von Schleicher became chancellor of Germany. His term of office was destined to last a mere fifty-nine days.

Schleicher was faced with a naggingly familiar problem. He had to put together a government which would have the support of all the right-wing and centre parties, and of the Nazis. The Nazi Party had been virtually bankrupted by a year of constant campaigning, but Hitler had no intention of getting into bed with Schleicher who was now putting out feelers to Gregor Strasser.

Unlike Goebbels, Strasser had never been an unreserved convert to the Hitler myth, although in many ways he took the same line as Hitler. He was an out-and-out racist and a vigorous apostle of political violence, but he had reached the conclusion that Hitler's absolute inflexibility would permanently exclude the Party from power. Strasser was not an all-or-nothing man, and was prepared to contemplate joining coalitions as a way of gaining political purchase in Weimar's convoluted jostling for power. Moreover, he had never wholly abandoned his Socialist leanings – a philosophical underpinning which was anathema to Hitler – and had strong links with the German trade unions. After the November elections, Strasser became increasingly semi-detached from Hitler's inner circle, a lonely voice urging Hitler to abandon his strategy of holding out for the chancellorship.

Papen recognized that, inevitably, Hitler would be the next chancellor. He saw his main task as ensuring that Hitler was ring-fenced by conservatives.

The qualities which estranged Strasser from Hitler were precisely those which recommended him to the embattled Schleicher. At the beginning of December, Schleicher offered Strasser the posts of Vice-Chancellor and Minister-President in Prussia. Inevitably this brought Strasser into direct conflict with Hitler, and at a meeting two days later there were heated exchanges between the two men. Strasser then backed down. He knew that he was outgunned by Hitler, resigned all his Party offices and retired from politics. His departure produced an immediate and all too familiar result.

The organizational framework of the Party, which Strasser had in large part created, was dismantled, and Hitler himself assumed political control with Robert Ley as his deputy. Declarations of loyalty to Hitler were elicited from all sections of the Party across Germany. There was much shaking of hands with the Führer, and the backs of wavering loyalists were stiffened by the gaze of his deep blue eyes. Goebbels wrote triumphantly, 'Strasser is isolated. Dead man!'

Schleicher's failure to enlist Strasser and the Nazis in his struggle to stay in power fatally wounded his faltering chancellorship. Then Hitler received help from an unexpected quarter. A Cologne banker, Baron Kurt von Schroeder, engineered a meeting on 4 January between Papen and Hitler. At this and several subsequent meetings, the two men agreed to shelve their differences and work together for the overthrow of Schleicher. Papen harboured hopes of once again becoming chancellor and, foolishly, believed that Hitler could be kept in check. For his part, Hitler was well aware that the man to unlock the door to Hindenburg's approval was the president's favourite, Papen.

On 28 January Schleicher and his cabinet tendered their resignations. By now, Papen recognized that, inevitably, Hitler would be the next chancellor. He saw his main task as ensuring that Hitler was ring-fenced by conservatives who were held in high esteem by Hindenburg but were nevertheless willing to work with the new man. On the night of 28 January, his work done, Papen met Hindenburg, who withdrew his objections to a Hitler chancellorship. The door had been unlocked.

In discussions with Hitler and Göring on 29 January, Papen divided the spoils. All the cabinet posts bar two (and the chancellorship) were to be held by conservatives. Frick was to be nominated as Reich Minister of the Interior; Göring would be Papen's deputy at the Prussian Ministry of the Interior, a key appointment giving the Nazis control over the police in Germany's biggest state. There was no place for Goebbels, who was needed to mastermind the election campaign which Hitler was insisting must follow his appointment as chancellor. Hugenberg, who in November had warned Hindenburg that Hitler was wholly untrustworthy, was bought off with the Economics Ministry. Given a sniff of power, Hugenberg had put aside his misgivings, concluding, 'We have boxed him in.' When Papen was warned that he was placing himself in Hitler's hands, he replied, 'You are mistaken. We've hired him!'

—ɯ—

Shortly after midday on 30 January 1933, the Hitler cabinet filed into the rooms of the Reich President. They had kept Hindenburg waiting while they bickered outside the door over the final composition of the cabinet. Even at this stage, the cracks were showing. A visibly annoyed Hindenburg congratulated the nationalist Right on having at last come together. After swearing to carry out his obligations for the good of the entire nation, Hitler gave a short and unexpected speech, vowing to uphold the constitution, respect the rights of the president and, following the next election, to restore Germany to parliamentary government. There was a long pause before Hindenburg replied, 'And now, gentlemen, forwards with God.'

3

THE DICTATOR

THE DEATH OF DEMOCRACY

'Hitler is Reich Chancellor. Just like a fairytale,' was the reaction of Josef Goebbels to the Führer's appointment as chancellor. Hitler's waiting game had paid off. The Linz mummy's boy, the Vienna dreamer and down-and-out, the World War I regimental runner, the police spy, the beer-hall ranter on the outer limits of Munich's political lunatic fringe – a man with no qualifications for heading a national government – was now at the helm of one of the most important states in Europe. From the moment he was released from Landsberg prison, Adolf Hitler's message had been clear to all those who listened: Marxism would be crushed; the Jews would be removed; parliamentary government would be suspended; a re-armed Germany would break the bonds of Versailles; *Lebensraum* in the East would be seized, by force of arms if necessary. He had not minced his words.

Opposite: Hitler at Nuremberg, in Franconia, the geographical and cultural centre of the Third Reich, where the *Gauleiter* was Hitler's old comrade Julius Streicher. Josef Goebbels called the Nuremberg rallies the 'high mass' of the Nazi Party. From 1933, the rallies were held in early September under the title of National Congress of the German People, a deliberate attempt to underline the solidarity between the German people and the Nazi Party. By the late 1930s, the rallies were attended by over half a million people from all sections of the Party, armed forces and the state. In September 1939, the eleventh Party Congress, the 'Rally of Peace', was cancelled at the last minute as Hitler prepared to invade Poland.

On the Left, few had taken him seriously; on the Right he had been underestimated by those who imagined that they could muzzle him and use him for their own ends. It was these grave political miscalculations, rather than Hitler's genius as a demagogue – the one political skill he possessed in super-abundance – which ensured that in January 1933 he was placed at the heart of government in Germany. At every step along the way he had enjoyed the Devil's own luck: coming within a hair's breadth of death in the Munich putsch and then getting away with a ludicrously lenient sentence in the subsequent trial; the arrival of the Depression at a time when the NSDAP's fortunes were at a low ebb; and the machinations and miscalculations of right-wing politicians who levered him into power at the very moment when there was an upturn in the German economy.

> 'I solemnly prophesy that this accursed man will cast our Reich into the abyss and bring our nation inconceivable misery.'
>
> ERICH LUDENDORFF

Perhaps democracy never stood a chance in postwar Germany. By 1932 it was dead on its feet, and with it the Weimar Republic. It was this unique combination of circumstances – national humiliation after World War I, chronic fear of Bolshevism, yearning by many for authoritarian government, institutional racism – which enabled Hitler to preach national redemption and allowed his followers to build a personality cult around him. For Germany in 1933, and for Europe, it represented a terrifying leap in the dark.

From the outer reaches of the German Right echoed the voice of a now forgotten hero, Hitler's fellow conspirator in the Munich putsch, Erich Ludendorff, who wrote to his wartime colleague Hindenburg about the new chancellor: 'I solemnly prophesy that this accursed man will cast our Reich into the abyss and bring our nation inconceivable misery. Future generations will damn you in your grave for what you have done.'

—⟶⟶⟶—

In Berlin, on the evening of 30 January, there was an indication of what the future held in store. Goebbels seized the opportunity to organize torchlit processions of SA and SS men through the capital. He claimed that a million took part, although some onlookers estimated that the numbers were as few as fifteen thousand. In any event, when the marchers passed under the balcony from which Hitler was viewing the spectacle, the chancellor was greeted with furious acclaim. Hitler had not seized power, as one sometimes still reads, he had acceded to the highest office in government at the invitation of the Reich President, standing a few feet away and acknowledging the more restrained cheers of the crowd, just as his predecessors had done. However, after 30 January 1933, Germany would never be the same again. To Vice-Chancellor Papen, standing behind Hitler on the balcony that evening, Hitler's appointment signalled the transition 'from a moribund regime to the new revolutionary forces'.

That evening Hindenburg was persuaded to grant Hitler a dissolution of the Reichstag and thus enable the German people to confirm their support for the new government in elections, set for 5 March. Strictly, this measure should have first been put to the vote in the Reichstag. A decision which properly should have been parliament's was thus being placed directly before the people. It smacked of a plebiscite.

Above: Hindenburg and Hitler, one a former German warlord and the other already contemplating his role as the future *Felderr*. Hindenburg had taken office in May 1925 but had declined to be drawn into the bear-pit of German politics. He first met Hitler in October 1931 and took an instant dislike to him, referring to the leader of the Nazi Party as 'the Austrian corporal'. Hitler considered Hindenburg a senile reactionary, but the old soldier remained in office until the day of his death, 2 August 1934, at the age of eighty-six.

Hitler opened his campaign on 10 February with his first speech in the Sportpalast since becoming chancellor. It was also carried live on radio – Goebbels, who introduced the broadcast, claimed that there were twenty million listeners that night: 'Amid the tones of the German anthem the flags are borne through the wide hall. The entire mass is rapturously singing the German anthem ... The Sportpalast offers a wonderful, imposing picture of a mass demonstration. The people stand and wait and sing with raised hands. You see only people, people, people. All around, the galleries are decked with swastika flags. The mood intensifies, the expectancy is full of tension ... Any moment the Reich Chancellor can arrive ...'

—⁂—

Hitler was at his most mesmerizing but the message was familiar. Weimar had ransacked the nation ... Rebuilding would be a ground-up operation... it could only be accomplished by the German people themselves, abiding by eternal laws rather than class theories ... Gradually, Hitler upped the tempo. This was a struggle for the very existence of Germany, in which political parties and class divisions would disappear and the menace of Marxism would be vanquished. Germany would emerge victorious, and national unity, based on an alliance between German workers and peasants, would triumph. There would be stern resistance to all forms of parliamentary democracy in the process of national revival and absolute intolerance towards anyone who worked against it. At the climax of his speech, Hitler made an appeal: 'German people, give us four years, then judge and sentence us. German people, give us four years, and I swear that as we and I entered into this office, I will then be willing to go.'

The election campaign ushered in an orgy of political violence from which Hitler, as chancellor, was able conveniently to disassociate himself, hypocritically urging 'extreme discipline' on the SA thugs who had been brought in by Göring as 'auxiliary police' to terrorize the Nazi Party's opponents and authorized 'where necessary to make ruthless use of firearms'. In Prussia and other Nazi-controlled states, Communist meetings and demonstrations were banned, along with their newspapers. This, and the blatant terror tactics which left the SA's calling cards of broken bodies and lives, were the first signs that the state itself had lifted all constraints on violence. The actions were, if nothing else, even-handed; along with the Communists and the SPD, the right-wing Centre Party did not escape the attentions of the SA. Faced with this lawlessness, Papen and the cabinet were quite happy to accept Hitler's repeated reassurances that he would rein in the more radical elements in the Party: 'We all agreed that there was no reason to doubt Hitler's intentions, and hoped that experience in the cabinet would have a beneficial effect on him.'

THE REICHSTAG FIRE

On 27 February 1933, as the election campaign moved towards a blood-bolstered climax, a twenty-four-year-old Dutch Communist, Marinus van der Lubbe, a modern Herostratus if ever there was one, set fire to the Reichstag as an act of protest against what he termed the 'Government of National Concentration'.

Van der Lubbe was arrested at the scene of the crime, which had gutted the Chamber of Deputies and went on to consume much of the building. Göring, in his capacity as President of the Reichstag, was first to arrive, followed by Hitler and Goebbels who had been dining together that night. Göring told Hitler, 'This is a Communist outrage, and one of the culprits has been arrested.' Hitler, who was in a state of manic excitement, declared that the fire was 'a sign from heaven' – a signal to mark the beginning of a Communist putsch. The Communist pests would have to be crushed with an iron fist. Later, the mood verged on the hysterical as Göring issued a stream of frenzied orders – a full police alert, wholesale use of firearms, and the mass arrest of Socialists and Communists. Rudolf Diels, a protégé of Göring's and the first head of the Gestapo,[17] was present, and recalled that the atmosphere was like that in a madhouse.

The day after the fire, the Reich Minister of the Interior, Wilhelm Frick, using as a model a draft scheme for a state of emergency prepared during Papen's chancellorship, presented Hitler with a decree 'For the Protection of the People and State'. This extended emergency powers to the whole of Germany and gave the Reich government powers of intervention in the state legislatures. Significantly, the powers provided by the decree were vested in the Reich government and not in the Army.

The decree was signed into law by Hindenburg using Article 48 of the Weimar constitution. At a stroke, the individual freedoms enshrined in the constitution – freedom of speech and association, of the press, and of the privacy of postal and telephone communications – were suspended indefinitely. It was a charter for the Third Reich, and in the hysterical mood of the time was widely welcomed throughout Germany. A Bavarian newspaper, the *Miesbacher Anzeiger*, reflected the views of many when it commented that the emergency decree had 'finally got the centre of the German disease, the ulcer which had for years poisoned and infected the German blood, Bolshevism, the deadly enemy of Germany'.

Like many others, the Hamburg schoolteacher Luise Solmitz returned to the Nazi fold. Nazi propaganda had convinced her that Germany was on the verge of a Communist takeover: 'They [Communists] wanted to send armed gangs into the villages to murder and start fires. Meanwhile, the terror was to take over large cities stripped of their police. Poison, boiling water, all tools from the most refined to the most primitive, were to be used as weapons. It sounds like a robber's tale – if it were not Russia that had experienced Asiatic methods and orgies of torture that a Germanic mind, even if sick, cannot imagine, and if healthy cannot believe.'

---

17 The Gestapo was the German secret police, an internal police force created in 1933 under Göring, then Minister-President of Prussia, to replace the existing state police. In 1934 Reinhard Heydrich assumed command under the general direction of Himmler. In the process, the Gestapo became a totally independent arm of the Nazi Party. No appeal was permitted against its decisions and it possessed sweeping powers to deal with any act which it considered inimical to the interests of the state. In 1939 it was combined with the criminal police to form the *Sicherheitspolizei* (State Security Police, or 'Sipo' under the control of the *Reichsicherheitshauptamt* (Reich Security Office, or RHSA)) commanded by Heydrich. Rudolf Diels, the Göring protégé who headed the precursor body to the Gestapo in Prussia and was van der Lubbe's chief interrogator after the Reichstag fire, made an enemy of Heydrich and narrowly escaped execution in the Night of the Long Knives. He was dismissed in 1934 but turned up at the Nuremberg trials, at which he was a defence witness for Göring.

In fact, the horrifying violence which was stalking Germany was not perpetrated by scheming Communists against a helpless civilian population but by the SA and the Steel Helmets against the defenceless Jews and the German Left. It mattered little to Luise Solmitz, who now resolved to cast her vote for Adolf Hitler, 'the saviour of a wicked, sad German world'.

—⚏—

When the results of the election were declared, the Nazis had won 43.9 per cent of the total votes cast. With their allies, the nationalists and the Centre Party, this gave them a slim majority but one that was insufficient to ensure the passing of an enabling act, an 'Act for the Removal of Distress from People and Reich', which would transfer the power of law-making from the Reichstag to the cabinet, that is to Hitler, who could then rule by decree.[18] To do this, a two-thirds majority was required. Frick found a simple solution to the problem. The Communist deputies would be simply deducted from the total membership of the Reichstag. Göring suggested that, if necessary, some SPD members could also be ejected from the chamber (relocated in the Kroll Opera House since the fire). To make doubly certain of the desired result, Frick made a further suggestion: deputies who were absent without leave should now be counted as present. All too ominously present for the vote, would be squads of SA men inside the chamber and outside the opera house.

On 23 March 1933, the Reichstag voted itself out of existence as a democratic body. Only the SPD voted against the Enabling Act, which became law on 27 March. Political power had now passed into the hands of the NSDAP. It was not the first time that Hitler had got his own way with a combination of bullying and pseudo-legality, and it would not be the last. He no longer needed to rely on the Reichstag or on the Reich President.

CONCENTRATION CAMPS AND CO-ORDINATION

The Nazi takeover was also under way outside Berlin. One by one, the state governments had been taken over by the Nazis. The pattern in every case was similar: pressure on those not controlled by the NSDAP to place a Nazi in charge of the police department; the mounting of ominous SA marches through large towns and cities, and the raising of a swastika banner at the town hall. The finishing touch in each case was the appointment of a Reich Commissar on the pretext of maintaining order. In Bavaria, for example, Heinrich Himmler was appointed Reich Commissar for Police and Reinhard Heydrich, the head of NSDAP security, became commissar for the state's political police.

---

18 The Enabling Act was renewed in 1937 and 1941. In 1942 the Reichstag passed a law giving Hitler the power of life and death over every citizen, effectively extending the provisions of the Act for the duration of the war. It was finally renewed, 'by order of the Führer', in 1943.

Both men went to work with a will, arresting some ten thousand Communists in March and April. By June, there were twenty thousand political prisoners in Bavaria, many of them arrested after denunciations by neighbours or fellow workers, a measure sanctioned by the Malicious Practices Act of 21 March 1933. On the same day, Himmler held a press conference at Dachau, twelve miles outside Munich, to announce the opening of Germany's first concentration camp. He told the attentive journalists that its purpose was to hold five thousand Communists and Social Democrats and was intended as a deterrent.

—ɯ—

The day of the Dachau press conference also saw the opening ceremony of the new parliament. The date marked the anniversary of the meeting of the first Reichstag after Chancellor Otto von Bismarck had founded the First Reich in 1871. The venue was the garrison church in Potsdam, in whose crypt lay Frederick the Great. The ceremony was staged to demonstrate reconciliation between the revolutionary Nazi movement, represented by Hitler in a dark morning suit, and the 'Old Prussia', embodied by Hindenburg wearing the uniform of a field marshal and raising his baton to the empty throne of the exiled Kaiser.

A French observer called the ceremony the 'comedy of Potsdam'.

Here was Hitler the consummate actor, now cast as the humble servant of the war hero and president, bowing deeply and offering his hand. The theme of Hitler's

Above: Heinrich Himmler (second left) and Reinhard Heydrich (second right) in Prague in 1941 after the latter's appointment as the Reich Protector of Bohemia-Moravia. In this role Heydrich moved ruthlessly against the Czech Resistance. He was assassinated on 27 May 1942 by Czech agents trained by the British Special Operations Executive (SOE).

address was national unity. In a deeply ambiguous phrase, he vowed that those who formed no part of that unity would be rendered 'unharmful'. An unaligned observer reflected that 'it can't be denied that he has grown. Out of the demagogue and party leader, the fanatic and agitator, the true statesman seems – for his opponents surprisingly enough – to be developing.'

One by one the bastions of political opposition, and former allies, yielded to the Nazis, usually without a fight. The Communist Party (KPD) had already been smashed, and there was no longer any need to take formal steps to outlaw it. It was time to deal with the rest, on the Left and on the Right. On 2 May, the Social Democratic trade union movement, the largest in the world, was wound up within a few hours and its members incorporated into the German Labour Front (*Deutsche Arbeitsfront,* DAF) led by Robert Ley. By the end of the year, the DAF itself had been reduced to the status of a propaganda machine for mobilizing the German workforce in the service of the new regime. Workers now faced a confident, increasingly aggressive management, backed by the full powers of the state.

Since 1929, the Social Democratic Party, the SPD, had compromised itself to death. Now it needed only the gentlest of pushes to send it toppling into the grave. Its paramilitary arm, the Reichsbanner, was dissolved in April, and many of its activists had fled abroad. The publication in Prague of an SPD magazine, *Neuer Vorwärts*, was used as the pretext for the banning of all SPD activities in Germany, the abolition of its parliamentary representation and the confiscation of its assets. The Nazis' coalition partner, the DNVP (now renamed the DNF), whose leader Hugenberg had become an isolated figure in Hitler's cabinet, went the same way as the SPD at the end of June. Hugenberg, who many had confidently predicted in January 1933 would be the dominant figure in the cabinet, was forced to resign. Far from 'boxing in' Hitler, Alfred Hugenberg was now yesterday's man. Tomorrow belonged to the Führer. The parties of the Catholic Right were the next to go. On 5 July the last, the Centre Party (*Zentrum*), dissolved itself, a turkey voting for Christmas. A week later, the Law Against the New Construction of Parties made the NSDAP the only legal party in Germany. The penalty for breaking this law was three years' imprisonment.

The so-called co-ordination of Germany (*Gleichschaltung*) extended far beyond the dissolution of political parties. It affected every aspect of society, from town councils to gardening clubs, and the intellectual life of the nation. Mayors and town councillors who had been members of the left-wing parties were quickly driven from their posts. Their conservative counterparts were happier to join the NSDAP, whose membership grew by one 1.6 million after Hitler became chancellor, prompting a ban on new entrants imposed on 1 May.

Opposite: Magda and Josef Goebbels and three of their children with Hitler at the Berghof. Goebbels was probably the most intelligent of the Nazi hierarchy and totally committed to Hitler. His skills as an administrator and orator were of immense importance in promulgating Nazi ideology. His flair for propaganda never deserted him. In the closing stages of the war, Goebbels's fabrication of a 'Last Redoubt' in Bavaria became a fixation of the Allied Supreme Commander, General Eisenhower.

Many associations, clubs and societies already had a majority of members who belonged to the NSDAP. Nevertheless, the Party now took under its wing every voluntary grouping imaginable, from business associations to choral societies and sports clubs. Indeed, if you wanted to form a club to pursue any form of social activity whatsoever, it had to be done under the aegis of the NSDAP. Everything was seen through a Nazi filter. There were many artists who were eager to clamber aboard the NSDAP bandwagon, the reins of which were in the hands of Josef Goebbels, who had been appointed Reich Minister of Public Enlightenment and Propaganda on 13 March. The role of the new ministry, which was housed in handsome offices in the Leopold Palace on Wilhelmstrasse, opposite the Reich Chancellery, was the centralization of state control over all aspects of German cultural and intellectual life: the press, the radio and the visual and performing arts

Goebbels was the Reich's master of spectacle and had organized and staged the National Day of Labour on 1 May, which preceded the destruction of Germany's trade unions. Now his canvas was the reconfiguring of German cultural life. Those who signed up for the programme were often idealists, sooner or later to be disillusioned, or careerists flattered by the attention given them by the new regime and eager to repay the favour.

The stage and screen star Emil Jannings, who had played the pompous professor enslaved by Marlene Dietrich's immortal Lola-Lola in *The Blue Angel* (1930) was recruited by Goebbels and, although not a Party member, was only too eager to endorse Nazi ideology. In 1938 he became head of Tobis, the company which distributed his films. In contrast, Dietrich travelled in the opposite direction, emigrating to Hollywood in 1930. In 1937, while filming in England, she turned down an offer, allegedly made by Hitler himself, to return to German cinema. The Allies later awarded her the Medal of Freedom and created her Chevalier of the French Legion of Honour for her war work.

However, for every Hollywood exile, like Dietrich or Peter Lorre, there was a Gustav Gründgens or Werner Krauss who, in the Nazi years, was made an Actor of State. The careers of composer Richard Strauss and the conductors Wilhelm Furtwängler and Herbert von Karajan, however, indicate the pressures brought to bear on individuals by the Nazi state. Without any consultation, Goebbels appointed Strauss president of the State Music Bureau in November 1933. Much of the composer's subsequent behaviour can be explained if not necessarily excused by his desire to protect his Jewish daughter-in-law, an endeavour in which he succeeded by enlisting the help of Baldur von Schirach, former head of the Hitler youth, later the *Gauleiter* of Vienna, and a man with the blood of many Jews on his hands. Throughout the war Furtwängler was kept on a very tight rein by the Nazis and only managed to escape to Switzerland in January 1945. Of the three, Karajan seems the most culpable, a Party member from 1933 who opened every concert with the '*Horst Wessel Lied* ', a Nazi anthem composed by an SA man who was killed by a communist in January 1930.

Opposite: First books are burned, then men. The book-burning campaign, led by German students, was a key element in Nazi 'co-ordination'. On 10 May 1933, students burned over 30,000 volumes of 'un-German' books, ushering in an era of rigid censorship and control. The burnings continued through June and were covered by German radio, which broadcast many of the speeches and much of the communal singing which accompanied the bonfires.

For modernists and Jews, exile beckoned. Arnold Schoenberg and Kurt Weill were no longer welcome in Germany, nor were conductors Bruno Walter and Otto Klemperer. In 1933, the Jewish film director Fritz Lang found himself in an invidious position. His film *The Testament of Dr Mabuse* (1932) was banned by Goebbels, who then summoned him to the Wilhelmstrasse. Goebbels apologized for the banning of the film and, to Lang's stupefaction, extended an offer from the Führer himself to supervise and direct Nazi film productions. Lang, whose mother was Jewish, caught the train to Paris that evening, leaving everything behind including his wife, Thea von Harbou, who divorced him the same year and went on to make propaganda films for the Nazis. Like Harbou, others had no problem with the Nazis, notably Leni Riefenstahl, director of *Triumph of the Will* (1935), a documentary record of the Nuremberg rally of 1934 and one of the most brilliant and chilling examples of propaganda on film. Perhaps the foremost Nazi film propagandist was Veidt Harlan, whose *Jud Süss* (1940) was a savage anti-Semitic distortion of an anti-Fascist book by the Jewish author Lion Feuchtwanger.

The distinguished philosopher Martin Heidegger, the author of *Time and Being* (1927) joined the Nazi Party in 1933. That same year, in his inaugural lecture as Rector of Freiburg University, he talked of German students being on the march, leaving behind questionable academic freedom in the service of the *völkisch* state. It was the National Socialist German Students Association and its rival, the German Students Association, which were the driving forces behind the notorious burning of twenty thousand books unacceptable to the new regime in Berlin's Opernplatz on 10 May 1933. This was a thoroughgoing demonstration of co-ordination. The police and the local authorities had volunteered to clear out public libraries of the books to be burned. There was hardly a squeak of protest. The poet Heinrich Heine, whose works were among those consigned to the flames, once wrote: 'Where books are burnt, in the end people are also burnt.'

CHURCH AND STATE

One significant section of the German establishment, the churches, contrived to escape the full effects of the policy of co-ordination. Hitler's reflex was always to dominate and control, and this led to the appointment of Ludwig Müller, a former naval chaplain and head of the pro-Nazi German Christians in East Prussia, as Reich Bishop to bring all the Protestant churches under NSDAP control. But the installation of Müller, after a campaign marked by chicanery and terror tactics, proved a Pyrrhic victory. There was mounting opposition to Müller, led by Pastor Martin Niemöller, a World War I submarine commander and postwar *Freikorps* commander, and the Confessing Church was established to oppose the Nazis. For his pains, Niemöller was imprisoned in Sachsenhausen concentration camp, then Dachau, between 1938 and 1945.

The Roman Catholic Church, with its substantial membership, strong discipline and efficient organization threatened to be an even tougher nut to crack. In July 1933 Hitler signed a concordat with the papal nuncio, later Pope Pius XII (ratified the following September), the aim of which was to protect the Catholic Church in Germany. The concordat was a poisoned chalice, but as the Catholic leader of Bavaria, Cardinal Michael von Faulhaber of Munich, observed, 'With the concordat we are hanged, without the concordat we are hanged, drawn and quartered.'

'As a Catholic bishop, I may not remain silent when the preservation of the moral foundations of all public order is at stake.'

CARDINAL MICHAEL VON FAULHABER

At the time, the bishops of Austria, which was still an independent country, expressed their view of the concordat in a letter written in December 1933: 'The concordat recently concluded between the Holy See and Germany does not mean that the Catholic Church approves of the religious errors of Nazism. Everybody knows how tense is the situation between the Church and State in Germany … The Catholic Church has never agreed with the three fundamental errors of Nazism which are first, race madness, second violent anti-Semitism and third extreme nationalism.'

Like some of Nazi Germany's most distinguished writers and musicians, Faulhaber was obliged to pick a path through the moral minefields of the Third Reich. He had greeted the concordat with the warmest of praise for Hitler: 'What the old parliament and parties did not accomplish in sixty years, your statesmanlike foresight has achieved in six months … May God preserve the Reich Chancellor for our people.'

Subsequently Faulhaber's sermons contained veiled but nevertheless pointed criticisms of the Nazis, prompting some Party diehards to call for his assassination. In 1938, after he had condemned the racism of *Kristallnacht*, a mob broke the windows of his episcopal palace. He was also an opponent of the euthanasia programme. In a letter to the head of the Reich Chancellery, he wrote: 'I have deemed it my duty to speak out in this ethico-legal, non-political question, for as a Catholic bishop I may not remain silent when the preservation of the moral foundations of all public order is at stake.'

However, the Cardinal was an enthusiastic supporter of Operation Barbarossa, Germany's 1941 invasion of the Soviet Union. In December 1941, in a pastoral letter, he wrote:

> We attend our soldiers with our prayers and commemorate in grateful love the dead ones, who gave their life for our nation. We have repeatedly, have insistently, appealed to our believers for faithful fulfilment of their duties, to persevere boldly, for self-sacrificing work and for fighting in service of our country in the hardest times of war … We gave warning to the German Catholic of Bolshevism and called for vigilance in many pastoral letters from 1921 to 1936, as the German government well knows, and so we observe this fight against Bolshevism with great satisfaction.

THE NIGHT OF THE LONG KNIVES

Although he was now chancellor, Hitler's daily routine had still not noticeably changed since the late 1920s. Only Göring, Goebbels and Himmler saw him with any degree of regularity. Access for anyone else was all but impossible. Hitler rose late and often chose to spend much of the day with his disreputable crew of *chauffeureska* cronies and hangers-on, among them the photographer Heinrich Hoffmann, his driver Julius Schreck (Emil Maurice's successor) and adjutant Julius Schaub. They were happy stooges, sounding boards for Hitler's interminable monologues. Lunch, the high point of the day, was a moveable feast, which could never be strictly scheduled because Hitler remained a creature of whim and sudden impulse. He stayed up late at night, often enjoying films in his private cinema – one of his favourites was *King Kong*. Only his personal authority could sustain such an unconventional regime, although, as Goebbels observed, this routine encouraged and enabled subordinates to embark on the implementation of radical policies on the mere understanding that they were in line with the Führer's thinking and wishes, but without his direct authorization.

On many major issues, Hitler remained a great prevaricator. Action was endlessly delayed until he made a sudden and irrevocable decision. One such, perhaps the most dramatic of the early years of his chancellorship, concerned the thorny problem of the SA, which by 1934 was presenting a growing threat to the sway that Hitler held over the NSDAP.

By the spring of 1934, relations between the Army and the SA had reached crisis point. The SA, which had been responsible for most of the violence and disorder in the year of five elections, was now some four and a half million strong. Its leader, Ernst Röhm, had been appointed a cabinet minister without portfolio, but his ambition lay elsewhere. He wanted to initiate an era of 'permanent revolution' which would transform the SA into a people's army, supplanting the Reichswehr and reducing it to a mere feeder organization for the *Sturmabteilung*.

Both the Army and Röhm lobbied Hitler strongly for his support, the former attempting to curry favour by introducing for the German officer corps the notorious Aryan Paragraph which, in April 1933, barred Jews from the civil service. However, forced to choose between the Army, which was backed by Hindenburg, and the SA, the Party army, Hitler stayed his hand. This was not a posture he could maintain indefinitely; as one of his generals reminded him in a pointed reference to Röhm, 'Re-armament is too serious and difficult to permit the participation of speculators, drunkards and homosexuals.'

Hitler waited on events while, from February 1934, Röhm was kept under surveillance by the Prussian Gestapo (*Geheimestaatspolizei*, or secret police established in 1933) which had now passed into the hands of Heinrich Himmler and Reinhard Heydrich, who were both itching to expand their embryonic SS empire which was still subordinated to the SA. It was decidedly in the interests of this predatory duo, and their boss in Prussia, Hermann Göring, to see the SA emasculated. Röhm was rapidly acquiring a portfolio of determined enemies, while Hitler was finessing his position. Early in 1934, with his eye on the current disarmament negotiations, he indicated in a meeting with Anthony Eden, then the British government's Lord Privy Seal, that he was determined to demilitarize the SA.

It was left to Heydrich to set the ball rolling. In concert with Himmler, he concocted a plot whereby by the SA would appear to launch a putsch against Hitler. The conspiracy was wholly imaginary, but by now Röhm had antagonized too many powerful players in the Party. Röhm and his senior lieutenants were ordered to meet Hitler in Bad Wiessee on the morning of 30 June. The Army was placed on alert while Hitler travelled to Bad Godesberg, there to be joined by Goebbels and Sepp Dietrich, head of Hitler's SS bodyguard. Goebbels was under the impression when he arrived that a move was imminent against Papen and a conservative cabal who were, belatedly and wholly ineffectually, attempting to sideline Hitler. He was quickly disabused of this notion. Röhm was the target.

Hitler flew on to Munich in the company of his adjutants, Goebbels, Viktor Lutze, an SA officer loyal to the Führer, and Sepp Dietrich. They landed at dawn, to be greeted by news that the SA had been demonstrating against Hitler in the city's streets. This was the last straw for the Führer. He and his entourage sped on to the Bavarian Ministry of the Interior, where two local SA leaders were summoned, stripped of their rank, and carted off to prison. Hitler then raced to Bad Wiessee, arriving at 6.30 a.m. to find Röhm and his lieutenants sleeping off a night of heavy drinking.

Hitler, waving a pistol and followed by his entourage, burst into Röhm's room and accused the SA chief of treachery. Röhm was led away under arrest to Munich's Stadelheim prison while, in a neighbouring room, Edmund Heines, the SA chief in Breslau, was discovered in bed with a young man, a fact from which Goebbels was subsequently to gain much mileage. Arrests followed thick and fast as Hitler and his party made their way back to Munich's Brown House, where he addressed a gathering of SA leaders in the Senators' Hall. The Führer was incandescent with rage, saliva dribbling from the corners of his mouth, as he launched himself on an arc of hyperbole. In the 'worst betrayal in world history', he declared, Röhm had taken bribes from the French to have him arrested and killed, but now the boot was on the other foot and the SA traitors would be executed.

In Munich the executions began shortly afterwards, but Röhm's was not among them. While Hitler's cronies, notably among them Rudolph Hess, clamoured for the honour of despatching the SA chief, Hitler dithered. This was partly out of of lingering loyalty, but also, perhaps, because of fear of embarrassment. It was no simple matter to order the shooting, out of hand, of one of your principal lieutenants.

In Berlin, Göring and Goebbels had no such inhibitions. The code-word for the death squads – *Kolibri* – was issued and the executioners went about their work. They were taking no chances. Anyone who was considered a threat to Hitler, real or potential, was executed after a one-minute 'trial'. Many of the victims had nothing to do with the SA but died in the settling of old scores. Among them were Gregor Strasser; the former Chancellor, General Schleicher and his wife; one of Schleicher's right-hand men, General Bredow; and Hitler's old adversary of the 1920s, Ritter von Kahr, who was hacked to death near Dachau by a squad of SS men. Father Bernhard Stempfle, one of the men who had laboured to turn *Mein Kampf* into readable prose, was also killed by the SS. Perhaps his death was a case of mistaken identity which, as the blood-letting raced out of control, sealed the fate of the music critic Wilhelm Eduard Schmid, whose executioners had confused him with Dr Ludwig Schmitt, a former associate of Gregor Strasser.

Ernst Röhm, however, was still alive when Hitler's plane touched down at Tempelhof airfield at 10 p.m. on the evening of 30 June. Göring and Himmler urged Hitler to order Röhm's execution, but it was not until Sunday 1 July, during a garden party at the Reich Chancellery, that he agreed to the liquidation of the SA chief, who, as a final grisly courtesy, was to be offered the chance to shoot himself. The pistol was presented to Röhm in his cell by Theodor Eicke, the commandant of Dachau, but the veteran front fighter declined to do the decent thing. After ten minutes had elapsed, the pistol was removed and Röhm was despatched by Eicke and his deputy, SS-Sturmbahnführer Michael Lippert, as he stood before them, bare-chested and still struggling to speak.

—m—

On 2 July, Hitler halted the so-called cleansing action, and Göring ordered the burning of all police files connected with the affair. The weeding out was insufficiently rigorous to cover all the tracks, however, and surviving documents list eighty-five victims, of whom fifty were SA men. It is likely that during the Night of the Long Knives, some two hundred people were killed by the SS. The action marked the end of the *Sturmabteilung* as an alternative power base in Nazi Germany and its demise was not mourned by many. The SA's arrogance and undisciplined behaviour had alienated the German middle class, who applauded Hitler's apparent readiness to grasp the nettle. Within a year the SA's numbers had been slashed by 40 per cent and many of its senior officers had been disciplined or dismissed. The SA still had its uses, as was to be shown in 1938 on *Kristallnacht*, but it had been cut down to size with a swiftness and brutality which no one could ignore.

The Army, which had supplied weapons to the SS death squads and then stood back during the slaughter, was unstinting in its praise. The Defence Minister, General von Blomberg, thanked Hitler for his 'resolute and courageous action ... [which] called forth a pledge for attainment, loyalty and devotion in this difficult hour'. The fact that two generals had died in the bloodbath counted for little. The Army, too, believed that it could deal with Hitler. It was only later that the terrible implications of the deal it had struck with him dawned on the Army high command.

Hitler covered his own tracks with the Law for the Emergency Defence of the State, which was agreed by the cabinet on 3 July and which read, 'The measures taken on 30 June and 1 and 2 July for the suppression of high treasonable and state treasonable attacks are, as emergency defence of the state, legal.' On 13 July, Hitler addressed the Reichstag, which had lost thirteen deputies on the Night of the Long Knives. To a storm of cheering, he justified the abandonment of the rule of law and the adoption of a policy of state-backed murder with the following words:

> Mutinies are broken according to eternal, iron laws. If I am reproached with not turning to the law courts for sentence, I can only say: in this hour, I was responsible for the fate of the German nation and thereby the supreme judge of the German people ... I gave the order to shoot those men most guilty of this treason and I further gave the order to burn out down to the raw flesh the ulcers of our internal well-poisoning and the poisoning from abroad.

Hitler had got away with murder, and so had the SS, which was now free from its subordination to the SA. Henceforth it would be responsible to Hitler alone. The unruly mass of the SA had been replaced by an elite praetorian guard whose sinister empire inexorably expanded. By 1944 the Waffen (armed) SS was seven hundred thousand strong and made up 10 per cent of the German Army.

The ailing President Hindenburg died on 2 August 1934. The old man had been ill for months and Hitler was well-prepared for the inevitable. Scarcely an hour after Hindenburg had breathed his last, an announcement was made that henceforth the office of the chancellor would be merged with that of president. Hitler was now the sole and undisputed head of the German Reich.

The Army was now keen to turn over a new leaf. Acting on his own initiative, General von Reichenau, General von Blomberg's deputy, devised a new oath to the head of state to be sworn the moment he took office. Hitler was delighted with it, and on the afternoon and late evening of 2 August, the anniversary of German mobilization in 1914, at ceremonies throughout Germany, soldiers and sailors took their oath of allegiance to their new Head of State and Supreme Commander with the words: 'I swear by God this holy oath, that I will render to Adolf Hitler, Führer of the German Reich and People, Supreme Commander of the Armed Forces, unconditional obedience, and that I am ready, as a brave soldier, to risk my life at any time for this oath.'

By this oath, every serviceman in Germany's armed forces placed himself at the sole disposal of one man, Adolf Hitler, in his position as Reich Chancellor and President, the power of which offices had been extended by the Enabling Law which swept away all legal or constitutional constraints. Henceforth, Hitler was not obliged to render account to any man for the use to which his soldiers were put.

Hitler was, if anything, pathetically grateful for the manner in which Germany's armed forces had acknowledged him as head of state. In a letter to Blomberg, he wrote: '... I wish to express my thanks to you, and through you, to the Armed Forces, for the oath of loyalty which has been sworn to me. Just as the officers and men of the Armed Forces have obligated themselves to the new state in my person, so I shall always regard it as my highest duty to intercede for the existence and inviolability of the Armed Forces, in fulfilment of the testament of the late Field-Marshal, and in accord with my own will to establish the Army formally as the sole bearer of arms of the nation.'

The Army and the Führer were now as one. As supreme commander, Hitler ordered the Army to appear at the Party rally at Nuremberg in September 1934, where it delighted the audience with its displays of drill, tactics and weaponry. There was one more brick to lay in the wall. In a mid-August plebiscite, the merging of the offices of chancellor and president, and Hitler's assumption of the role of supreme commander, were approved by 84.6 per cent of the electorate. Now there were no checks and balances left on Hitler's power. He was ready to roll.

HITLER AND THE GENERALS

The German Army was long accustomed to following an autocratic ruler. Until the end of World War I, the rule of the Kaiser, theoretically circumscribed by parliament, was in practice absolute. The Kaiser enjoyed the absolute privilege to conduct foreign affairs, hold supreme command of the armed forces and declare war. In periods of acute internal crisis he could assume the powers of a military dictator, and it was to the Kaiser that, under the 1871 constitution, the Army pledged its loyalty. The personal bond between soldier and Emperor was the source of great pride to the Army and underlined the deep commitment of the officer corps to the monarchy; any open criticism of the monarchy was considered a serious offence, punishable before a military Court of Honour. The men of the officer corps inhabited a world which was deeply inimical to the concepts of democracy and Socialism.

This stern world of order and authority was turned upside down by Germany's defeat in 1918. In its immediate aftermath it led to the formation of the *Freikorps* and the crisis of the Kapp putsch. The situation had been stabilized

by General Hans von Seeckt, the C-in-C of the one-hundred-thousand-strong army, the Reichswehr, which the Allies permitted Germany to retain under the terms of the Treaty of Versailles. Seeckt restored discipline, re-establishing the Army's apolitical credentials (*Überparteilichkeit*), and the officer corps was instructed to avoid the unpredictable, often chaotic ebb and flow of politics in the Weimar Republic. Seeckt's view was absolutely straightforward: 'Hands off the Army! is my cry to all parties. The Army serves the state and the state alone.' In 1930, as the Republic was entering its prolonged death throes, the then defence minister, Wilhelm Gröner, reasserted the concept of unconditional obedience as the fundamental requirement of military service.

In the Weimar years the Army had become a reliable, albeit unthinking pillar of state. It had been no friend of the Nazi Party and declined to come out to support it during the abortive Munich putsch in 1923. After the 1930 trial in Leipzig of young officers for distributing National Socialist literature, at which Hitler appeared as a witness, Gröner felt it necessary to issue a special circular to senior officers, asserting that the actions of the three lieutenants had shattered his 'faith in the Reichswehr as an unshakeable rock of obedience and devotion to duty, on which is founded the whole edifice of the state'. The Army was to be a bulwark against threats to the Republic whether from the Left or the Right.

Nevertheless there were many in the Army, particularly among the officer class, who were attracted to aspects of National Socialism, not least Hitler's denunciation of the Versailles settlement and his promises of a general rearmament. They had a natural sympathy with a politician who could declare: 'We will see to it that, when we have come to power, out of the present Reichswehr shall rise the great Army of the German people.' The appointment of Hitler as Chancellor released them from the strain of *Überparteilichkeit* and enabled them to return to a policy of vigorous patriotism, rearmament and the reintroduction of conscripton.

Hitler signalled his intentions towards the Army within twenty-four hours of his appointment as Chancellor. He addressed, without invitation, the leading officers of the Berlin garrison. In a two-hour speech, he promised rearmament and the 'strengthening of the will to defence by all possible means'; confirmed their vital position within the state against the rival claims of the SA, and also confirmed that they were to remain 'unpolitical and above parties'.

At the opening of the new Reichstag on 21 May, held at the old garrison church at Potsdam, Hitler had bowed low before the aged President Hindenburg, his wartime commander-in-chief, in a symbolic gesture that united Prusso-German tradition with the new political wind blowing through Germany. Field Marshal Eberhard von Mackensen, one of the most able field commanders of World War I,

Left: Military manoeuvres – Hitler confers with Generals Fritsch (left) and Blomberg in 1935. In 1938 he removed them from their posts as, respectively, commander-in-chief of the Army and head of the armed forces (Wehrmacht) and replaced them with men more inclined to back without reservation his plans to pursue an increasingly aggressive foreign policy.

enthused over Germany's new chancellor: 'We German officers used to be called representatives of reaction, whereas we were really bearers of tradition. It is in the sense of that tradition that Hitler spoke to us, so wonderfully, and so directly from the heart, at Potsdam.'

The Army high command, and indeed many Germans, both believed and backed Hitler's assurances that he would restore national honour. In March 1933 he had argued that Germany had been the only country to disarm in accordance with the Treaty of Versailles. If other nations would not disarm, then Germany should be allowed to rearm. Later, in October 1933, Germany withdrew from the League of Nations' disarmament talks and then walked out of the League of Nations itself. In a plebiscite held on 12 November 1933, Hitler's actions were approved by 95 per cent of the electorate.

So far, so good. Hitler continued to move cautiously in his relations with the Army, scrupulously avoiding interfering with internal Army affairs. The Army saw only his charming side. He gracefully accepted Hindenburg's rejection of his recommendations for senior appointments, accepted the advice he was given by military subordinates, and did not participate in the planning of operations or the considering of promotions. He tried to allay fears about the SA expressed – not unreasonably – by senior officers, telling them: 'I know that you accuse me of many wrongs which exist in the Party. I admit that you are one hundred per cent correct, but you must remember … I still have to work with persons of low quality.' In May 1933, he sanctioned an agreement between the Army and the SA which provided for the Army's unquestioned superiority. Using a tried and trusted tactic, he asked Röhm, and his Defence Minister, General von Blomberg, to sign an agreement confirming Hitler's statement of policy. This enraged Röhm, who subsequently told his SA lieutenants, 'What the ridiculous corporal [Hitler] says in this brutal jostling of egos, means nothing to us … I have not the slightest intention of keeping this agreement. Hitler is a traitor and at the very least must go on leave … If we can't get there with him, we'll get there without him.'

In June 1934, with the Night of the Long Knives Hitler had the last word. The Army, which had been careful to avoid direct entanglement in the gruesome bloodletting, was relieved that it was not to be absorbed into the Brownshirt empire. Hitler's half-formulated promise that the stormtroopers would become the new soldiers of Germany was to be made good only in one sense: after March 1935 when, in a breach of the Treaty of Versailles, he announced the reintroduction of conscription, the younger members of the SA received call-up papers and found themselves in the armed forces alongside hundreds of thousands of others who had never worn the brown shirt.

By 1936 the reintroduction of conscription had given Hitler an army with a skeleton strength of thirty-six divisions, a five-fold increase on the Reichswehr's seven. The elimination of the SA as the armed wing of the Nazi Party earned Hitler high favour in the military, but these feelings were not necessarily reciprocated.

Hitler was enough of a military snob to see that the SA was little more than a disorderly militia – the army which he intended to recreate was to be modelled on the one in which he had served on the Western Front in World War I. And this personal experience, which had won him the Iron Cross (First Class), had deeply marked him and placed limits on his loyalty to the Army with which he had to deal as chancellor and subsequently as commander-in-chief. The men who were now in many of the most senior positions in the Army had, in the main, not fought in the front line in 1914-18 – their brains were considered too valuable to be risked beyond headquarters, the inside of which Corporal Hitler never saw.

Hitler, however, was also a combat snob and no worshipper of rank or title for its own sake. He had never forgotten the trial which followed the failed Munich putsch, at which the head of the Bavarian Army, General von Lossow, had slightingly referred to him as a mere 'political drummer boy', a wound salted by the state prosecutor's assertion that the drummer boy had 'allowed himself to be carried beyond the position assigned to him'. Now he felt keenly that many of the Army's new elite were inclined to patronize him. It was now he who assigned positions everywhere – except in the Army, which jealously guarded its own promotional structure. But Hitler wanted to move into a higher gear, and for this he needed commanders who were more combative than those with whom he had been obliged to deal when he became chancellor.

In June 1934, with the Night of the Long Knives Hitler had the last word.

At the head of the German Armed Forces, or Wehrmacht, was General Werner von Blomberg, who had been appointed Reich Minister of Defence on 29 January 1933, having been manoeuvred into position by Hindenburg with the object keeping Hitler under control. Blomberg, a much-decorated veteran of World War I, was an imposing figure who nevertheless had been nicknamed the 'Rubber Lion' because his character did not measure up to his impressive physical presence. Hindenburg believed that Blomberg epitomized the 'soldier above politics' but, alas for Hindenburg, the Rubber Lion became an devoted admirer of Hitler. When he was questioned on the unqualified support he gave the Führer, Blomberg's reply was that he was acting in the best interests of the country and the Army: 'The Führer is cleverer than we are, he will plan and do everything correctly.' In May 1935 Blomberg was appointed commander-in-chief of the three armed services in addition to his ministerial responsibilities, elevating him to a position of military authority surpassing any other German general in peacetime history. In 1936, on the occasion of Blomberg's fifty-seventh birthday, he was made field marshal.

The commander-in-chief of the Army was General Werner von Fritsch, another Hindenburg appointment and an exceptionally fine military professional who, however, possessed no political skills or interest in politics. A man of immense reserve, never known to talk about himself, Fritsch's only interest outside the military was horses. His monocle, needed to correct a weakness in his left eye, was also a feature of his personal defences. He once confessed, 'I wear a monocle so that my face remains stiff, especially when I confront the Führer.'

Both Blomberg and Fritsch were to clash with Hitler over rearmament and foreign policy. On the face of it, rearmament should have been the strongest link between Hitler and the Army. Soldiers recognized that the new regime would provide the means by which they could regain their former prestige and ensure the defence of their homeland, while Hitler considered the creation of a large and powerful army as crucial to the success of his foreign ambitions. However, the soldiers were increasingly alarmed by the scale and pace of the rearmament programme. In five years the Army grew from one hundred thousand men to three million, three hundred and forty-three thousand. Senior generals complained that this was more like a mobilization than a peacetime build-up. Fritsch grumbled that Hitler's policy was 'forcing everything, overdoing everything, rushing everything far too much and destroying every healthy development'.

The military leaders urged caution, fearing the reaction of the major powers to Germany's defiance of Versailles. In the event, they need not have worried. The major powers remained inert. Hitler had taken their measure. The announcement of the reintroduction of conscription in March 1935 had been prompted by a French government announcement that, because of France's falling birth rate, it was doubling the length of conscripts' military service. Hitler then offered the French a pact which would limit the size of the German Army to three hundred thousand men and that of his new air force, the Luftwaffe, to 50 per cent of theirs. France's refusal of his offer enabled him to go for larger totals. The French, and Germany's generals, were powerless against Hitler's will. He had already realized this in the matter of the military reoccupation of the Rhineland in March 1936, which proved to his satisfaction that his willpower and intuition were immeasurably superior to the combined expertise of his military advisers, a theme to which he would return time and again in later years.

> **'The Führer is cleverer than we are, he will plan and do everything correctly.'**
> GENERAL WERNER VON BLOMBERG

Worse was to come over sending the Army to war. Hitler's grand strategy was aggressive and expansionist, while his generals, as so often happens in peacetime, were horrified by the thought of war. In June 1937, Blomberg issued the following directive:

The general political situation justifies the supposition that Germany does not have to reckon on an attack from any side. This is due mainly to the lack of desire for war on the part of all nations, especially the Western powers. It is also due to the lack of military preparedness on the part of a number of states, notably Russia. Germany has just as little intention of unleashing a European war. Nonetheless, the international situation, politically unstable and not exclusive of surprising incidents, requires readiness for war on the part of German Armed forces (a) so that attacks from any side may be countered; and (b) so that any favourable political opportunities may be militarily exploited.

The German Army's preparations for war remained wholly defensive, and fearful of aggressive action. Blomberg had opposed the introduction of general conscription and the rearmament programme and, during the reoccupation of the Rhineland, had behaved, in Hitler's words, like 'a hysterical maiden'. In 1941 Hitler reminisced: 'Before I became chancellor I thought that the General Staff was like a mastiff which had been held tight by the collar because it threatened all and sundry. Since then I have had to recognise that the General Staff is anything but that. It has consistently tried to impede every action that I have thought necessary … It is I who have always had to goad on this mastiff.'

'FOR GOOD OR ILL'

At the beginning of February 1933, within a month of assuming power, Hitler had aired with the military the topic of the establishment of a Greater Germany and the acquisition *Lebensraum*, by force of arms, in the East. The generals received the latter part of Hitler's proposal – one of the key elements in his world view – with less than enthusiasm. Nor did this change on the occasions when Hitler returned to this theme.

He raised it again in a significant confrontation with his military advisers at a conference at the Reich Chancellery on 5 November 1937, minuted by Hitler's military adjutant, Colonel Count Friedrich Hossbach. A Greater Germany, he announced, would be created by amalgamating into the Reich German-speaking Austrians, the Germans of the Czech Sudetenland, and the areas lost in post-World War I plebiscites. He also indicated that he would turn East to acquire *Lebensraum*, warning that Germany would have to launch an outward expansion by 1943 at the latest because, by then, the nation's war-making capacity would have been over-taken by those of its future enemies. If the Western powers would not permit this eastward drive, they would have to be dealt with first. Hitler stressed that history had shown that such expansion was vital to Germany's survival and could not be achieved without risk. The only questions to be answered were when, and how.

Blomberg and Fritsch forcefully opposed this line of thinking. Any move against Czechoslovakia might drag France, an ally of the Czechs, and Britain into war with Germany. An all-out war with such opponents was unthinkable. Four days later, on the anniversary of the Munich putsch, Fritsch again attempted to impress on Hitler, in no uncertain terms, the unpalatable military realities of this line of thinking. His words fell on deaf ears.

Hitler did not abandon hope of winning over his senior military commanders but he badly bungled his last attempt at a meeting at the War Ministry on 22 January 1938. This time he directed his appeal over the heads of Blomberg and Fritsch to their subordinates. However, on this occasion the Führer fluffed his lines. Talk of replacing Christianity with National Socialism, the securing of living space as the only solution to Germany's problems, and world domination by the Aryan peoples, might have gone down well with the Party faithful but struck all the wrong notes with this audience. Frustrated, Hitler ended the address by reproving the generals for their conservatism and lack of foresight.

Hitler no longer had any use for Blomberg and Fritsch. The fundamental elements of his future policy were anathema to the men upon whom Hitler had relied for their execution, and they had forfeited his confidence. They would have to be removed. They also had other powerful enemies in Göring (commander of the Luftwaffe since 1935), who considered them his rivals and had been accused by Fritsch, not without reason, of being a dilettante; and in Himmler and his associates who saw the Army as an important sector of German society which as yet remained free of their influence.

Blomberg was the first to fall, and by his own hand. In January 1938 the widowed War Minister had married Erna Gruhn, a twenty-six-year-old shorthand typist who worked in the Reich Egg Marketing Board and was already carrying his child. Hitler had been a witness at the wedding. Unfortunately for Blomberg, Erna had had a previous life as a prostitute, and there were photographs and a police record to prove it. The Berlin Police President, Count von Helldorff, took the photographs to Göring, giving him the means to destroy Blomberg and succeed him as Defence Minister, a coveted post which both Blomberg and Fritsch had actively prevented him from acquiring.

On 26 January, Blomberg was forced to resign on the grounds that he had brought the officer corps into disrepute. At their final meeting the next day, Hitler told him that 'when Germany's time comes you shall be at my side'.[19] Fritsch was removed a few days later, although this proved a harder task. As a middle-aged and unmarried man, he was a ripe target for a charge of homosexuality. In 1935 Otto Schmidt, a petty criminal, alleged during a police interrogation that he had witnessed a homosexual act between a man with a monocle and a youth. Now he was wheeled out to testify that he had subsequently blackmailed the middle-aged man, who was none other than the commander-in-chief of the Army. In fact, the middle-aged homosexual, if he was indeed involved in this farrago at all, was apparently another man with a similar-sounding name.

It was a flimsy frame-up, and at first Hitler refused to accept it. However, Fritsch's fate was unwittingly sealed by Blomberg when he met Hitler on the day he left office. Hitler had asked him to suggest a successor, and the departing field marshal had observed that the Führer himself should take over the post of Defence Minister and C-in-C of the armed forces. Thus the disgraced Blomberg had unwittingly presented Hitler with the perfect answer to his problems in reordering the top of the military chain of command. Hitler then asked Blomberg who had been his chief of staff. Blomberg told him that it was General Wilhelm Keitel, adding the rider, 'He's only the man who runs my office.' Hitler realized in an instant that the subservient Keitel, a conscientious yes-man to his fingertips, was exactly the officer he was looking for. And, with that, Blomberg departed into oblivion, having performed his last service for the Führer and his greatest disservice to the German Army. Hitler could now start looking for a compliant Army chief.

---

19 Hitler lied. Blomberg spent World War II in obscurity and re-emerged to give evidence at Nuremberg, where he died in detention.

REOCCUPATION OF THE RHINELAND

The military reoccupation of the Rhineland was a move which radically changed Hitler's relations with not only the German Army's high command but also with the British and French. Hitler and his generals believed that the move was essential to secure the vital strategic, economic and communications centres of the Ruhr and the Rhine valley. But the generals were fearful that such an operation, in contravention of the Versailles Treaty and the Locarno Pact, would prompt an overwhelming military response from Britain and France for which Germany was ill-prepared. The General Staff regarded Hitler as a roulette player, prepared to gamble everything on a single throw of the dice. Hitler's nerve held, and he was proved correct in his assumption that the British and French would do nothing and the League of Nations, preoccupied with Mussolini's occupation of Abyssinia, would remain inactive. The reoccupation, code-named Winter Exercise (*Winterübung*), went ahead on 7 March 1936, initially conducted by only three battalions of German infantry but reinforced later that day by four divisions of state police (*Landespolizei*). Hitler later observed that 'the first forty eight hours of the march ... were the most nerve-racking of my life'. The peaceful reoccupation of the Rhineland was celebrated by the Germans, consolidated Hitler's dictatorship, and confirmed his belief that his own intuition outweighed the professional expertise of his commanders. He was able to embark on an aggressive foreign policy. In the summer of 1936, German 'volunteers' and much materiel were despatched for combat testing in the Nationalist cause in the Spanish Civil War.

The hapless Fritsch, his services no longer required, was now to appear before a special court convened by the Gestapo. Before this, Hitler had confronted him in the Chancellery in the company of Göring and Himmler. Fritsch, who thus far had maintained a stony silence in this sorry affair, succumbed to a paroxysm of rage when the blackmailer was produced. Afterwards, Göring collapsed on a sofa, shrieking, 'He did it! He did it!'

Göring was appointed the court president at Fritsch's trial, which opened on 10 March. The verdict, however, was a surprise that temporarily wiped the smile off Göring's face: 'Acquitted on the grounds of proven innocence.' But the moment passed. There was no protest from the Army, most of whose officers were unaware of the details behind the removal of Blomberg and Fritsch. Those who knew more could not bring themselves to believe that Adolf Hitler, the Army's friend and ally in the fight against the SA, could have turned so swiftly against its commanders without reason. After the war, General Heinz Guderian reflected: 'These serious allegations against our most senior officers, whom we knew to be men of spotless honour, cut us to the quick. They were quite incredible, and yet our immediate reaction was that the first magistrate of the German state could not simply have invented these stories out of the air.'

Pressure from the Army, and many threats of resignation, obliged Hitler to make Fritsch an honorary colonel in his old regiment. Fritsch retreated ever deeper into his austere shell, from which he occasionally emerged to shower Hitler with derisive praise: 'This man [Hitler] is Germany's destiny for good or ill, and this destiny will run its course to the end; if it leads us into the abyss he will take us all with him – there is nothing to be done about it.'

The enforced retirement of Blomberg and Fritsch did not immediately bring Hitler generals of the bellicose temper he required, but it provided him with the pretext to replace the Defence Ministry with an over-arching stratum of command, the *Oberkommando der Wehrmacht* (OKW), headed by the pliant Keitel, who was answerable to Hitler. OKW was given responsibility for strategic planning, a move which inevitably placed it on a collision course with the separate *Oberkommando des Heeres* (OKH, the German Army High Command) and led to a great deal of unproductive jostling in the war years.

There was no recall for Blomberg, but in September 1939 Fritsch went to war with his regiment in Poland and was killed by a sniper's bullet. A memorial was erected on the spot, only to be destroyed later in the war, as was his grave. The news of his death was given to Hitler on the evening of 22 September, when General Alfred Jodl, OKW chief of staff, delivered his daily report: 'Today there fell one of the finest soldiers Germany has ever had, Generaloberst Baron von Fritsch.' Hitler started but remained silent. He later declined to attend Fritsch's funeral.

The removal of Fritsch was followed by the appointment of General Walther von Brauchitsch as his successor. Hitler had a considerable moral hold over Brauchitsch, having personally secured his divorce and financed his marriage to the divorced wife of a fellow officer, a woman with an extremely shady past. Blomberg's replacement was indeed General Wilhelm Keitel, although he held a post of much lower status than his former boss. Keitel was little more than a tirelessly efficient clerk, totally subservient to the Führer, and exercised no influence over the conduct of operations; he was simply a functionary, faithfully carrying out his master's orders.

Friday, 4 February 1938 was a day of immense importance both to the Army and to Germany. It was a day which marked a crucial shift in the balance of power within the Third Reich and began the concentration of military leadership into Hitler's hands. At midnight on 3 February, a Führer decree was broadcast on German radio:

> From henceforth I exercise personally the immediate command over the whole Armed Forces. The former Wehrmacht Office in the War Ministry becomes the High Command of the Armed forces [OKW] and comes immediately under my command as my military staff. At the head of the staff of the High Command stands the former chief of the Wehrmacht Office [Keitel]. He is accorded the rank equivalent to that of Reich Minister. The High Command of the Armed Forces also takes over the functions of the War Ministry, and the chief of the High Command exercises, as my deputy,

the powers hitherto held by the Reich War Minister. The task of preparing the unified defence of the Reich in all fields, in accordance with my instructions, is the function of the High Command in time of peace.

At the same time, Hitler seized the opportunity presented by this dramatic reshuffle to remove and retire a large number of senior officers, including sixteen generals, on whom he could not rely. Göring, Fritsch's nemesis, had been denied the Defence Ministry but was nonetheless rewarded by being given the rank of General-Field Marshal (*Generalfeldmarschall*). As Brauchitsch was only a Colonel-General (*Generaloberst*), this made Göring the senior officer of the armed forces. Finally, on the day the announcement was made, in one of his several acts of supreme cynicism Hitler also announced the elevation of Walther Funk, Goebbels's Secretary of State, to the post of Minister of Economics. Funk was a notorious homosexual.

At the centre of the third Reich's military direction after February there was only one reality – Adolf Hitler. He was the sole military and political authority, from whom all power flowed. General Guderian later wrote: 'Up to that time Hitler had been receptive to practical considerations, and had at least listened to advice and been prepared to discuss matters with others; now, however, he became increasingly autocratic. One example of his change in behaviour is furnished by the fact that after 1938 the cabinet never met. The Ministers did their work in accordance with instructions issued by Hitler to each of them singly. There was no longer any collective examination of major policy … The national administration was emasculated.'

ANSCHLUSS

Within eighteen months of becoming chancellor, Hitler had turned his attention to three foreign policy goals which were central to his aim of restoring German national prestige. First, the military restrictions imposed by the Treaty of Versailles were to be lifted. Second, Germany was to be restored to its rightful place as the strongest European power, and a 'Greater Germany' was to be created to include German-speaking Austria, the Czech Sudetenland and the territories lost after World War I. The removal of Blomberg and Fritsch, and the Army reorganization announced in February 1938 enabled Hitler to pursue the Greater Germany part of his programme without opposition or obstruction.

The first target in Hitler's sights was Austria, the scene of a grave political embarrassment for him in 1934. The Austrian chancellor, Engelbert Dollfuss, was a Fascist, but also a vigorous opponent of union with Germany. In May 1933 he had dissolved parliament and banned political parties, including the Austrian NSDAP. Like their German counterparts, the Austrian Nazis were wedded to political violence, but resented Hitler's apparent closeness to the Italian dictator Mussolini, who was an ardent supporter of the Dollfuss regime. For his part, Hitler was unwilling to ruffle Mussolini's feathers and attempted to muzzle the Austrian Nazis, who were itching for a fight.

In Austria, political violence worsened. In May 1934 Dollfuss put down an

ANTI-SEMITISM IN GERMANY

In the nineteenth century, anti-Semitism was a European-wide phenomenon, and in Germany after 1918 the Jews became scapegoats for the country's defeat and humiliation at the hands of the Allies. In 1933 there were approximately half a million Jews living in Germany, just under one per cent of the total population. However, the proportion of Jews in the professions was higher (16.6 per cent of lawyers and 10.9 per cent of doctors) which fuelled a general popular resentment but in no way confirmed the Nazi propaganda picture – a picture relentlessly retailed in rabid publications like Julius Streicher's *Der Stürmer*, of a deadly Jewish threat to German society. Indeed, most German Jews were culturally assimilated, seeing themselves as Germans of Jewish faith.

The early years of Nazi rule, however, witnessed an escalating campaign against Germany's Jews. In part it was orchestrated from the top by Hitler and his lieutenants, notably Josef Goebbels, who lost no opportunity to portray the Jews as an alien menace; but pressure also came from below, from violent and undisciplined elements in the Nazi apparat, notably, regional *Gauleiter* and the SA, both acting on their own initiative but nevertheless taking their cue from the top, provided a striking example of 'working towards the Führer'(see p. 91).

On 1 April 1933 there was an official one-day boycott of Jewish shops. The fact that the boycott was limited to one day was the result of the lobbying of Hitler by cabinet colleagues, notably Foreign Minister Neurath and Reichsbank President Schacht, that an all-out boycott of Jewish businesses would lead to a retaliatory boycott of German goods in important markets in the United States and Britain. In April 1933 Jews were banned from the civil service and the legal and medical professions. In the same month, a decree was passed identifying non-Aryans as any

people who had a Jewish parent or grandparent. They were presumed to be Jewish if they practised the Jewish religion. If there was any doubt, there would be recourse to an opinion delivered by 'an expert on racial research'. Limits were placed on the number of Jews teaching in higher education institutions and all Jewish business enterprises had to be identified as such. By the end of 1933, nearly forty thousand Jews had left Germany, among them twenty Nobel Prize winners, the most celebrated being Albert Einstein.

Preoccupations with foreign policy and the task of cutting the SA down to size meant that the Nazi leadership temporarily took its foot off the pedal. This led to a growing number of spontaneous outbursts of grassroots violence against the Jews. In turn, these prompted more protests from Hjalmar Schacht about the damage this was doing to Germany's image abroad. However, Himmler's deputy, Reinhard Heydrich, approached the problem from a different angle, observing that 'the methods of rowdy anti-Semitism are to be rejected. One does not fight rats with a revolver, but with poison and gas. Foreign political damage has no relationship to local success.' The debate was resolved at a meeting of the Reichstag in Nuremberg on 15 September 1935, when Hitler announced the hastily drafted Nuremberg Laws. These prohibited marriage, and sexual relations outside marriage, between Jews and ethnic Germans, and the employment of Aryan women aged under forty-five in Jewish households. Jews were also deprived of citizenship and political rights.

In 1936, the year of the Berlin Olympics, there was a temporary slackening of anti-Jewish pressure, but the momentum was stepped up thereafter. In November 1937 the dismissal of Schacht removed another stumbling block to the hardening of policy. From 1934, Schacht had added the post of Minister of Economics to his portfolio, and had continued to counsel against the more extreme forms of actions against the Jews, principally on the utilitarian grounds of disruption to industry and the closing of export markets. In December 1937, Göring, now in charge of the Four-Year Plan, issued a decree restricting the ability of Jews to buy raw materials or deal in currency, part of a strategy to 'Aryanize' Jewish businesses.

Anschluss with Austria in March 1938, which incorporated another two hundred thousand Jews into the Reich, was followed by an unbridled eruption of looting and violence. In Vienna,

Heydrich and his subordinate, Adolf Eichmann, established the Central Office for the Emigration of Austrian Jewry to encourage emigration and hasten the de-judaization of the Austrian economy. By the end of the year, thousands of Jewish homes had been forcibly expropriated and the psychological green light given for the events of *Kristallnacht* in November 1938. *Kristallnacht* was sparked on 7 November by the shooting in Paris of a German embassy official by a young Polish Jew, Herschel Grynzspan, who was protesting against the expulsion of thousands of Jews from Germany. Encouraged by Goebbels, hundreds of Jews were murdered, business premises and synagogues were ransacked and destroyed, and over thirty thousand Jews arrested and sent to concentration camps. Although the SS and SA were involved at local level, neither Himmler nor Heydrich was informed of the pogrom until after it had started. Göring, who was nominally in charge of Jewish affairs, also felt that his turf had been invaded by Goebbels. However, along with Himmler and Heydrich, he was obliged to bite his tongue as Hitler had given Goebbels's initiative his full support.

In the immediate aftermath of *Kristallnacht*, Göring presided over a meeting, attended by Goebbels and Heydrich, to discuss further measures against the Jews. On the urging of Goebbels, the breathtakingly cynical decision was taken to impose a massive fine – 1.25 thousand million Reichsmark – on the Jews for the damage which had been inflicted on them. It was to be a demonstration of how all Jews were to be held collectively guilty of any crime. Three days later, all Jewish pupils were expelled from German schools. In December, a decree was issued excluding Jews from all aspects of Germany's economic life. By assiduously working towards the Führer, Goebbels had pushed the persecution of the Jews into an ominously higher gear.

A poster put up by the National Socialist Workers' Party for a 1930 election. A Nazi sword is shown slaying the Jewish menace, represented by a serpent.

armed uprising and subsequently unveiled a new constitution modelled on Fascist
Italy. Then, in July 1934, Dollfuss was assassinated by the Austrian Nazis in a hare-
brained attempted putsch. Mussolini, who saw Austria as a useful buffer between
Italy and Hitler's Germany, despatched three divisions towards the Brenner Pass.
The gesture made it clear that if Germany came to the aid of the Austrian Nazis
there would be war. Hitler could only watch as the new Austrian government, led
by another autocrat, Kurt von Schuschnigg, slapped a new ban on the Austrian
NSDAP and executed the putschists.

—m—

Hitler had to wait four years to turn the tables. The new Austria was a shadow of
the empire into which Hitler had been born, with its population of fifty-four million shrunk to seven million, two million of them in Vienna. Nevertheless, the union
of Germany with Austria (*Anschluss*) had been stated in the NSDAP programme of
1920, and on the first page of *Mein Kampf* Hitler had stated that Austria must be
reunited with the German mother country, not for economic reasons but because
'one blood demands one Reich'. However, it was undeniable that Austria's strategic
position, industries and mineral resources would give an enormous boost to a
German economy now struggling to meet the demands of its Four-Year Plan.

Hitler had clearly stated his position on Austria in November 1937 and it had
been noted in the Hossbach memorandum. That same month Hitler had discussed
'possible alterations in the European order' with the British Lord Privy Seal Lord
Halifax, but had left Halifax with the impression that 'Germany did not want to
annex Austria or to reduce her to political dependence – her desire was to bring
about by peaceful means full economic, cultural, commercial, and possibly mone-
tary and currency union with Austria, and to see in Austria a Government really
friendly to Germany and ready to work hand in hand for the common welfare of
both branches of the Teutonic race'.

Hitler had his own way of dealing with the problem. On 12 February,
Schuschnigg accepted an invitation to meet him at the Berghof. Waiting for the
small Austrian party were Hitler, Joachim von Ribbentrop – former champagne
salesman and diplomat, now Hitler's foreign minister – Keitel, and two of the
Führer's most intimidating-looking generals, Reichenau and Sperrle, who in 1937
had commanded the Kondor Legion in Spain. By the time Schuschnigg arrived,
Hitler had worked himself up into a towering rage and subjected the Austrian chancellor to a protracted rant in his study, threatening to turn up unexpectedly in
Vienna, 'like a spring storm'.

Meanwhile, Ribbentrop was presenting Guido Schmidt, an official of the
Austrian Foreign Ministry, with a set of demands that included an end to all
restrictions on the Austrian NSDAP and the appointment of a Nazi sympathizer,

Opposite: Hitler addressing a vast crowd in the Heldenplatz in Vienna during the *Anschluss*, or reunification, of Germany and Austria on 15 March 1938. The Anschluss demonstrated that Britain and France were unwilling to stand up to him and that Mussolini was happy to accept the sacrifice of his Austrian buffer for the sake of friendship with Germany.

HITLER AND EVA BRAUN

Hitler, Eva Braun, and one of Eva's terriers, Negus, on the terrace at the Berghof. Braun became Hitler's mistress in 1932, after the death of Geli Raubal, and remained discreetly in the background until late in the war, a position which she bitterly resented but over which she had no control. In the 1930s she made two suicide attempts, after the second of which Hitler bought her a villa in the suburbs of Munich with some of the royalties from Heinrich Hoffmann's photographs. Braun was a great lover of cosmetics and nude sun-bathing, neither of which was to Hitler's taste. It was not until late in the war that she made public appearances, and then only because in June 1944 her sister Gretl had married SS *Gruppenführer* Hermann Fegelein, the ex-jockey who was Himmler's representative with Hitler and who was summarily executed in the last mad days in the Führerbunker. Loyal to Hitler to the end, Braun was nevertheless an unexceptional woman – in the postwar words of Albert Speer, who knew her well, all the historians coming to the subject of Eva Braun were doomed to find her 'a great disappointment'.

Artur von Seyss-Inquart,[20] as Minister of the Interior. Remarkably, all was sweetness and light at lunch, with the generals, then Hitler and Schuschnigg returned to the Führer's study, where Hitler threatened to march into Austria if his demands were not met in full.

Schuschnigg did not buckle, but informed Hitler that only the Austrian president could sanction such measures. However, he had been left in no doubt whatsoever as to Hitler's deadly seriousness, and before he departed he signed the list of demands. He declined Hitler's offer of dinner. Three days later Hitler's demands were implemented.

But Schuschnigg had one more card to play. On 9 March he announced, out of the blue, that within four days he would hold a referendum on Austrian autonomy, a measure for which the Austrian Nazis had long been agitating. But the wording of the referendum, asking the electorate to back 'a free and German, independent and social, Christian and united Austria…' was calculated to produce the worst

---

20 Seyss-Inquart became the Austrian chancellor after the *Anschluss*. In October 1939 he was appointed governor-general of those areas in Poland which had not been absorbed into either Germany or the Soviet Union. In May 1940 he became the Reich Commissioner of the Netherlands with almost absolute power, being responsible only to Hitler for his actions. During his time in office he imposed fines and confiscations, inflicted reprisals, compelled five million Dutch citizens to work for Germany, and deported some hundred and twenty thousand Jews. He was captured in 1945 and executed for war crimes the following year.

possible result for the Austrian Nazis. The biter had been bitten. Hitler was dumbfounded, then seized by rage at what he considered a betrayal of the agreement signed at the Berghof.

Goebbels and Göring were summoned, as was Seyss-Inquart, who was visiting southern Germany. Hitler sat up with Goebbels, outlining his plans. At midnight on 11 March, Goebbels wrote in his diary, 'The die is cast. On Saturday march in. Push straight to Vienna. Big aeroplane action. The Führer is going himself to Austria. Göring and I are to stay in Berlin. In eight days Austria will be ours.' On the 10th Hitler had ordered General Ludwig Beck, the Army chief of staff, and Becks' deputy, General Erich von Manstein, to prepare for an immediate invasion of Austria. This they did with some reluctance, telling Hitler that in their opinion the Army was not ready for such a task. But as Keitel later observed, 'their objections were summarily brushed aside by Hitler.' On 11 March OKW issued a directive which included the announcement that the Führer himself would take charge of operations. And on the 12th, German troops proceeded to incorporate a recalcitrant Austria into the Greater German Reich.

Hitler had snatched triumph from disaster. Mussolini did not intervene, prompting Hitler to shower him with extravagant thanks: 'Please tell Mussolini I will never forget him for it, never, never, never, come what may.' Schuschnigg, whose pleas to the British for help had fallen on deaf ears, had been replaced by Seyss-Inquart, and his cabinet was succeeded by an Austrian Ministerial Council. In a final broadcast to the Austrian people, Schuschnigg declared that Austria had yielded to force and, to spare bloodshed, the Austrian Army would offer no resistance.

Shortly before 4 p.m. on 12 March 1938, Hitler crossed the Austrian border over the bridge at his birthplace, Braunau am Inn. Church bells pealed as his cavalcade of grey

THE BERGHOF

The Berghof was Hitler's residence in the Obersalzberg of the Bavarian Alps near Berchtesgaden. It had started life as a small chalet, Haus Wachenfeld, owned by a Buxtehude businessman, Otto Winter. In 1928 Winter's widow rented the house to Hitler, who bought it in 1933 with royalties from the sales of *Mein Kampf*. In the mid-1930s he embarked on a substantial expansion of the premises which reflected his tastes in domestic architecture. The Berghof's Great Hall groaned with heavy Teutonic furniture and hid a projection booth behind one of its walls to screen the Führer's favourite movies. A huge picture window afforded stunning views of the mountains of his native Austria. The British *Homes and Gardens* magazine described Hitler as 'his own decorator, designer, and furnisher, as well as architect', and noted that many of the rooms contained caged canaries and were hung with Hitler's own watercolours. Silent home-movie footage, shot by Eva Braun in the late 1930s, caught Hitler relaxing on the Berghof's massive terrace while his German shepherd, Blondi, and Eva's terriers mingled with the Führer's lieutenants, Himmler, Heydrich, Goebbels, Göring and Ribbentrop. Braun herself posed for the camera, laughing coquettishly in a dirndl skirt. Hitler spent much time in the Berghof, obliging the Nazi paladins to acquire or build residences in the area. The site of Göring's house now boasts the Intercontinental Hotel. A landing strip was built to ease the entourage's comings and goings. From the mid-1930s, public access to the area was prevented by heavy security restrictions. Hitler's final visit to the Berghof was in July 1944. On 25 April 1945 it was bombed by RAF Lancasters; on 4 May it was set on fire by its withdrawing SS guards, and it was subsequently sacked by Allied troops.

Mercedes limousines inched their way through streets packed with delirious crowds. The convoy pushed on to Linz, where a vast crowd halted its progress. Hitler reached the town hall on foot. Tears streaked his cheeks as he addressed the heaving mass from the balcony. He told them that they were witnesses to the accomplishment of his mission, adding, 'I do not know on which day you will be called. I hope it is not far off.'

He remained in Linz for the next day, Sunday, taking rooms with his party in the Hotel Weinzinger on the banks of the Danube. The hotel's single telephone was reserved for his use alone. He told a British journalist that Austria would become a German province, 'like Bavaria or Saxony'. He went to Leonding to lay flowers on the graves of his parents. He used the hotel's telephone to pour a second paean of praise on Mussolini, and that evening signed the law by which Austria became a German province.

On the morning of 14 March, Hitler drove to Vienna. The crowds massed in front of the hotel in which he was staying, the Imperial, drew him out on to his balcony time after time, chanting, 'We want our Führer.' The next day he gave a speech to a colossal crowd, estimated at a quarter of a million, in Vienna's Heldenplatz. But there was a terrible ugliness lurking behind the unbridled enthusiasm on display.

THE FOUR-YEAR PLAN

Hitler had no time for received ideas about the structure of government and the development and implementation of policy. From 1933, the Nazi state was characterized by the emergence of new and competing agencies advancing radical agendas tailored to coincide with or anticipate the Führer's world view. In 1936 Hitler personally wrote a memorandum setting out the goals of the so-called Four-Year Plan, to be implemented under the direction of Hermann Göring who was handed sweeping powers in the economic sphere. Anticipating war, Hitler stipulated a timetable for rearmament which would give the Wehrmacht an operational capability and the German economy a degree of self-sufficiency to enable it to weather wartime conditions. Autarky was to be secured by German expansion and the securing of vital raw materials. Great emphasis was also placed on the development of synthetic materials and the control of labour. Important industrialists were recruited to develop and administer the Plan, for example Carl Krauch of IG Farben the chemical giant, which had worked closely with Nazi officials during the take over of Czech chemical plants in 1938–39. During World War II, IG Farben also built plants – one of them in the Auschwitz complex – to produce synthetic oil and rubber (from coal). IG Farben held the patent for Zyklon B, a cyanide compound originally developed for fumigation. It was first used against human victims in 1939 in the euthanasia programme, and again later in the extermination camps. The steady expansion of Göring's sprawling empire forced the resignation in November 1937 of Economics Minister Hjalmar Schacht, who was replaced by the more compliant Nazi, Walther Funk. During the war the powers vested in Göring were extended to the industries and economies of occupied countries, whose resources were, as a matter of policy, ruthlessly plundered for the benefit of the Third Reich. Göring also directed the deportation of millions of people from the occupied territories to forced labour camps.

Himmler, Heydrich, and their subordinate Adolf Eichmann, had arrived in Vienna on the 12th, and a wave of arrests had begun.

The violence which they set in train was of a ferocity and on a scale far greater than in 1933 when Hitler came to power. The Gestapo immediately got their hands on Vienna's police records and began hauling in Socialists, Communists and Jews. Many of the Jews were subjected to brutal beatings, during which their valuables were plundered at will. Some were forced to scrub the pavements while they were drenched with water by crowds jeering 'work for the Jews at last'. A seventeen-year-old Jew watched, horrified, from his apartment window in the Nussdorferstrasse, when 'I suddenly heard a muffled shout from right below … I craned my neck and saw an Austrian policeman, a swastika brassard already over his dark green uniform, his truncheon in his fist, lashing out with berserk fury at a man writhing at his feet. I immediately recognised that policeman. I had known him all my life …'

THE SUDETENLAND

The *Anschluss* had immensely strengthened Hitler's position. The groundswell of opposition in the Army high command, stirred by the Blomberg–Fritsch affair, had been stilled by the triumphant reception of the troops in Austria. The overwhelming majority of army officers were, like the German people, firmly behind the Führer. Moreover, Hitler had pulled off the coup without bloodshed – that is, if you chose to ignore the barbaric treatment of thousands of terrorized and brutalized Jews.

The German takeover of Austria left Czechoslovakia horribly exposed. The Czechs, Slavs whom Hitler had despised since his days in Vienna, offered an even greater prize than Austria. However, any move made by Germany would be fraught with danger. A Franco-Czech treaty bound the French to support Czechoslovakia in the event of aggression and, since Britain was allied with France, armed conflict with the Czechs risked lighting the touchpaper for a European conflict. Looming ominously in the background was the Soviet Union, which also had treaty obligations to the Czechs and had indicated its willingness to help the French. But the Red Army had no direct access to Czech territory. Poland, deeply hostile to the Soviets, and Romania, extremely pro-German, blocked its passage westward.

Hitler put his foot down on the accelerator. The web of alliances between the Czechs and his enemies to the east and west made it imperative to move quickly. And, just as with Austria, there were compelling economic reasons to press ahead. Czechoslovakia had a thriving industrial base, with important armaments factories, notably the Skoda works in Pilsen, and was an important source of raw materials.

The three million ethnic Germans living in the Sudetenland, on Czechoslovakia's western border with Germany, gave Hitler a ready-made pretext for demanding that they be brought home to the Reich. In the summer of 1938 he steadily increased the pressure on the Czechs, instructing the local Nazi leader, Konrad Henlein, to campaign for greater autonomy for the Sudeten Germans. Every time the Czech government offered concessions, Henlein came back for more. The Czech president, Edvard Beness, prepared for war.

War seemed likely, but this was not a prospect which struck a chord with the German people. Too many of them remembered the Great War. They were only happy with bloodless conquests, and the Army, as usual, was dragging its heels. The Chief of the General Staff, General Ludwig Beck, urged the military leadership to take a collective stand, and on 16 July sent a memorandum to General von Brauchitsch, summarizing the views of many of the generals: 'There was no doubt that an attack on Czechoslovakia would bring France and Britain into the conflict at once ... the outcome would be a general catastrophe for Germany, not only a military defeat. The German people did not want this war, the purpose of which they do not understand. Similar thoughts were abroad in the Army ... Military preparations have attracted foreign attention ... Any hope of achieving surprise had thereby been dashed.'

Brauchitsch wriggled around on the hook but agreed to hold a secret meeting where the military foolishness of a war with Czechoslovakia was discussed, but no decision was taken on a plan of action. Hitler faced down the generals on 15 August after attending manoeuvres, telling them of his absolute determination to smash the Czechs in the autumn. He warned them that, despite all advice to the contrary, he had been proved right in the past. The generals remained silent. By the end of August, Beck[21] had resigned.

The generals still had the most profound misgivings about Hitler's plans.

The generals still had the most profound misgivings about Hitler's plans and some may have entertained hopes, however faint, of removing Hitler should he order the Army to move against Czechoslovakia. These hopes were destroyed by the British prime minister, Neville Chamberlain. Sadly for the Czechs, Chamberlain believed he could deal with Hitler. Somewhere in this extraordinary creature, he thought, there must lurk a man of reason, and this creature could be coaxed, blinking into the sunlight, if only Chamberlain could convince him that he could get his way by negotiating rather than going to war. Chamberlain felt he was the man to convince him.

Chamberlain, who had never flown before, now embarked on the first example of shuttle diplomacy. On 15 September he flew to meet Hitler at Berchtesgaden, then a week later at Bad Godesberg. The only result was that Hitler increased his demands. Chamberlain pressed on, persuading himself that Hitler was speaking the truth in desiring no more than 'racial unity' with the Sudeten Germans, but his personal appeal to the Führer cut no ice. War seemed inevitable.

Then Hitler backed down. The British, supported by the French, pressed the Czechs into ceding the Sudetenland to Germany. Chamberlain was unable to contemplate a war like that of 1914–18, and had been advised by his military chiefs that Britain's forces were not ready for a new armed conflict. Mussolini then stepped forward, appealing to Hitler to postpone a mobilization and accept a negotiated settlement along the lines proposed by the British. This was the last thing Hitler wanted, but he reluctantly had to accept when what he fervently wanted was war, and the complete destruction of Czechoslovakia. However, as Goebbels reminded him, 'We have no jumping off point for war. You can't carry out a world war on account of modalities.'

—⁓—

In Munich at the end of September 1938 a four-power conference was held. Attending were the Germans, British, French and Italians – but not the Czechs. They were to have no say in the mutilation of their own country. Chamberlain had, admittedly, been dealt a very poor hand, but had then proceeded to play it disastrously because of his mistaken assessment of Hitler's aims and his over-eagerness to placate the Führer with territorial concessions.

Nevertheless, Chamberlain was given a hero's welcome when he returned from Munich, brandishing in his hand the famous piece of paper signed by the Führer. Hitler later said that Chamberlain was such a nice old gentleman that it would have been impolite not to sign it, but the truth was staring everyone in the face. Peace had been secured, but probably temporarily and only at the expense of sacrificing the Czechs. It was clear that Hitler would make more demands. Lord Halifax (British foreign secretary 1938–40) was cheerfully of the opinion that Poland, and other nations in Eastern Europe, would inevitably be drawn into the German orbit. It was not long before the hopes raised at Munich were dashed.

> **The browbeaten Hacha gave the order that Czech troops were not to fire on the invading Germans.**

On the night of 14–15 March 1939, Hitler received Emil Hacha at the Chancellery in Berlin. The elderly, frail Hacha, president of Czechoslovakia since the previous November, was kept waiting until the small hours of the 15th while Hitler enjoyed watching a movie called *A Hopeless Case*. The same could now be said about Czechoslovakia. The wretched Hacha, who was accompanied by his foreign minister and the Czech ambassador in Berlin, was subjected to a brutal haranguing by Hitler in front of intimidating ranks of Nazi paladins. Hitler ranted and raved. German troops were on the march and would cross the border at 6 a.m., information which was conveniently confirmed by General Keitel; Hacha must telephone Prague immediately if he wished to avoid bloodshed. Göring then threatened Hacha with the Luftwaffe, which was poised to level the historic city of Prague.

At this point Hacha fainted, only to be revived by an injection from Hitler's personal physician, Dr Morell. When a telephone line was established with Prague, the browbeaten Hacha gave the order that Czech troops were not to fire on the invading Germans. Shortly before 04:00 hours he signed the document which placed the fate of his nation in the hands of Hitler. The Führer was overcome, telling the two secretaries who were on duty that night, 'I will go down as the greatest German in history.'

—⁓—

Czechoslovakia had been swallowed whole, and later that day Hitler drove into Prague, accompanied by the SS and the Gestapo. Snow was falling and no crowds lined the streets, only a sullen smattering of onlookers, some of whom were bold enough to shake their fists at the Führer. He spent the night in the Hradschin Castle, ancient home of the kings of Bohemia, dotting the 'I's and crossing the 'T's on the document that transformed Czechoslovakia into the protectorate of Bohemia-Moravia. Its preamble, dictated by Hitler, stated that, 'the Bohemian and Moravian lands had belonged to the living space of the German people for a thousand years'. For the Czechs, it was the start of six long years of subjugation.

On 31 March the British government guaranteed to protect Poland against aggression. From this moment, Britain and France were on the hook. In reality, neither could do anything effective to aid the Poles if they were attacked, nor could they wring concessions from Poland as they had done with Czechoslovakia. They could only hope that nothing would happen. But they knew something would.

POLAND

At the same time that he was swallowing Czechoslovakia, Hitler was putting pressure on Poland, the next country on his list. Poland had no effectively defensible frontiers, a strategic problem which gave rise to the aphorism, 'Poland has no history, only neighbours.' In the Middle Ages, Poland's Baltic littoral was settled and taken over by German crusaders, the Teutonic Knights. This territory became the state of Prussia, which was later dynastically united with Germany by the Hohenzollern rulers of Brandenburg, the last reigning incumbent of which was Kaiser Wilhelm II. In the late eighteenth century, Poland had been partitioned out of existence by the central European powers, only to rise like a phoenix from the ashes as an independent state in the Versailles settlement after World War I.

Versailles gave Poland access to the sea by extending her boundaries to include the mouth of the Vistula river. This Polish corridor cut Prussia off from Germany. As a concession to the Germans, the German-speaking city of Danzig, at the mouth of the Vistula, was established as a free city under the supervision of the League of Nations. Even before he had digested Czechoslovakia, Hitler was demanding an adjustment of the corridor and the status of Danzig. With the sorry example of Czechoslovakia staring them in the face, the Poles ignored Hitler's demands and continued to do so even when, on 23 March 1939, as an earnest of his intentions, he occupied the Lithuanian port of Memel. It was the last 'peaceful' German conquest.

The Poles had an inflated belief in their own power, further sustained by the knowledge that Britain and France were preparing to extend them a guarantee of protection. On 31 March 1939, a week after announcing that they would defend Belgium, Holland and Switzerland if they were attacked, Britain and France issued a joint declaration guaranteeing the independence of Poland. This did nothing to deter Hitler, who had profited from French and British inaction over Czechoslovakia. In August 1939 he told his generals, 'Our enemies are small worms. I saw them in Munich.'

Poland now became the epicentre of the gathering storm. The British and French attempted to take the heat out of the crisis by drawing the Soviet Union into a protective agreement, even though they were well aware that the Poles were reluctant in the extreme to enter into an agreement with the Russians. The Poles hated the Russians more than they feared the Germans and suspected, rightly as it turned out, that the Soviet Union, given the chance, would annex large parts of Poland as part of the price for their intervention. The British and French were also hobbled by their own deep distrust of the Soviet dictator, Josef Stalin, who returned the feeling with interest.

Throughout the summer of 1939, British and French negotiations with the Soviets inched painfully forward. Hitler, on the other hand, had a freer hand. That spring and summer he, too, had been negotiating with Stalin, encouraged by hints that the Soviet Union had no desire to risk war, even over the future of a nation on its western border. However, neither the German nor the Russian dictator would show his hand.

Hitler broke the logjam in late July when he dangled a thinly veiled offer to hand Stalin a slice of eastern Poland if he agreed not to impede a German invasion of Poland from the west. The Russian eagerly responded, and on 22 August the German and Soviet Union foreign ministers, Ribbentrop and Molotov, signed a non-aggression pact in Moscow. It contained secret clauses which permitted the Soviet Union, in the event of a war between Germany and Poland, to annex eastern Poland up to the line of the Vistula, as well as the Baltic states of Latvia, Lithuania and Estonia.

There was nothing more that diplomacy could do. Poland was now doomed. By mid-June OKH, the Army high command, had settled on a plan which provided for two Army Groups, North and South, to attack simultaneously. Their objective was the Polish capital, Warsaw. Poland was deeply vulnerable along the entire length of its two most important borders. Northern Poland was dominated by East Prussia while in the south it was threatened from Czechoslovakia, which was now an extension of German territory. The Polish government did not know the secret provisions of the Nazi-Soviet non-aggression pact and the new threat it posed to its rear. And, in the event of war, it counted on the French, aided by the British, to attack Germany's western frontier to draw off German divisions from the east.

Hitler's calculations ran on different lines. He was convinced, correctly as it transpired, that the French would make no aggressive moves in the west, which he left defended by only forty-four divisions to oppose the nominal hundred of the French Army; and he was also sure that the British could do little or nothing to hurt Germany during the short time he needed to overrun Poland. Moreover, he was fully mobilized; the British and French were not. Finally, the German Army and the Luftwaffe were immeasurably better armed than their Polish opposite numbers. Between them, Army Groups North and South fielded sixty-two divisions, six of them armoured and ten mechanized, supported by thirteen hundred modern

Above: German infantry march into Poland, 1 September 1939. Three of the five armies used in the operation employed armoured spearheads but the dominant force remained the infantry divisions, which formed approximately 75 per cent of all participating formations. The German high command concluded that in the campaign, 'German infantry formations added one more to their list of triumphs'.

combat aircraft. As war loomed, the Poles had begun to mobilize, but by 1 September 1939 they had not fully deployed their forty divisions, none of which was armoured. The tanks they did field were obsolete, as were half of the nine hundred and fifty aircraft of the Polish air force.

The rush to war had now gained a seemingly irresistible momentum. There was a brief pause following the announcement, on 25 August, that the British had entered into a formal alliance with the Poles which guaranteed protection against aggression by a third party. A flurry of inconclusive diplomatic sparring followed, and on 28 August Hitler abrogated Germany's 1934 non-aggression pact with Poland, which had been signed at a time when Poland's and Germany's relative military strengths had been reversed.

Hitler still expected France and Britain to flinch from taking any military action, as they had done over Czechoslovakia. To give them a means of doing so without losing face, he created a 'border outrage', in fact staged by a unit of the SS, to make

it appear as if the Poles were the aggressors.[22] Responding to this 'provocation', German troops crossed the border into Poland at 4.30 a.m. on 1 September. Britain and France immediately attempted to avoid the unavoidable. They mobilized but said they would negotiate with Germany if Hitler pulled his troops back. There was a last exchange of notes but the German Army was not reined in.

At 11.15 on the morning of 3 September, a weary Neville Chamberlain announced to the British people that they were at war with Germany. As he finished his speech the air raid sirens began to wail. Within a few hours, the French, too, had declared war.

When the news was given to Hitler, he listend to his interpreter, Paul Schmidt, translate the diplomatic language. He sat, slumped in his chair, for a few moments. Then he looked up and asked, 'Well … what do we do now?'

---

22 Heydrich oversaw the staging of a fake Polish attack on a German radio station at Gleiwitz, a mile from the Polish border.

4

THE WARLORD

BLITZKRIEG

Before dawn on 1 September 1939, the Luftwaffe began a bombardment of strategic points inside Poland. It was the prelude to the first full-scale demonstration of the speed and striking power of Blitzkrieg tactics developed in Germany during the 1930s and based on deep armoured thrusts supported by dive – and level – bombers.

The Polish Army was dispersed in seven concentrations along its borders, with little in reserve, inviting swift envelopment by Army Groups North and South. In the opening exchanges there was also a dramatic demonstration by German Ju-87 Stuka dive-bombers of their ability to shatter troop formations caught in the open. In an attempt to block the left wing of the German Tenth Army advancing in the south, the Polish C-in-C, Field Marshal Rydz-Smigley ordered a cavalry brigade some three thousand strong to drive westward from the town of Wielun, twelve miles from the frontier with Germany. The dust raised by the cavalry – an echo of an earlier age – was quickly spotted by one of the many German reconnaissance aircraft flying over the battlefields. Thirty minutes later the column came under heavy Stuka attack. The carnage inflicted by the dive-bombers was completed by level bombers. After ninety air sorties the cavalry brigade ceased to exist as a fighting unit.

Opposite: Hitler takes the salute at the victory parade in Warsaw at the conclusion of the Polish campaign. The role of the German armoured formations in the victory was not to act independently of the infantry but to spearhead the general advance of the Army and protect the flanks of the great double encirclement which destroyed the Polish forces in a classic battle of annihilation.

BLITZKRIEG UNLEASHED

Norway was strategically important to Hitler as a springboard for aerial attack against Britain, and against the British naval blockade. The blockade threatened the route taken by the ships bringing Germany vital iron ore from Sweden through the port of Narvik in northern Norway. On 4 April 1940, the British prime minister, Neville Chamberlain, confidently announced, 'Hitler has missed the bus.' Four days later, British warships encountered German vessels escorting troop transports towards five Norwegian ports: Hitler was invading Norway. Only at Oslo, the Norwegian capital, did the Germans encounter serious resistance before airborne troops took the city on 9 April. On the same day Denmark was overrun. Between 10 and 13 April the Royal Navy inflicted heavy damage on the German naval force ferrying troops to Narvik, where the British and French came ashore on 15 April. The Allies also landed north and south of Trondheim, but these footholds were eliminated by the Germans as they swept inland and evacuations followed at the beginning of May. An Allied force captured Narvik in late May but was obliged to evacuate on 8–9 June because of events in the Low Countries and France.

Within two days the Luftwaffe had gained total air superiority and the Polish cordon defences had been splintered into uncoordinated groups. The German plan involved a double pincer movement. The inner pincer (Fourth, Eighth and Tenth Armies) was to close on the Vistula near Warsaw, while the outer pincer (Third and Fourteenth Armies) was to meet on the River Bug at Brest Litovsk, a hundred miles east of the Polish capital.

The outer encirclement was completed on 14 September. Three days later Poland's fate was sealed when the Red Army invaded from the east. Warsaw surrendered on 27 September, and the fortress city of Modlin fell on the following day. The last Polish resistance was overcome at Kock, south-east of Warsaw on 5 October. Polish casualties totalled some sixty-six thousand dead and over two hundred thousand wounded, while nearly seven hundred thousand prisoners were taken by the Germans and another two hundred thousand by the Red Army. German casualties were light – some fourteen thousand dead and thirty thousand three hundred wounded.

The German Army immediately turned westward to man the West Wall and prepare for a campaign against the British[23] and French, who had made no attempt to help the Poles, apart from a small demonstration in September, dubbed the Saar Offensive.

On the evening of 3 September, Hitler had boarded his special armoured train in Berlin and left for the front. For the next three weeks it was to be the first Führer headquarters. Hitler's carriage, at the head of the train, contained a spacious lounge, sleeping compartment and bathroom, together with compartments for his adjutants. In addition, the carriage held communications equipment and a conference room for meetings with his commanders. Martin Bormann, the Nazi Party organizer and now a permanent fixture in the Führer's entourage, had his quarters in the next carriage.

---

23 After declaring war, the British moved an expeditionary force (BEF) across the Channel to France. By May 1940 it consisted of ten infantry divisions, one under-strength tank brigade and an RAF component of five hundred fighters and light bombers.

On 19 September, Hitler entered Danzig to scenes of wild jubilation. Twice, on the 22nd and the 25th, he flew to the outskirts of Warsaw to witness at first hand the bombing and shelling he had ordered. By 27 September he was back in Berlin.

LOOKING WESTWARDS

On 12 September 1939, Hitler had told Colonel Schmundt, his chief Wehrmacht adjutant, that he intended attacking in the West immediately after the conclusion of the Polish campaign. On 27 September, the day the defenders of Warsaw capitulated, he held a meeting of the commanders-in-chief of the three Wehrmacht services in the map room of the new Chancellery.

Hitler got straight to the point: France was to be attacked as soon as possible to pre-empt a threat to the industrial region of the Ruhr. The offensive would slice through neutral Belgium and Holland. After a short discussion, Hitler threw into the fire the scrap of paper on which he had scribbled his notes for the meeting.

The Führer's army group commanders were dumbfounded. Such an offensive, they argued, would have little chance of success. The motorized and armoured divisions which had fought in Poland could not possibly be reorganized before mid-November; the troops stationed defensively on the Rhine were simply not up to scratch, and there were serious shortages of ammunition and equipment. The OKH view ruled out any possibility of an offensive against France until the spring of 1942.

Hitler would not be deflected. On 9 October, OKH was informed that he had chosen 25 November as the date on which the offensive would begin. The next day OKH received a fifty-eight-page memorandum pressing it to commence detailed planning. Nothing less was at stake than the 'destruction of the predominance of the Western powers in order to leave room for the expansion of the German people'.

Führer Directive No.6[24] described how that destruction was to be achieved: 'An offensive will be planned … through Luxembourg, Belgium and Holland [and] must be launched at the earliest possible moment [since] any further delay will … entail the end of Belgian and perhaps of Dutch neutrality to the advantage of the Allies. The purpose of this offensive will be to defeat as much as possible of the French Army and of the forces of the Allies fighting on their side, and at the same time to win as much territory as possible in Holland, Belgium and northern France to serve as a base for the successful prosecution of the air and sea war against England and as a wide protective area for the economically vital Ruhr.'

At this stage in the war Hitler, as Supreme Commander-in-Chief, was content to lay down broad strategic aims but did not involve himself in the details of planning. That would eventually change, but for the moment the plan of attack, code-named Case Yellow (*Fall Gelb*), was to be developed in detail by OKH, the Army's high

---

24 Hitler's Directives of World War II run from the plans to attack Poland (31 August 1939) to his last orders to German troops on the Eastern Front (15 April 1945) to choke the Red Army in a 'bath of blood'. They reveal the state of Hitler's mind throughout the war, from Germany's initial triumphs to stalemate, retreat and imminent disaster.

command. The OKH chief of staff, General Franz Halder, a devout Christian and a cautious artilleryman, delivered a plan which conformed to the OKH projection of spring 1942 as the earliest prudent moment at which Germany could tackle France and Britain. He acknowledged the letter of Führer Directive No.6 but not its spirit. The British Expeditionary Force (BEF) would be split from the main body of the French Army and sufficient ground won in Belgium to provide ports and airfields from which the Kriegsmarine (the German navy) and the Luftwaffe could operate against the British. It was a modest plan to achieve a limited victory.

A frustrated Hitler attempted to work round the obstacles which Halder had laid in his path. But the General Staff would not budge. Late autumn was no time to launch a campaign in the sodden plains of north west Europe. Hitler tried another tack, suggesting to General Jodl, the OKW chief of staff, on 20 October that the Wehrmacht's tanks be committed to an attack launched through the hills and forests of the Ardennes. Once more Hitler was balked, but he was about to acquire an important new ally.

The commander-in-chief of Army Group A, General Gerd von Rundstedt, had retired in 1938, the year of the purging of Blomberg and Fritsch, but had been recalled to the service in 1939 at the age of sixty-four. Rundstedt and his chief of staff, Erich von Manstein, who possessed one of the most incisive brains in the Germany armed forces, knew nothing of Hitler's dissatisfaction with Halder's plan but considered Case Yellow, which they did know about, a thoroughly pusillanimous attempt to address a problem which cried out for a full-blooded solution.

As the autumn weather worsened into winter, forcing one postponement of Case Yellow after another, Hitler, Rundstedt and Manstein converged, like men playing a game of blind man's buff, until their eventual collision led to the formulation and application on the ground of one of the great strategic triumphs of World War II. It was, however, a triumph which would lead inexorably to disaster.

Nevertheless, Hitler was growing increasingly frustrated by OKH's delaying tactics. On 5 November he clashed angrily with Brauchitsch at the Chancellery. When Brauchitsch warned the Führer against underestimating the French, Hitler interrupted him: 'Herr Generaloberst, I should like to interrupt you immediately here, because I hold quite different views. First, I place a low value on the French Army's will to fight. Every army is a mirror of its people. The French people think only of peace and good living, and they are torn apart in parliamentary strife. Accordingly, the Army, however brave and well trained its officer corps may be, does not show the combat determination expected of it. After the first setbacks, it will swiftly crack up.'

Thoroughly discomfited, Brauchitsch blundered on, pointing out that, in his opinion, the assault troops in Poland had not matched up to the men of 1914. Hitler exploded. Brauchitsch was making monstrous accusations about his, Hitler's, Army. His high command had never been loyal to him and, worse, they were defeatists. Brauchitsch, who had been stunned into silence by the outburst, left the room, and Hitler dictated a letter sacking him, which he later destroyed. Brauchitsch's humiliation was another nail in the coffin of the OKH. Hitler, however, had by no means finished with his generals.

POINT OF NO RETURN

At a meeting at the Chancellery on 23 November, attended by all the senior Wehrmacht officers down to corps commanders and their equivalents in the Luftwaffe and Kriegsmarine, Hitler delivered a scalding lecture, treating his top commanders like so many feckless schoolboys. He reminded them that they owed their status entirely to the Nazi Party and that, thanks to his leadership, for the first time in nearly seventy years they would have to fight on only one front. He was determined to launch a crushing offensive on this front, and anyone who thought other-wise was irresponsible. Fretting about Belgian and Dutch neutrality was pointless – nobody would raise the issue if Germany emerged victorious over the French. The British, moreover, would be brought to heel by U-boat warfare.

The generals, Hitler continued, were little more than cowards. If they imagined that he had created the Wehrmacht in order not to fight, they were fools as well. Anyone who stood in his way would be annihilated. In a reference to the hapless Brauchitsch, Hitler declared that he had been 'infuriated' by the suggestion that his soldiers had been inadequate. 'Everything,' he said, 'depends on the military leaders. With the German soldier I can do anything, provided he is well led.' He ended by calling for total commitment: 'If we emerge from this struggle as victors – and we shall be victors! – then our epoch will enter into the history of our people. As for me,' he added prophetically, 'I shall stand or fall in this struggle. I shall not survive the defeat of my people. No surrender abroad! No revolution at home!'

Manstein was now enlisting support from other middle-ranking generals, like the tank expert Heinz Guderian, to endorse his concept of a knockout blow delivered in northern France. Guderian supported him, saying that if the tank force was strong enough, he could negotiate the heavily forested and supposedly 'untankable' Ardennes, cross the River Meuse, and deliver such a blow. Meanwhile Hitler, for all his fine words, had seemingly reconciled himself to the Halder plan in spite of its limitations. Only bad weather prevented its immediate implementation. The final 'A-Day', which would set the wheels in motion, was set for 17 January. Then fate took a hand.

On 10 January, two Luftwaffe officers crash-landed in Belgium with parts of the Case Yellow plan in a briefcase. They survived the crash but failed to burn all the documents, a fact which was immediately uncovered by the German military attaché in Holland. Case Yellow was now fatally compromised and the Army was obliged to make a clean breast of it to Hitler. He promptly dismissed the commander of Second Air Fleet and replaced him with Albert Kesselring, one of the most able German commanders of World War II and, once his rage had subsided, postponed Case Yellow indefinitely. Hitler then demanded a new plan 'to be founded particularly on secrecy and surprise'.

This presented Manstein with a window of opportunity, which was promptly slammed shut by Halder, who had thus far received six lengthy memoranda from Manstein on the invasion of France. Manstein was shunted off to command a corps in East Prussia, theoretically a promotion but in effect a way of preventing him from exercising any influence. However, protocol required that, on appointment, corps commanders should pay their respects to the head of state. This was a mere formality, but by chance Hitler's Wehrmacht adjutant, Colonel Rudolf Schmundt, visited Manstein's headquarters, where he heard of the plan. It was so like Hitler's concept, although 'in significantly more precise form', that Schmundt secured for Manstein an entire morning with the Führer on 17 February. Hitler immediately adopted Manstein's ideas as his own. Planning could begin.

—m—

Within a week OKH had produced its own plan, code-named Sickle Stroke (*Sichelnitt*), which transformed the embryonic proposal with which Manstein had fired Hitler's imagination into a detailed operational plan. This involved an invasion of Holland and Belgium designed to draw the BEF and much of the French strength north. The bulk of the German armour would then break through the weakly held Ardennes sector, cross the Meuse and cut a swathe across northern France to the Channel, trapping the Allied forces in the north inside a huge pocket. The attack on the Low Countries would be delivered by Bock's Army Group B with two Panzer Corps under his command; the *Sichelnitt* blow would be executed by Rundstedt's Army Group A, spearheaded by three Panzer Corps; in the south, Leeb's Army Group C would mount holding attacks on the Maginot Line and along the Upper Rhine.

'Everything depends on the military leaders. With the German soldier I can do anything, provided he is well led.'

ADOLF HITLER

The Allied high command also played a willing albeit unwitting part in *Sichelnitt*. On the eve of the launching of the invasion of the Low Countries and France, the French General Maurice Gamelin, the Allied commander-in-chief, clung to the belief that the German attack, when it came, would be a mechanized version of the Schlieffen Plan of 1914, outflanking the Maginot Line with an attack through Holland and Belgium. Gamelin planned to order the thirteen divisions of the British Expeditionary Force and twenty-seven of the best divisions in the French Army to move up to support the eleven Dutch and twenty-two Belgian divisions along the line of the River Dyle.

The BEF had at its disposal two hundred light tanks and a hundred of the heavier infantry tanks, but its order of battle contained no dedicated armoured formations – Britain's only tank division, the First Armoured, was not yet combat-ready. The French armoured and motorized formations were of better quality than their infantry, and were mostly equipped with tanks superior to and more numerous, by almost five hundred, than those in the German armoured divisions. However, the French armour was distributed haphazardly among Gamelin's army groups, and over half were tied to the slow-moving infantry. In contrast, all ten of the German

Panzer (armoured) divisions and all six of its motorized divisions were deployed in the West, along with a hundred and eighteen infantry divisions.

Unlike the Allies' complicated and overlapping command structure, the German command arrangements in 1940 were models of effectiveness. Authority over the Army's formations ran down from Hitler through OKW, his personal headquarters, to the Army high command, OKH, and then directly to the army groups. Hitler dealt personally with the General Staff from his separate but nearby headquarters; at this stage in the war, he left operational control to OKH, which also closely co-ordinated operations with the Luftwaffe high command.

The Panzers were ready to move off from their start lines. On 9 May the Luft-waffe announced that the weather on the 10th would be fine, earning the head of the meteorological service a present of a gold watch from the Führer. That evening, Hitler and his entourage embarked on his special train from a small railway station near Berlin and headed north. Only after darkness had fallen would the train turn westwards to bring Hitler to his specially prepared battle headquarters, the Crag's Nest (*Felsennest*) at Munstereifel, midway between Bonn and the Belgian Ardennes. That night, at 21.00 hours, OKW transmitted the code word 'Danzig' to all the for-mations tensely waiting behind the western frontiers of the Reich, signifying that the offensive would begin at 05.35 hours the next morning.

The scene was set for the last great battle of World War I. On one side, the British and French, led by politicians who had been outfoxed at every turn by Adolf Hitler and whose armies faced the confrontation with divided loyalties and purpose. On the other, a superb military machine willed into existence and given purpose by a daemonic prophet, brimming with a self-confidence not universally shared by his own high command. It was not, of course, the Kaiser's Army of 1914 with which the young Adolf Hitler marched to war, but it was an army about to execute one of the most brilliant war plans of all time. Everything would depend on its firmness of purpose.

The German offensive was launched on 10 May as German paratroops and air landing formations seized strategic locations in Holland. A single Panzer division drove west from the frontier to relieve them, isolating the Dutch Army from the French Seventh Army, which was moving ponderously forward in support. The British and French reacted like a bull drawn by the matador's cloak. Hitler was ecstatic: 'I could have wept for joy; they had fallen into the trap … The birds in the morning, the view over the road up which the columns were advancing, the squadrons of planes overhead. There, I knew just what I was doing!'

The Dutch were then presented with an ultimatum by the Germans – if they did not surrender, every city in Holland would be destroyed. To prove the point, on 14 May the Luftwaffe bombed the centre of Rotterdam, killing a thousand of its inhabitants and making seventy-eight thousand homeless. The Dutch capitulated the next day. On 10 May, the linchpin of the Belgian defences, the supposedly impregnable Fort Eben Emael guarding the confluence of the Albert Canal and

'Nothing but a miracle can save the BEF now.'

Commander of II Corps,
General Alan Brooke

River Maas, had been neutralised in a daring *coup de main*. Following Gamelin's plan, the BEF and French armies wheeled north east on to the Dyle Line while, in the Gembloux Gap on the BEF's right flank, the first major tank battle of World War II was fought on 12–13 May between the German XVI Panzer Corps (Third and Fourth Panzer Divisions) and the French First Cavalry Corps (II and III Light Mechanized Divisions) which was covering the deployment of the French First Army along the Dyle Line.

However, the real danger for the Allies loomed to the south. Army Group A, spearheaded by Panzer Group Kleist, advanced through the Ardennes and, with heavy support from the Luftwaffe, secured three bridgeheads across the Meuse between 13 and 15 May. During these operations, the French Ninth Army was destroyed and their Second Army badly mauled. Bursting out of the Meuse bridgeheads, German armoured formations drove through northern France on a fifty-mile front between 16 and 21 May. For the Allies, the Battle of France was now lost.

At 7 p.m. on 20 May, German armoured formations reached Abbeville, at the mouth of the River Somme, effectively dividing the Allied armies into two. An hour later, tanks of XIX Corps were on the Channel coast at Noyelles. On the same day, General Maxime Weygand, a soldier who had never commanded troops in action, succeeded Gamelin as Allied commander-in-chief. The same day, Hitler was also busy, reviewing plans for Case Red, the drive into the heart of France which would complete the destruction of the French Army.

—⁓—

The British war cabinet was also making an important decision. Part of the BEF might have to be evacuated from the Channel ports. Accordingly, the Admiralty was instructed to begin assembling small ships on the south coast to take the troops off. The operation, code-named Dynamo, was not as yet intended to be a full-scale evacuation – the war cabinet still hoped that the greater part of the BEF would be able to break through the Panzer corridor in northern France to join hands with the surviving French armies on, and south of, the River Somme.

Lord Gort, the commander of the BEF, which was now conducting a fighting withdrawal in Belgium, was more realistic. On 23 May he received an assurance from War Minister Anthony Eden that the British government would arrange the evacuation of the entire BEF from the northern coast of France, should it have to withdraw. The commander of II Corps, General Alan Brooke, wrote, 'Nothing but a miracle can save the BEF now.'

There was a miracle, of sorts, on 24 May. On the morning of that day Hitler paid a visit to Rundstedt's headquarters at Charleville. Rundstedt was anxious about the vulnerability of his flank and the fact that two days earlier, in the Arras sector, General Erwin Rommel's Seventh Panzer Division had been mauled by the Matilda infantry tanks of the British First Army's Tank Brigade.[25] Rundstedt was concerned that in the marshy terrain of Flanders, which both he and Hitler knew so well from World War I, the Matildas, and British artillery, might inflict another severe reverse on German armour. In turn, this might compromise the second part of Case Red: the defeat of the French forces south of the Somme.

Hitler and Rundstedt agreed that the capitulation of the encircled Allied forces in the north was only a matter of time, and that the preparations for Case Red must take top priority. Hitler was also fretting about the vulnerability of his Panzer formations in the coastal lowlands of north-west Europe, laced with dykes and canals. He issued a Führer Order which, by its nature, was mandatory, and halted the German armour for two days. This enabled the BEF, and a substantial number of French troops, to withdraw behind the Canal Line to the port of Dunkirk. The task of destroying them was left to the Luftwaffe.

On 25 May Boulogne was taken by the Germans, and Calais fell a day later. At midnight on 27 May, Belgium capitulated. Behind the heavily defended perimeter at Dunkirk the evacuation was under way. Planned by Vice-Admiral Bertram Ramsay, the Flag Officer, Dover, it commenced at 19:00 hours on 26 May. For Operation Dynamo, Ramsay had assembled a fleet of over a thousand vessels, including destroyers and smaller warships, cross-Channel ferries, pleasure steamers, coasters, fishing trawlers, and craft as small as cabin cruisers manned by their civilian owners. When the evacuation ended on 4 June, some three hundred and thirty-eight thousand men — one third of them French — had been taken off the beaches.

THE FALL OF FRANCE

After the Dunkirk evacuation, French hopes rested on the so-called Weygand Line,[26] an imaginative attempt to carry out a last-ditch defence of France. The line ran from the Channel coast, following the Rivers Somme and Aisne, to the Maginot Line[27] at Montmédy. It was to consist of a linked checkerboard of heavily defended 'hedgehog' positions (a system later copied by NATO in the 1970s to deal with an attack by the Red Army) which could continue to resist even if bypassed.

In practice many of the hedgehogs collapsed on their first brutal contact with the enemy. Their defenders lacked anti-tank weapons and had no air cover. The Luftwaffe dominated the skies. Some hedgehogs held on with great courage, even

---

25 In the action the British First Army's Tank Brigade had lost all but twenty-six of its Matilda Mark 1 infantry tanks and all but two of its Matilda Mark 11s. The tracks of the remaining tanks were breaking with wear, and they fell back under heavy attack from dive-bombers. Nevertheless, the shock they had delivered to Seventh Panzer Division on 21 May, and the subsequent delay in the German drive to the coast, contributed materially to the success of the Dunkirk operation.

26 General Maxime Weygand succeeded Gamelin as the Supreme Allied Commander on 20 May 1941. He was seventy-three years old and in his long career had never commanded troops in action. He later served as commander of the Vichy French troops in North Africa, was arrested during the German occupation of Vichy in 1942 and was imprisoned in Germany for the rest of the war. The taint of 1940 still clung to him at the end of the war, and in 1948 he was tried and acquitted of treason. He died in 1965 at the age of ninety-eight.

27 The Maginot Line was a French fortification system built between 1929 and 1940. It was intended to provide a fixed defensive line along three hundred and eighty-five miles of the Franco-German border, behind which manoeuvre armies could form and deploy. In 1940 it had been simply bypassed by the main thrust of the German invasion, driving through the Ardennes and Sedan. The garrison of the Maginot Line was some four hundred thousand strong, and only one section of blockhouses fell to German attack. It was named after André Maginot, Minister of War 1929–32, who authorised its construction.

when isolated from the main body of the retreating French Army. On 9 June Army Group A, led by Panzer Group Guderian, went on the attack on the River Aisne. It encountered heroic resistance from the French Fourteen Division, led by General Lattre de Tassigny, but the German drive rolled on. General Guderian recalled that First Panzer Division advanced 'as though this were a peacetime manoeuvre'.

The aged Marshal Pétain, the hero of Verdun who had been brought out of retirement as France's deputy prime minister, was now begged by his former chief of staff, Bernard Serrigny, to bring President Roosevelt into the imminent armistice negotiations before Italy joined the war. But Roosevelt had already told the French prime minister, Paul Reynaud, that he had no power to influence the situation in France and could offer no more material aid.

On 10 June, Italy declared war on France and Reynaud moved the government from Paris to Tours on the River Loire. There, on the following day, he and the British prime minister, Winston Churchill, met for a final conference. Churchill, who had succeeded Neville Chamberlain on 10 May, urged Reynaud to defend Paris, but the latter had already taken the decision to declare the capital an open city. Many Parisians were now fleeing the Germans, who arrived in the city on 14 June. Two days later, Churchill offered to declare an indissoluble union between England and France, an idea which had also been proposed by the junior French defence minister, General Charles de Gaulle, who arrived in London as an exile on 17 June. The French cabinet rejected Churchill's proposal, seeing acceptance as a humiliating subordination to the British. Now they would have to submit to the Germans.

In the small hours of 17 June, Pétain, now France's new president, approached the Germans, via the Spanish ambassador, to open armistice negotiations (Pétain had until recently been the French ambassador in Madrid). A new humiliation awaited Pétain's emissaries. They had to sign the armistice in the railway coach near Compiègne in which Marshal Foch had dictated peace terms to the Germans in 1918. An exultant Hitler observed the arrival of the French delegation and stamped his feet in excitement. The defeat of 1918, and its consequences, had seared themselves on Hitler's consciousness. They would now be blotted out by repaying the humiliation.

At 15.15 hours on the afternoon of 21 June, Hitler, accompanied by Göring, Admiral Raeder, Brauchitsch, Keitel, Ribbentrop and Hess, gathered at the Great War memorial recording the French victory over the 'criminal arrogance of the German Reich'. The Führer took his place in the carriage, greeting the French delegation in stony silence and listening without speaking as Keitel read out the preamble to the armistice terms. Inwardly, as he later recounted, he was relishing the revenge for the humiliation of November 1918. Then he returned to his headquarters. The debt had been expunged.

The terms presented by Keitel were harsh. Although Pétain's government – shortly to be removed to the spa town of Vichy – was to remain notionally sovereign, Paris, northern France and its borders with Belgium, Switzerland and the Atlantic were to become a German occupation zone, the cost to be met by the French. France's colonies were to remain under Vichy control along with the French navy, which was to be demilitarized. Germany would retain indefinitely all French prisoners taken during the six-week campaign, including the garrison of the Maginot Line. The armistice was signed on 22 June and, along with the separate armistice signed with Italy, would come into force on the morning of 25 June.

Germany's victory in the West, brilliantly conceived and ruthlessly executed, cost the Third Reich twenty-seven thousand killed, hundred and ten thousand wounded and eighteen thousand missing. France suffered ninety thousand dead and two hundred thousand wounded, and 1.9 million of her soldiers had been taken prisoner or were missing – one-quarter of her active manhood. Total British losses were sixty-eight thousand. The French were prostrate, but the British monarch, George VI, comforted himself with the observation, 'Personally, I feel happier that we have no allies to be polite to or to pamper.' Winston Churchill, was less sanguine. On 18 June he told the House of Commons, 'The battle of France is over. I expect the battle of Britain is about to begin.'

The advantage of hindsight enables us to see that in this, the moment of his greatest triumph, lay the seeds of Adolf Hitler's downfall and that of the Third Reich. After the defeat of the French and the humiliation of the British, Hitler believed that no nation on earth could withstand the Wehrmacht, a weapon he had forged himself. He was soon to convince himself that, even while cutting back German war production and demobilizing part of that magnificent army, he could nevertheless deal with the Jewish-Bolshevik ogre in the Soviet Union in another lightning campaign. What he failed to take into account was the tyranny of distance. In the summer of 1941, the Red Army, like that of the French, would crumple at the first impact but, unlike the French, would be able to make a retreat equivalent to a French withdrawal from Sedan across the Pyrenees and down to Zaragoza on the Ebro, before launching a counter-offensive. But Hitler now considered himself infallible. In the Low Countries and France his audacity had trumped the caution of the military professionals, and he now turned his gaze to the East.

PARIS, BERLIN, MOSCOW . . .

Meanwhile, after the signing of the armistice at Compiègne, Hitler awarded himself a vacation from responsibility. He became a tourist, revisiting the battlefields in Flanders where he had won his Iron Cross. In addition to his regular entourage, he was accompanied by two World War I comrades, Max Amann (the Party publisher) and Ernst Schmidt, his closest wartime friend, who had been with him on the detail which guarded Trauenstein prisoner-of-war camp in 1919.

Then, on 28 June, the Führer paid his first and last respects to Paris. He and his entourage – which included the sinister and ever-present Martin Bormann, Hitler's court architect Albert Speer, and the sculptor Arno Breker – landed at Le Bourget at 5.30 a.m., an unusually early time for Hitler, and long before most Parisians were awake. He was in the capital for a little over three hours, and came as a sightseer rather than a conqueror. His first port of call was the Opéra, where all the lights were blazing as if for a gala performance as the Führer party, riding in three large Mercedes limousines, swept up to the handsome entrance. Hitler was ecstatic, happily demonstrating to his companions his intimate knowledge of the building's details. The elderly guide who showed the party round was deferential but declined the large tip offered by Hitler's adjutant.

The limousines were soon gliding up the deserted Champs-Elysées, stopping at the Tomb of the Unknown Warrior, below the Arc de Triomphe, before viewing the Eiffel Tower and Napoleon's tomb in Les Invalides. The tour ended in Montmartre at the church of Sacré Coeur, a nineteenth-century monument to Catholic piety. From the hilltop of Montmartre, Hitler gazed over the slowly stirring city, and then he was gone. He told Speer that the visit had fulfilled a lifelong dream, but he later informed Goebbels that he had been disappointed by the French capital and had toyed with the idea of razing it to the ground before deciding to spare it. Soon it would be overshadowed by the rebuilt Berlin.

Hitler arrived back in Berlin on the afternoon of 6 July. His car drove from the Anhalter Station through cheering crowds and flower-strewn streets to the Chancellery. He appeared on the balcony to acknowledge the adulation, and the crowds would not let him go. For perhaps the only time in the war, Berlin was gripped by war fever. Now, it seemed, only the British stood in the way of total victory. Behind the triumphalist cheers, there was nevertheless an almost universal desire in Germany for a quick end to the war.

—⁓—

The British and their new prime minister, Winston Churchill, were not about to oblige. The mood in Britain was sombre and the threat of a German invasion was taken in deadly earnest. Early in July, Churchill told the House of Commons, 'We shall defend our island, whatever the cost may be. We shall fight on the beaches, we shall fight on the landing grounds, we shall fight in the fields and in the streets, we shall fight in the hills. We shall never surrender.'

Nevertheless, the situation was desperate. After the Dunkirk evacuation, the British could muster some two hundred thousand operational troops in recognizable formations, plus almost a million poorly armed Home Guard volunteers. But the home defence forces were virtually without tanks or artillery. In the Berghof, Hitler began talks with his high command about an invasion of Britain should his peace feelers, which had been extended through various neutral channels, be rejected.

On 11 July, Hitler was reminded by Admiral Raeder, C-in-C of the German navy, of an OKW directive of 2 July which stated that a successful naval landing could be made on the southern coast of England only after the Luftwaffe had defeated the Royal Air Force's Fighter Command. On 16 July, Hitler issued Führer Directive 16, which began, 'Since England, in spite of the hopelessness of her military situation, shows no sign of being ready to come to an understanding, I have decided to prepare a landing operation against England and, if necessary, to carry it out.' The operation was given the code name Sealion (*Seelöwe*) and the scene was set for the opening phase of the Battle of Britain. The attempted elimination of RAF Fighter Command by the Luftwaffe was under way by mid-July.

Hitler was convinced that the British could not defeat him, but he ran the risk of humiliation if he launched a cross-Channel invasion against the opposition of his advisers. He clung stubbornly to the dream that he could enlist the co-operation of Britain. He did not want to bludgeon the British into submission. In any event, he had other things on his mind. With his gaze already turned eastwards, the outlines of another military adventure were taking shape in his mind: the defeat and subjection of the Soviet Union.

He was well aware of the colossal dangers inherent in such an undertaking. The first rule of military history was 'Do Not Invade Russia', a warning which the Emperor Napoleon, before whose tomb Hitler had only recently stood, had ignored to his cost. In 1940 the Soviet Union appeared militarily strong, and its sheer size could swallow armies whole, just as Imperial Russia had devoured France's *Grande Armée* in 1812. However, fear that the passage of time would only make the Red Army stronger was a powerful motivating factor in Hitler's urge to incorporate the vast territories of European Russia – which Germany had fleetingly possessed in 1918 – into the Third Reich.

GLORIFICATION

Hitler's immediate response to these anxious calculations was to make a gesture which was Napoleonic in scale. On 9 May 1804, when he was at the height of his power, the French Emperor had made eighteen of his generals Marshals of the Empire. It was a move designed to glorify the head of state rather than honour his military servants. On 19 July 1940, Hitler convened the Reichstag in the Kroll Opera House to witness the creation of a new German marshalate. His three army group commanders in the Battle of France, Generals Bock, Leeb and Rundstedt, were created field marshals, as were the three Luftwaffe commanders now fighting the Battle of Britain, Milch, Sperrle and Kesselring. Hitler's personal chief of staff, Keitel, and his army commander-in-chief Brauchitsch were also on the roll, as were four of the most successful field commanders in the campaign in the West, Kluge, Reichenau, Witzleben and List. Göring was appointed to the unique rank of *Reichsmarschall*, which gave him the opportunity to sport an extravagant new uniform decorated with the Great Cross of the Iron Cross, an honour which had previously been conferred by the kings of Prussia on Blücher, Moltke and Hindenburg.

The principal purpose of the occasion, however, was for Hitler to review the course of the war and to outline the terms on which it might be brought to an end. His speech was thus intended as an invitation, mediated by world opinion, to the British to make peace with the Third Reich. William Shirer, who had witnessed many of Hitler's speeches, thought that it was one of his finest: 'The Hitler we saw in the Reichstag tonight was the Conqueror, and conscious of it, and yet so wonderful an actor, so magnificent a handler of the German mind, that he mixed superbly the full confidence of the conqueror with the humbleness which always goes down so well with the masses when they know a man is on top.'

Hitler's appeal to the British came at the end of the speech: 'In this hour, I feel it is my duty before my own conscience to appeal once more to reason and common sense in Great Britain as much as elsewhere. I consider myself in a position to make this appeal since I am not the vanquished begging favours, but the victor speaking in the name of reason. I see no reason why this war must go on.'

By the end of July 1940, the Battle of Britain was moving into a higher gear. Shortly before the stakes were to be raised yet again, Hitler reconvened discussions with his high command in the Berghof. The focus, however, was not on the air fighting boiling up over the English Channel and south-east England, but on moving forces eastwards to the border with the Soviet Union. Hitler, despite the agreement in the Molotov-Ribbentrop pact of August 1939, was deeply uneasy about the Soviet occupation of the Baltic states – Latvia, Lithuania and Estonia – and by the Soviet annexation from Romania of Bessarabia and North Bukovina. While he did not believe that the Soviet Union was planning to attack Germany, these acquisitions of territory nevertheless restricted his own freedom of manoeuvre in Eastern Europe and the Baltic, and also threatened two of Germany's client states, Finland and Bulgaria.

Opposite: Hitler with Wilhelm Keitel (left) and Alfred Jodl (centre) on board his command train. Keitel had succeeded Werner von Blomberg as chief of OKW (*Oberkommando der Wehrmacht*, the German high command) in 1938 but with a much lower status than his predecessor. Jodl, head of the Operations Section of OKW, was the effective commander of all German operations in all theatres in World War II except the Soviet Union, and was the instrument of turning Hitler's ideas into practical orders for the armies. In 1942 Jodl realized that the war was lost but kept his views to himself.

THE FRITZ PLAN

Hitler decided that he could no longer defer a trial of strength with the Soviet Union. As early as the time of his 'vacation' after the French armistice, he told Rudolf Schmundt, his principal Wehrmacht adjutant, that he was considering an attack on the Soviet Union and had asked Colonel Bernhard von Lossberg, one of OKW's operations officers, to draft a study, which Lossberg code-named 'Fritz', after his son. Now Hitler set OKH the same task. OKH's Foreign Armies East, the intelligence section which monitored Soviet capabilities and intentions, had reported in May 1940 that the Red Army, although capable of raising some two hundred infantry divisions for war, remained gravely disorganized and demoralized by Stalin's purges of the late 1930s. It estimated the size of the Soviets' tank fleet at ten thousand vehicles (it was in fact some twenty-four thousand). Hitler was unfazed by these figures. He aimed to have at least a hundred and twenty divisions close to the Soviet border by the spring of 1941, with some three and a half thousand tanks. The odds still looked good to him.

When, on 14 August, the twelve newly created field marshals arrived at the Chancellery to collect their batons, Hitler informed them of his intention to move against the Soviet Union. The notes taken at the meeting by Field Marshal Wilhelm Ritter von Leeb convey the thrust of Hitler's geopolitical thinking:

> Probably two reasons why Britain won't make peace. Firstly, she hopes for US aid; but the US can't start major arms deliveries until 1941. Secondly, she hopes to play off Russia against Germany. But Germany is militarily far superior to Russia ... There are two danger areas which could set off a clash with Russia; number one, Russia pockets Finland; this would cost Germany her dominance of the Baltic and impede a German attack on Russia. Number two, further encroachments by Russia on Romania. We cannot permit this because of Romania's gasoline supplies to Germany. Therefore Germany must be kept fully armed. By the spring there will be 180 divisions ... Germany is not striving to smash Britain because the beneficiaries will not be Germany but Japan in the east, Russia in India, Italy in the Mediterranean and America in world trade. That is why peace is possible in Britain.

On the last point, events were swiftly to prove Hitler wrong. A day after Hitler's meeting with his senior generals in the Berghof, the Luftwaffe launched its main attack, code-named Eagle (*Adler*), to provoke and win a decisive battle with RAF Fighter Command. In fierce air fighting the Luftwaffe lost seventy-two aircraft on what became known as Black Thursday.

From early July, the Luftwaffe had fatally switched back and forth between targets – the RAF's coastal radar chain, Fighter Command's sector stations, Britain's aircraft factories – without knocking out any of them. On 25 August, RAF Bomber Command had flown its first raid against Berlin. In retaliation, Hitler sanctioned the bombing of London, which began on 7 September. The Luftwaffe believed, wrongly, that attrition had reduced Fighter Command to a hundred aircraft, but on 15 September it suffered a heavy defeat when two heavily escorted waves of bombers ran into nearly three hundred British fighters in the skies over the British capital. Air superiority was decisively denied to the Luftwaffe, and on 12 October Hitler ordered the indefinite postponement of Operation Sealion.

———※———

At the end of August, Hitler had despatched Schmundt and Dr Fritz Todt, his chief of war construction, to East Prussia to find a suitable location for a new headquarters from which the campaign in the East might be conducted. The site they chose was a few miles east of the town of Rastenburg (now Ketzryn), in the gloomy Görlitz forest. Here was to be built the Wolf's Lair (*Wolfsschanze*) from which Hitler would direct much of the war. Behind the barbed wire and minefields which were to surround Security Zone One, the Führer would retreat into self-imposed exile, moving in an airless world of maps, tables and military conferences.

On 15 September, Lossberg submitted his Fritz plan to Jodl. The transfer of German divisions to the east continued apace and a military mission was despatched to Romania, soon to become a member of the Tripartite Pact, which had been signed between Germany, Italy and Japan on 27 September 1940. Having abandoned plans for Sealion, Hitler now sought to widen the war against the hard-pressed but defiant British. On 13 September the Italians had opened an offensive from Libya into British-garrisoned Egypt. On 4 October, when the Italian offensive still promised success, Hitler met Mussolini at the Brenner Pass on the German-Italian border to discuss opening a front in the Mediterranean, which for over two hundred years the Royal Navy had treated as a British lake.

Hitler was also eager to coax Spain's dictator, General Francisco Franco, into the Axis, a move which would provide Germany with access to Gibraltar at the mouth of the Mediterranean. On 20 October, Hitler boarded his command train, *Amerika*, to meet Franco, and Pétain, the head of the French Vichy government.

The meeting with Franco, which took place three days later at Hendaye on the Franco-Spanish border, proved a great disappointment – Hitler subsequently observed that he would rather have several teeth extracted than repeat the experience. He had been warned by Admiral Canaris, head of the German Armed Forces Intelligence Service (*Abwehr*) that Franco was 'not a hero but a little pipsqueak', and had been kept waiting by the late arrival of the Caudillo's aged train, which had once been used by King Alfonso XIII.[28] During the subsequent talks, Hitler was further irritated by Franco's relentless impertubability and droning, sing-song voice, 'like a muezzin calling the faithful to prayer', according to Paul Schmidt, Ribbentrop's press secretary and interpreter.

---

28 Alfonso fled Spain in 1931 after the proclamation of the Second Spanish Republic. He settled in Rome, where he died in 1941.

BALKAN INTERLUDE

Smarting at Hitler's successes in the West, the Italian dictator Benito Mussolini invaded Albania and Greece in October 1940. The Italians soon ran into stiff resistance, were driven back into Albania by the Greeks and had to be rescued by the Germans. Hitler was determined to protect his southern flank before launching his long-planned invasion of the Soviet Union. When the pro-German Prince Paul of Yugoslavia was overthrown in a coup encouraged by the arrival of sixty thousand British troops in mainland Greece, Hitler went on the offensive. In Operation Punishment, which was launched on 6 April 1941, the Germans overran Yugoslavia in only ten days. The conquest of Greece took just over two weeks. The British evacuated some eighteen thousand troops to the island of Crete, which was captured by the Germans at the end of May after an airborne invasion. The German victory in Crete was gained at the cost of nearly ten thousand casualties. Horrified at the losses, Hitler cancelled a proposed airborne seizure of the major British Mediterranean naval base in Malta.

The two dictators discussed the possibilty of a Spanish–German attack on Gibraltar, to be followed by the seizure of the Azores, the Canaries, Madeira and Cape Verde. Franco's price for co-operation, however, was Morocco, and other French North African territory which Hitler was reluctant to offer for fear of harming relations with Vichy. After the meeting, as they rattled away in their train with rain leaking through the roof, Franco told Serrano Suner, his brother-in-law and foreign minister, 'These people are intolerable. They want us to come into the war in exchange for nothing.'

Marshal Pétain, whom Hitler met on 24 October, proved equally unresponsive but nevertheless convinced Hitler, who was impressed by the old soldier's military bearing, that they had enjoyed a meeting of minds and were united in hostility to the British. The dismantling of the British Empire was one of the subjects on the agenda when Hitler met the Soviet foreign minister, Vyacheslav Molotov, in Berlin on 12 November. Before the meeting he had minuted his high command that, 'Political discussions have been initiated with aim of establishing what Russia's position will be ... Irrespective of the outcome of these discussions, all the preparations orally ordered for the East are to continue.'

Molotov proved an even more difficult customer than Franco. At a preliminary meeting, Ribbentrop had shown the Russian his hand. The Soviet Union was to share in the despoliation of the British Empire; it would be given free rein to expand southwards towards the Indian Ocean while Japan extended its conquests in Asia, and Germany moved into Africa. Molotov was singularly unimpressed by this windy geopolitical *tour d'horizon*. Soviet interests lay closer to home. He insisted on strict adherence to the terms of the Molotov-Ribbentrop pact and wanted to annex Finland (which had been Russian territory between 1809 and 1918), guarantee Bulgaria's borders (irrespective of Bulgaria's wishes), and improve Soviet access to the Black Sea, the Mediterranean and the North Sea – the last via the Baltic, which was the training ground for German U-boats.

The discussions were interrupted by a British air raid which forced Ribbentrop, Molotov and their entourages into an air raid shelter. Underground, the German foreign minister continued to press his opposite number on the benefits which would accrue to the Soviet Union from the dismemberment of the British Empire, which, he asserted, was on the verge of defeat. He received the silky reply, 'If that is so, then why are we in this shelter and whose are those bombs which are falling?'

For Hitler, it was the last straw. Five years later, within days of his death in the Berlin bunker, as T-34s ground through the shattered streets of Berlin, he was still raving about Molotov's impossibilist demands: 'He demanded that we give him military bases on Danish soil on the outlets to the North Sea. He had already staked a claim to them. He demanded Constantinople, Romania, Bulgaria and Finland — and we were supposed to be the victors.'

At the beginning of December 1940, at the Reich Chancellery under the chairmanship of Hitler, OKH and OKW initiated joint discussions of their plans for the invasion of the Soviet Union. The finishing touches to the OKW plan, still code-named Fritz, had been supplied by General Friedrich Paulus, who was later to surrender the Sixth Army at Stalingrad. Both plans identified, as a precondition of victory, the encirclement and destruction of the greater part of the Red Army in a succession of cauldron battles (*Kesselschlachten*) close to the borders of the Soviet Union.

The OKH plan stressed the need to strike for and capture Moscow at the earliest opportunity. Under the centralized Soviet system, power resided in Moscow, which OKH also estimated was the country's industrial and transport hub. In contrast, the Fritz plan downgraded the importance of Moscow. The final drive on the Soviet capital would have to wait until the Red Army had been chewed up in colossal cauldron battles on the edge of the Baltic in the north and in the Ukraine in the south. Hitler was instinctively drawn to the Fritz plan. He was dismissive of the Red Army's capabilities: 'In terms of the weapons, the Russian soldier is as inferior to us as the French. He has a few modern field batteries, everything else is old, reconditioned materiel … the bulk of the Russian tank forces is poorly armoured. The Russian human material is inferior. The armies are leaderless.'

> **The final drive on the Soviet capital would have to wait until the Red Army had been chewed up in colossal cauldron battles on the edge of the Baltic in the north and in the Ukraine in the south.**

The debate was translated into Führer Directive 21, which embodied the strategic view taken by Hitler that the drive on Moscow should only be launched after the destruction of the Red Army on the Baltic coast. To this end, the Directive provided for the diversion of forces from Army Group Centre, one of the three army groups tasked with the operation, to aid Army Group North's encirclement and destruction of the Soviet forces in the Baltic region. Army Group Centre was to 'swing strong units of its mobile forces to the north, in order to destroy the enemy forces fighting in the Baltic area, acting in conjunction with Army Group North … in the general direction of Leningrad'.

At the beginning of January 1941, at the Berghof, the Führer addressed his senior commanders on the reasons for his decision to turn east. His objectives now extended to Baku on the Caspian Sea, the centre of Soviet oil production which, significantly, the German Army had reached in 1918. Here, on these shores, the 'manifest destiny' of the German race was to be fulfilled. This was the staple ingredient of Hitler's stultifying table talk: an endlessly repeated conducted tour of the gallery of German history from the feats of the German tribes which defied successive Roman emperors, to the Varangian bodyguards of their Byzantine successors, and the Viking seafarers of the early Middle Ages. Their survival had been secured only by unrelenting struggle.

Now the German people were once more under threat, and the menace lay in the east, among what Hitler called 'the motley of Czechs, Poles, Hungarians, Serbs and Croats, etcetera'. The 'etcetera' referred to the many non-Slav peoples of the Soviet Union. Ever-present in this gallery of enemies was the 'bacillus which is the solvent of human society, the Jew'. It was Germany's mission to destroy, once and for all, 'Jewish-Bolshevism'.

BARBAROSSA

The invasion of the Soviet Union, code-named Barbarossa,[29] was planned to be the last of Hitler's Blitzkrieg campaigns. Nazi ideology ensured that the war in the East was fought with unparalleled savagery. Hitler's invasion of the Soviet Union was the culmination of the obsessions which had driven him throughout his career. German hegemony in Europe could be secured only by the seizing of *Lebensraum* in the East and with it the industry and agricultural land which would ensure Germany's survival as a world power. Just as in the Middle Ages people of Germanic stock had colonized the Baltic lands and pushed on into Russia, so their twentieth-century counterparts would repeat the process on a vastly greater scale.

In the process, the Jewish-Bolshevik government of the Soviet Union would be destroyed and its 'human material', both Slav and Asiatic, enslaved, or expelled into the wastelands beyond the battlements of German imperium. This was to be a colonial war akin to those of the nineteenth century, but directed against one of the great powers of Europe with the intention of utterly destroying it.

The language which described this struggle is saturated with the contempt and disgust which Hitler harboured for those he considered sub-human, the *Untermenschen*. This was reinforced by the German *Volk* race memory of the Mongol hordes which might once again threaten to submerge Europe under an 'Asiatic tide'. Thus, the Soviet enemy was seen, in John Keegan's words, as 'a nation of 200 million Calibans quailing under the eye of a Prospero corrupted by absolute power', a telling mirror image of the *Volk* itself. Victory against such an enemy could only be won by 'annihilation'.

---

29 Frederick Barbarossa was the twelfth-century Holy Roman Emperor who led the Third Crusade.

—ɯ—

Hitler's pitiless view of the war in the East was transmitted directly to the front line in an order to his men by Field Marshal Walther von Reichenau, commander of the Sixth Army, and later distributed to all troops of the German Army in the East:

> The essential goal of the campaign against the Jewish-Bolshevik system is the complete destruction of the sources of power and the eradication of the Asian influences on the European cultural sphere … The soldier in the East is not only a fighter by the rules of war but also the carrier of an inexorable racial concept and the avenger of all bestialities inflicted on the Germans …
>
> For this reason the soldier must have complete understanding for the necessity of harsh but just measures against Jewish sub-humanity … Only in this manner will we do justice to our historical task, to liberate the German people for once and for all from the Jewish-Asiatic danger.

Herein lay the justification for the barbarities committed during the German invasion of the Soviet Union, which began at 3.30 a.m. on 22 June 1941, the day after the hundred and twenty-ninth anniversary of Napoleon's attack on Russia in 1812. Seven German infantry armies, their advance spearheaded by four Panzer groups, opened the greatest land war in the history of military operations. Three million soldiers, supported by three thousand eight hundred and fifty tanks, seven thousand one hundred and eighty-four guns and nearly two thousand aircraft, were on the move along a front of a thousand miles, stretching from Memel on the Baltic to Odessa on the Black Sea.

Army Group North, commanded by Field Marshal Wilhelm Ritter von Leeb, was to attack from East Prussia towards Leningrad, aided by the Finns advancing into the Karelian isthmus. The strongest formation, Army Group Centre, under Field Marshal Fedor von Bock, was to drive north of the natural barrier of the freshwater Pripet Marshes to Smolensk, the route followed by Napoleon in 1812. To the south of the Pripet, Field Marshal von Rundstedt's Army Group South was to advance to the black-earth country of the Ukraine, the Soviet Union's bread basket, and the oil-rich industrial areas of the Donets, the Volga and the Caucasus. The cream of the German Army was poised to advance into a vast area – some one million square miles – of steppe, forest and swamp.

The soldier must have complete understanding for the necessity of harsh but just measures against Jewish sub-humanity.

The Red Army, which was in the middle of a wholesale reorganization and was deployed forward to cover every curve and crevice in the Soviet frontier, was trapped in a series of colossal cauldron battles. But two months of victory exacted its toll on the Wehrmacht. Deaths, wounds and sickness struck a million men from the German order of battle. At Minsk and Smolensk in July, Army Group Centre took 400,000 prisoners. On 11 July, the commander of Eighteenth Panzer Division expressed fears that the loss of men and equipment would prove insupportable 'if we do not intend to win ourselves to death'.

—⁓—

After the fall of Smolensk on 16 July, Army Group Centre halted to bring up supplies. Ammunition was running low and the tank strength had been halved. Meanwhile there were growing divisions within the German high command. Field Marshal von Bock wanted to drive on to Moscow behind a renewed Panzer thrust, but Hitler intervened – the first of his fatal interventions in the war. He had agreed to his commanders' proposals for Poland and Scandinavia and had acquiesced in the execution of their policy. Before and during the campaign in the West he had given his generals orders but had also been prey to bouts of near-disabling indecision and second thoughts, notably during the advance to Dunkirk. Since the launching of Barbarossa, however, he had been gripped with an overwhelming feeling of certainty. This was his war, and thus far it had achieved an undreamed of degree of success. His generals, on the other hand, became acutely aware of the Führer looking over their shoulders. Halder reflected:

> He's playing warlord again and bothering us with such absurd ideas that he's risking everything our wonderful operations so far have won. Unlike the French, the Russians won't just run away when they've been tactically defeated; they have to be defeated in terrain that's half forest and marsh … Every other day I have to go to him [OKH and Hitler had separate headquarters in East Prussia]. Hours of gibberish, and the outcome is that there's only one man who understands how to wage wars. If I didn't have faith [Halder was a devout Protestant], I'd go under like Brauchitsch [the Army C-in-C], who's at the end of his tether and hides behind a mask of manliness so as not to betray his complete helplessness.

Hitler's intervention cut across Bock's desire to go for Moscow. On 19 July, the Führer issued a new directive: one of Bock's two Panzer groups was to turn south to aid Army Group South in another huge encirclement in northern Ukraine. The other was to swing north to reinforce the advance of Army Group North on Leningrad and cut Soviet communications with Moscow. This meant that Bock now had only infantry formations with which to push on to the Soviet capital.

The ensuing argument over the priorities of the *Ostheer* (the German Army in the East) lasted a month before Hitler settled matters with an order, issued on 21 August, in which he shifted the emphasis to the south and the envelopment of four Soviet armies east of Kiev by Army Group South. With firm orders from Stalin not to withdraw, the Soviet troops in and around Kiev fought on grimly until 19 September when nearly six hundred and seventy-thousand were taken prisoner.

Torn between the competing options of the drive to Moscow, the advance to

Leningrad at the head of the Baltic, and the huge manoeuvre at Kiev, Hitler had opted for the third. However, in the final planning stages of Barbarossa he had given priority to the capture of Leningrad as the preliminary to a drive on Moscow from the north. By shuttling his forces up and down a vast front, Hitler was dissipating the stunning success of the early weeks of the campaign.

By 20 July, Leeb's Army Group North had been poised to take Leningrad, but the exhaustion of his troops, exacerbated by hardening Soviet resistance and Hitler's interventions, had destroyed the chances of the city's early capture. At the end of August, as Leeb's armour finally nosed into the outskirts of Leningrad, the Führer ordered a halt, possibly fearing heavy losses in a street-by-street battle for the city. At the beginning of September, he ordered the city to be besieged. The siege, in which over a million of Leningrad's citizens died from German bombs and shells or from starvation, was not lifted until 27 January 1944.

Above: German infantry struggle through the mud of the Russian *rasputitsa*, the spring and autumn quagmires which dictated the rhythms of campaigning on the Eastern Front. For all its vaunted armoured spearheads, the German infantry relied heavily on horses for much of its motive power. In the East the Army used some 2.5 million horses, losing about a thousand every day.

By October, Hitler's attention had belatedly swung back to Moscow. Buoyed by the encirclement at Kiev, he resisted Rundstedt's cautious advice to call a halt to operations on the Eastern Front. For the autumn drive to Moscow, Army Group North's Panzer spearhead was transferred from the Leningrad sector and joined Army Group Centre's Fourth Army. By now, Russia's vast spaces, primitive roads and harsh climate were punishing the *Ostheer*. Scorching summer heat gave way to seas of autumn mud – the Russian *rasputitsa*, or quagmire, caused by flooding – while Hitler sought to reconcile the push for Moscow with the securing of his extended southern flank to retain the raw materials and agricultural riches of the Ukraine.

Snow had fallen as early as the first week in October and by now most of the German front-line units had been in action since 22 June. Few had warm winter clothing, making it all but impossible for most troops to remain out in the open during the increasingly severe night frosts. Exhaustion aggravated minor wounds and increased the misery of depleted units with punishing workloads. Hot food seldom arrived in the front line, having frozen solid on its short journey forward. Lice thrived, and leather boots disintegrated in the musty air of earth dugouts. As the thermometer dropped, sentry duty was limited to a maximum of one hour and sentries' goggles froze to the flesh of their faces. Men survived by stripping the clothing from the corpses of the Soviet dead.

By 27 November, the leading Panzer units had reached the Volga canal, within twenty miles of Moscow's northern suburbs, from where patrols could see the sun glinting on the domes of the Kremlin. This was the limit of their advance. With great difficulty, the high command persuaded Hitler to sanction a withdrawal from Moscow to establish a secure winter line along the River Ugra. The troops had barely begun the withdrawal when, on 5 December, they were struck by a Soviet counter-offensive, launched with fresh and well-equipped divisions transferred from Siberia.[30]

By 25 December, the Russian armies had retaken almost all the territory won by the Germans in the final stages of the drive on Moscow. Hitler had ordered that the Fourth Army 'is not to retire a single step'. A blizzard of dismissals followed. Rundstedt had resigned his post at the end of November during the arguments over a withdrawal from Moscow, having urged a pull-back before the Red Army counter-blow fell. Bock had been removed from his post on 17 December, and three days later Guderian was dismissed as commander of the Second Panzer Group, for making unauthorized withdrawals. In the purge no fewer than thirty-five army corps and divisional generals were dismissed. On 17 December, Field Marshal von Brauchitsch was relieved of his command, to be succeeded by Hitler himself. From now on, operations in the Soviet Union, right down to battalion level, were to be executed according to directives and orders issued by the Führer. Blitzkrieg had met its match. Army Group Centre was shunted back two hundred miles before the Soviet offensive slithered to a halt in the glutinous mud of the spring thaw of 1942.

---

30 Stalin was able to act because of information supplied by Richard Sorge, a German journalist based in Japan, who was an active and highly effective Soviet agent with high-ranking Japanese contacts and privy to many secrets. He was able to confirm that Japan had no plans to acquire Soviet territory in the Far East, enabling Stalin to release the Siberian divisions.

OPERATION BLUE

In the summer of 1942, Hitler hoped to gain what had been denied him in 1941 and would not countenance any more talk of withdrawal. He discounted evidence of recovering Soviet strength and was also blind to waning German strength. On the Eastern Front there were more divisions – one hundred and seventy-seven as opposed to the 1941 figure of one hundred and fifty-eight – but a fall of three hundred and sixty thousand in the number of men to fill their ranks. Reducing German resources in the East in order to bolster German defences in the West was to dislocate plans for the 1942 summer campaign and oblige Hitler to depend more heavily on the unreliable troops of his allies on the Eastern Front: the Romanians, Hungarians, Italians, Spaniards and Slovaks. There were also intractable transport problems, a fuel shortage, and a crisis in the vaunted Panzer arm where the loss of tanks in 1941–42 outstripped new production – which, in any case, had been earmarked for the North African theatre which now demanded Hitler's attention, if not his wholehearted support.

> **Reducing German resources in the East in order to bolster German defences in the West was to dislocate plans for the 1942 summer campaign.**

Hitler had a grand strategic plan for 1942 which entailed sweeping southward from the Caucasus, and north-east from Egypt, in a colossal pincer movement, to seize the oil resources of the Middle East. In fact, the only part of the plan which was to see the light of day was Operation Blue, a drive aimed east to the city of Stalingrad and south to the mountain passes of the Caucasus, and then on to the oilfields on the western shores of the Caspian Sea.

The offensive opened on 28 June 1942. At first it seemed like business as usual. Army Group B struck through the Don–Donets corridor towards Stalingrad, an industrial town which straggled along the west bank of the Volga, while Army Group A drove on to Rostov and the Caucasus. By 6 July Army Group B had reached the Don River opposite Voronezh, but its reinstated commander, Field Marshal Bock, was concerned that Red Army reinforcements might attack his left flank from the city. He sought and gained Hitler's permission to secure Voronezh with armour detached from the Sixth Army, which was commanded by General Friedrich von Paulus. Bock was now sucked into a slogging match at Voronezh that threatened to dislocate Operation Blue's timetable. On 13 July Hitler intervened, replacing Bock with Field Marshal Maximilian von Weichs. Paulus was ordered to wheel east towards Stalingrad.

In the Don–Donets corridor the Red Army was now threatened with a series of encirclements on the scale of those executed by the Germans in Barbarossa. With huge difficulty, the recently appointed Chief of the Soviet General Staff (*Stavka*), Marshal Aleksandr Vasilevsky, persuaded Stalin that orders to stand fast regardless of the strategic situation invited further catastrophe, and that it was imperative for the Soviet forces to withdraw. On 23 July Rostov, which the Red Army had lost and then retaken in the winter fighting, fell to Army Group A almost without a fight. Hitler now ordered Army Group A and General Ewald von Kleist's First Panzer Army to drive for the Caucasus oilfields.

Meanwhile the Sixth Army, supported by the Fourth Panzer Army, was to thrust forward to Stalingrad to 'smash the enemy forces concentrated there, to occupy the town and to block land communications between the Don and Volga ... Closely connected with this, fast-moving forces will advance along the Volga with the task of thrusting through to Astrakhan.' Astrakhan lay in the far Caucasus and was a land fabled even to Russians. To men who had marched fifteen hundred miles from their homes in Germany it must have seemed like somewhere at the end of the world. For Hitler, the master of the bold vision, it was territory which had seen German troops in 1918. But in the summer of 1942, limitless space and a still unsubdued Red Army stood in the way of Hitler's dreams of empire.

On 9 August, just six weeks after the start of Operation Blue, Kleist's forces had reached Maikop, two hundred miles south-east of Rostov, and captured the Soviet Union's most westerly oilfields. The installations, however, had been wrecked by the retreating Russians, and the Germans were never to reach the principal sources of oil beyond the Caucasus. Ironically, they now had insufficient fuel to maintain the momentum of their advance and faced stiffening opposition from locally raised formations.

HITLER DECLARES WAR
ON THE UNITED STATES

In September 1940 Japan signed the Tripartite Pact with Germany and Italy. This bound the three nations to mutual support in the event of any one of them being attacked by a country not yet at war. In April 1941 Japan also negotiated a non-aggression pact with the Soviet Union. This would allow the planned Japanese operations in South-East Asia to go ahead without any fear of a Soviet attack in Mongolia and Manchuria. In June 1941, the harmony of the Tripartite Pact was temporarily disturbed by Hitler's invasion of the Soviet Union, of which the Japanese received no advance warning. The Japanese attack on Pearl Harbor on 7 December 1941 then transformed the war into a global conflict. The United States immediately declared war on Japan, and on 11 December Germany declared war on the United States. Hitler addressed the Reichstag, declaring jubilantly that the Japanese had followed the German precept of always striking first. He was utterly convinced that Germany could not possibly lose the war. In this he fatally underestimated the massive and as yet unrealized potential of the American war machine. At President Roosevelt's meeting with the British prime minister, Winston Churchill, at Placentia Bay, Newfoundland, on 9 August 1941, it had already been agreed that the destruction of Nazi Germany would be the first priority when the United States entered the war. Now that the Americans were plunged into the conflict, some 75 per cent of their war economy was devoted to that end.

STALINGRAD

While the First Panzer Army raced to Maikop, the German Sixth Army — much of whose transport had been temporarily transferred to Army Group A — was moving slowly down the Don–Donets corridor towards Stalingrad across a wide, treeless and desolate steppe. By 19 August it was poised to begin its assault on Stalingrad, while the Fourth Panzer Army moved up along a north-east axis.

On 23 August a total of six hundred aircraft of the Luftwaffe's VIII Air Corps attacked the city and reduced its centre to an inferno. Thousands of Soviet civilians, ordered to remain in Stalingrad so as not to hamper Red Army movements, were killed in the raid. On the same day, German troops pushed into the outskirts of Stalingrad and also carved out a salient to the north of the city along the western bank of the Volga. At Hitler's forward headquarters in Vinnitsa in the Ukraine, the mood was jubilant. The seizure of Stalingrad was expected within days as forward German units plunged into the heart of the city.

Here they were entombed in savage street battles where Blitzkrieg was replaced by attrition. The Red Army commander in Stalingrad, General Vasili Chuikov, ordered his men to fight 'as if there was no land across the Volga'. Beneath the hulks of collapsed and burning buildings, the German attackers of the Sixth Army and the defenders of the Soviet Sixty-second Army sheltered and lived in the cellars. They fought from the cover of masonry, scrambling and slithering over dunes of bricks from one position to the next. The front lines were fluid, often no more than a grenade-throw apart. Swarms of rats scurried through the carnage, feasting on the dead and dying. It was a nightmare world in which the sniper was king. At Stalingrad the Russian sniping ace Vasily Zaitsev killed a hundred and forty-nine German soldiers.

Hitler seemed to have forgotten whatever reason he may have had for committing his Sixth Army to the fight for Stalingrad. Perhaps he was bewitched by the notion of seizing a city which bore the name of his dictator rival, but the battle had unbalanced the strategy of seizing the Caucasus as more and more troops were sucked into the Stalingrad inferno. Hitler was a man lost in the detail of his twice-daily command conferences, poring over maps of Stalingrad and fretting over yards instead of miles, platoons instead of armies. Even if he had succeeded in sweeping Stalingrad's defenders into the Volga, it would have availed him no more than a local success and at hideous cost: half the fighting strength of the Sixth Army, the largest fighting formation in the *Ostheer*.

On 8 November, in his old haunt, the Burgerbräukeller in Munich, Hitler made a long speech to the Nazi 'Old Fighters'. The broadcast was heard by many men of the Sixth Army. Hitler stated, with heavy irony: 'I wanted to reach the Volga, to be precise at a particular spot, at a particular city. By chance it bore the name of Stalin himself. But I don't think I marched there just for that reason … I wanted to capture it and, you should know, we are quite content, we have as good as got it! There are only a couple of small bits left. Some say: "Why aren't they fighting faster?" That's because I don't want a second Verdun, and prefer instead to do the job with small assault groups. Time is of no importance. No more ships are coming up the Volga. And that is the decisive point!'

This must surely rank as one of the greatest examples of hubris in history. At the time, Rommel's Afrika Corps was retreating from El Alamein and Anglo-American forces had landed in Morocco and Algeria in Operation Torch. Ribbentrop took the opportunity to suggest to Hitler that he make an approach to Stalin through the Soviet embassy in Stockholm. Hitler's Luftwaffe adjutant noted that the Führer refused outright: 'He said that a moment of weakness is not the right time for dealing with an enemy.' The absurd boasts about Stalingrad proved not only to be hostages to fortune but were also to lock Hitler on a course to disaster. The political ranter had sidelined the Feldherr (warlord).

On 12 November, units of the Fourth Panzer Army reached the Volga, south of the city. Stalingrad was now encircled, but this was the last success the Germans would achieve at the easternmost point of the advance of the *Ostheer* into Russia.

On 13 September Stalin had been persuaded by Marshal Georgy Zhukov, his deputy supreme commander and in overall command of the Stalingrad sector, to agree to a wide encirclement of the Axis forces on the Lower Volga and the destruction of the Sixth Army in Stalingrad. By the third week in November, when the Sixth Army was on the point of exhaustion, the time was ripe to launch this crushing counterstroke, code-named Operation Uranus.

Uranus was launched on 19 November and within hours had torn away the flimsy north and south flanks of the Stalingrad front, principally held by Romanian armies. Some thirty thousand Axis troops were taken prisoner, and within five days Sixth Army and part of Fourth Panzer Army were separated from the rest of the German front by a hundred mile-wide corridor which was littered with cairns of frozen corpses and smashed artillery and armour. Inside the Stalingrad pocket, Sixth Army had rations for only six days and ammunition for just two days.

Below: Field Marshal Paulus surrenders at Stalingrad. Before January 1942, when he became commander of the Sixth Army, Paulus had never commanded a division, let alone a corps, and appeared 'more like a scientist than a general' to his fellow officers, who nicknamed him 'Cunctator' (procrastinator). In captivity he made radio broadcasts urging Germans to surrender. He gave evidence for the prosecution at Nuremberg and made his postwar home in Dresden in East Germany.

On 19 November Hitler had been at the Berghof, thirteen hundred miles away from Stalingrad. His immediate response was to dismiss a proposal that the Sixth Army should break out of the besieged city. The next day he ordered Paulus to hold firm at any cost. He then ordered a command reshuffle, appointing Manstein commander of Army Group Don with orders to break through to the Sixth Army.

On 24 November, Göring promised Hitler that the Luftwaffe would supply the trapped army from the air, a challenge which was far beyond its limited capabilities. As had happened at Dunkirk, the Luftwaffe was not up to the task. The temperature plummeted and with it German morale. Inside Stalingrad soldiers survived on horsemeat. Manstein, opposed by sixty Red Army divisions and a thousand tanks in the breakthrough sector, was faced with an impossible task. His problems were compounded as units were shuffled back and forth on the Don front to plug the cracks radiating from the Stalingrad debacle.

Nevertheless, Manstein struggled to within thirty-five miles of Stalingrad and then requested that the Sixth Army be permitted to break out. Once again the Führer refused; Sixth Army was to stay put. Manstein then sent one of his officers to Stalingrad to plead with Paulus. The commander of the Sixth Army, once a polished staff officer rather than a fighting soldier and now a sick and utterly demoralized man, declared that a breakout was out of the question; that, indeed, surrender had been expressly forbidden by his commander-in-chief, Adolf Hitler.

By Christmas Eve, Manstein's relief force was fighting for its life. It lost an armoured division, detached to plug another leak in the line, and with it all hope of relieving the Sixth Army, which was now trapped inside the Stalingrad pocket, starving and subjected to constant air and artillery bombardment. Soldiers took desperate risks, venturing into the no-man's-land beyond the defensive perimeter to search for scraps of food and, most precious of all, salt in the pockets of the Red Army fallen. Like the besieged population of Leningrad, they were reduced to eating rats.

On 8 January, the Red Army offered Paulus the chance to capitulate, an offer he declined. Four days later he reported that there were no reserves and that all his heavy weapons were immobilized. He anticipated that Sixth Army could only hold out for a few more days. On 22 January he made a personal appeal to Hitler that he be allowed to open negotiations with the enemy, but the Führer turned a deaf ear and a week later made Paulus a field marshal. No German field marshal had ever surrendered, and in effect Hitler was pressing a suicide pistol into Paulus's hand, but the field marshal did not pull the trigger. Rather, on 31 January, he and twenty-two German generals stepped into captivity. Two days later the last defenders of Stalingrad laid down their arms.

In the Stalingrad pocket, the *Ostheer* had lost twenty divisions and over two hundred-thousand men. Of the one hundred and eight thousand who marched into captivity, only five thousand returned home at the end of the war. Six more divisions had been destroyed outside the encirclement. Germany's allies in the East – the Italians, Hungarians and Romanians – had lost four armies, four hundred and fifty thousand men, and any desire they might have originally felt to play an active role in the Russian campaign. The German losses at Stalingrad pale in comparison with Soviet losses in the summer of 1941 – nearly half a million in the Kiev encirclement alone – but they represented the worst defeat the German military had suffered up to that time and delivered a heavy blow to morale at home.

Hitler had confidently expected Paulus, his newly created field marshal, either to commit suicide or to perish gloriously at the head of his troops. At the midday briefing on 1 February he had railed:

> When you think that a woman has got sufficient pride, just because someone has made a few insulting remarks, to go off and lock herself in and shoot herself right off, then I've no respect for a soldier who's afraid to do that but would rather be taken prisoner … I can't understand how a man like Paulus wouldn't rather die. The heroism of so many tens of thousands of men, officers and generals is cancelled out by a man like this who hasn't the character when the moment comes to do what a weakling woman can do … He could have freed himself and ascended into eternity and national immortality, but he preferred to go to Moscow.

The debacle at Stalingrad had dealt Hitler a heavy blow. On 6 February, at a meeting at Rastenburg, he told Manstein that he was 'deeply affected by the tragedy, not just because it amounted to a blatant failure of his own leadership, but also because he was deeply depressed in a purely personal sense by the fate of the soldiers who, out of faith in him, had fought to the last with such courage and devotion to duty'. The words may have been insincere – Hitler was expert at tailoring his moods to suit different audiences. However, in the immediate aftermath of Stalingrad, he was sufficiently unnerved to change his usual tune of 'never give an inch of ground', albeit temporarily, thus enabling Manstein to win acceptance for his proposal to respond flexibly to Uranus, to give ground, and then to disable an over-extended enemy with a carefully weighted counterpunch.

SHRINKING HORIZONS

On 10 March 1943, as the Fourth Panzer Army opened the fourth battle fought over the city of Kharkov since the German invasion of the Soviet Union, the Führer travelled to Manstein's headquarters at Zaporozhye, on the Dnieper in south-east Ukraine. There, he added an Oak Leaf Cluster to Manstein's Knight's Cross, then met, and took reports from, all the army and air corps commanders on the southern front.

During the meeting, Hitler jokingly addressed everyone as 'Herr Feldmarschall', doubtless causing some of the company to shift uneasily at the thought that one of the officers most recently promoted to that rank had been the unfortunate Paulus. At the same time, the Führer happily encouraged Manstein to make slighting remarks about his two neighbouring army group commanders, Kleist and Kluge, with both of whom the commander of Army Group South was conducting his own private war.

Hitler confided in Field Marshal Wolfram von Richthofen, commander of Luftflotte Four, that:' … he never wants to hear of the Romanians or our other gallant allies again; if he relies on them he only gets worked up because they don't stand firm; and if he arms them but doesn't use them, he gets just as worked up to see them standing around doing nothing.'

Three days later, on 13 March, Hitler repeated the performance in Smolensk for Field Marshal Günther von Kluge, commander of Army Group Centre, which was on the point of completing a phased withdrawal from the Rzhev salient to release sufficient forces to block any Soviet advance west of Kursk. That day the Führer signed an order instructing Manstein and Kluge to take the initiative again when the spring muddy season was over. He then flew back to Rastenburg, unaware that a bomb had been placed on his aircraft.

The device, made from slabs of British-manufactured nitrotetramethanium, armed with a one-hour setting and packed into a parcel, had been prepared by Major-General Henning von Tresckow and Major Fabian von Schlabrendorff, two of Kluge's staff officers. Tresckow had persuaded one of Hitler's staff officers, Colonel Brandt, to carry the parcel, telling him that it was a present of a couple of bottles of cognac for a friend at Rastenburg. The bomb failed to explode, but Tresckow was able to retrieve the parcel from the unsuspecting Brandt, and discovered that the detonator cap had failed.[31]

Meanwhile, in Russia the front had been stabilized. The holes torn in the southern front after the Battle of Stalingrad had been stitched together and the German line restored, but Hitler could draw scant comfort from these tactical successes. A whole year had passed, bringing with it a remorseless rise in casualties. By February 1943, Army and SS losses in Russia since 1941 exceeded one million either dead or missing. Goebbels confessed that merely to look at a map of the Eastern Front gave him the creeps; so much ground had been lost and the prospect of an Anglo-American invasion in the West 'hanging over all of them' left him uneasy. For his part, Hitler expressed bafflement that the millions of casualties the Russians had suffered since the launching of Barbarossa had not led to the collapse of Soviet resistance. Surely Stalin must be reaching the end of his reserves.

The extravagant ambition which had animated the plans for Barbarossa had now dimmed. The sweep of grand strategy had been succeeded by endless

---

31 Hitler had the Devil's own luck and avoided assassination on numerous occasions, often because of a sudden change of schedule. On 8 November 1939, George Elser planned to kill him with a bomb at the Burgerbräukeller celebrations to mark the anniversary of the beer-hall putsch. The bomb was planted and duly exploded at the time at which it was set. It would have killed Hitler but for the fact that he had left the hall thirteen minutes earlier. In the early months of 1944 plans were made by suicide bombers to kill Hitler while he was inspecting a new design of army overcoat. The first attempt was stillborn as the overcoats were destroyed in a bombing raid. The second attempt was thwarted when another raid caused the cancellation of the inspection.

discussion of the new weapons which would give the Third Reich the technical superiority to hang on to that which had been won since 1939. Walls were going up around Hitler's Fortress Europe: the Atlantic Wall along the west coast and, after August 1943, the East, or Panther Wall in Russia, stretching from near Leningrad due southwards to the line of the Dnieper.

OCCUPATION

By the end of 1942, German troops occupied the territory of fourteen European sovereign states and much of European Russia. German policy in the conquered territories of the East was based on the principle of coercion. The Nazis had no interest in winning the goodwill or even the co-operation of peoples whom they considered less than human. Hitler's New Order was designed solely to serve, in the most brutal terms, the interests of Greater Germany.

In Poland, under the rule of Hans Frank's General Government, the German aim was not only to dominate but also to destroy Polish national identity. The entire Polish nation would become German slaves, forming a huge pool of cheap labour. When the Red Army entered Warsaw in October 1944, it found a hundred and sixty thousand famished survivors from a pre-war population of 1.3 million.

In the Soviet Union, millions of captured Red Army soldiers and civilians, the majority of the latter Ukrainians, were forced to work as slaves in Germany. In October 1943 Heinrich Himmler observed, 'It is a matter of total indifference to me how the Russians fare ... Whether the other peoples live in plenty, whether they croak from hunger, interests me only to the extent that we need them as slaves for our culture. Otherwise it does not interest me.' By the same token, thousands died of starvation in Greece when the Germans commandeered the food stocks there.

In Western Europe the situation was more complicated. Denmark, the Nazis' showcase province, retained its elected government and monarchy under the supervision of the German Foreign Office and became a major provider of meat and dairy produce to the Third Reich. Norway and Holland were administered by Reich commissioners who were directly answerable to Hitler; their civil administrations remained in place, although their monarchies and governments had gone into exile. Belgium and north-east France were run by the Wehrmacht, although the Vichy government in France remained the nominal civil authority throughout the country, even after the Wehrmacht occupation of the 'Free Zone' in November 1942, following the Allied landings in North Africa.

Although occupation in the West was not as unremittingly brutal as that in the East, Hitler's European empire was administered entirely for Germany's benefit. For example, the iron, coal and steel output of north-east France and Belgium was co-ordinated with that of the Ruhr through purchasing arrangements dictated by the Reich's Economics and Armaments Ministries. In addition, the French were not only obliged to feed the sixty occupying German divisions but also had to make good Germany's domestic agricultural shortfall, which could be achieved only at the expense of its own population. In Western Europe there was still a market of a kind, albeit rigged overwhelmingly in Germany's favour. However, from 1942 no such regulation applied to the conscription of Western European foreign labour to work in Germany, a measure which did much to swell the ranks of the Resistance.

Within and without these walls, the tide of war was turning against Hitler. The Battle of the Atlantic had reached a crisis point in March 1943 when three of Grand Admiral Dönitz's U-boat 'wolf-packs' had scored one of their greatest successes, plundering two convoys and sinking twenty-one ships out of a combined total of ninety merchantmen and their escorts. That month the U-boats accounted for one hundred and eight ships in the North Atlantic, totalling nearly half a million tons and, as the British Admiralty put it, 'never came so near [again] to disrupting communications between the New World and the Old'. However, by May 1943, Allied technological superiority had driven the U-boats from the North Atlantic.

Defeat was also looming in North Africa, where the supply situation of Field Marshal Erwin Rommel's Army Group North Africa in Tunisia was now critical. On

MARTIN BORMANN

Bormann served as a gunner in World War I but saw no action. He joined the Freikorps in 1918 and was an early member of the NSDAP. In 1933 he became secretary to the deputy Führer, Rudolf Hess. After the defection of Hess to Britain in 1941, Hitler appointed Bormann head of the Party Chancery with the rank of minister, and in 1943 made him his personal secretary. A dedicated, hardworking, brutal and yet almost invisible bureaucrat, derided by Goebbels as a 'file-shitter' and fatally underestimated by the other Nazi paladins, Bormann acquired enormous power by controlling access to Hitler and filtering the news which reached him. Bormann's proximity to the Führer, and his control of the Party apparatus, cemented his indispensability. The 'Brown Eminence' was in charge of the appointment of all civil servants, and in 1943 joined Field Marshal Keitel and his successor as head of the Party Chancery, Hans Lammers, on the Committee of Three to mobilize all military, Party and state agencies for the war effort. After the failed Bomb Plot of July 1944, Bormann gained even greater power, and his own office was given sole responsibility for the training of all Party functionaries. Only Goebbels, another fanatical ideologue, remained a serious rival, although the two men collaborated effectively against the SS and the Wehrmacht. During the last days of the Third Reich, Bormann was made the head of the *Volkssturm*, the German equivalent of Britain's Home Guard. Along with Goebbels, he remained in the Führerbunker to the last, signed Hitler's Last Will and Testament, witnessed the marriage of Hitler to Eva Braun, and organized the burning of their corpses.

4 March Hitler, still preoccupied with Stalingrad, reflected, 'This is the end. Army Group Africa might just as well be brought back.' Five days later Rommel himself, haggard, depressed, and already labelled a defeatist, arrived at Hitler's headquarters (*Wehrwolf*) at Vinnitsa in central Ukraine. In talks over the next three days, Rommel attempted to persuade Hitler to authorize the abandonment of Army Group Africa's positions along the Mareth line and a withdrawal into a one hundred-mile perimeter around Tunis. Hitler agreed to some shortening of the Axis front but insisted that the Mareth Line be defended. He glibly assured Rommel that Mussolini would increase supplies to the First Italian and Fifth Panzer Armies by at least a hundred and fifty thousand tons a month. Hitler then awarded Rommel the Diamond to his Knight's Cross – the first such award to an army officer – and gave him a leave of absence, a decision which was kept secret lest it affect morale.

Rommel's successor as commander of Army Group Africa, General Jürgen von Arnim, was unable to hold the Mareth Line and by mid-April was clinging to the north-eastern tip of Tunisia. By 12 May Axis resistance was over. With the fall of Tunis, more than two hundred and thirty thousand Axis prisoners, nearly half of them German, tramped into Allied captivity. In spite of his gloomy forebodings, Hitler had once again been unable to bring himself to liquidate a front; as a result, he had presided over another Stalingrad on the southern shores of the Mediterranean.

Meanwhile, within the Reich itself, Fortress Europe had no roof to shield its civilian population from the increasingly heavy blows delivered by the British and American combined bombing offensive. The year had opened with a small but dramatic demonstration of the shortcomings of the Luftwaffe's air-defence system. On the morning of 3 January 1943, a 'nuisance flight' of three RAF Mosquitos arrived over Berlin to disrupt a speech given by Goebbels. During the afternoon, a second such flight arrived to wreck a rally attended by *Reichsmarschall* Hermann Göring.

These pinpricks were the preliminaries to the Battle of the Ruhr, which ended in mid-July 1943, and during which RAF Bomber Command dropped nearly sixty thousand tons of bombs on German industrial targets: more than the total delivered throughout 1942.

TOTAL WAR

Josef Goebbels was no military man, but he grasped that Germany, with its restricted capacity for the manufacture of aircraft, acute fuel and growing manpower shortages, and an incompetent Luftwaffe high command could not hope to retain air superiority against three enemies – the British, Americans and Russians – each of whose aircraft production figures exceeded those of the Reich (in the case of the Americans by many times). Perpetual air inferiority not only removed the essential condition of victory, it also precluded the conduct of a successful defensive strategy. The exposure of the German heartland, its population and its industries, to regular air attack, with the attendant effects on morale and war production, completed the vicious circle.

On 13 January 1943, Hitler issued a decree stating, 'The total war confronts us with tasks which must unequivocally be mastered.' But there was much that was indeed equivocal about the war effort in the Third Reich. Up to the end of 1942, economic planning had been governed by the assumption that the war would soon be won. The output of domestic product was only 12 per cent less than in 1938. In 1942 the armaments minister, Albert Speer, had increased war production by 40 per cent in spite of the fact that the work force in war industry between 1939 and 1942 had declined by almost 10 per cent. The German war economy was a mass of contradictions, with six million workers still producing consumer goods and one and a half million women still employed as maids and cooks.

Also on 13 January, Hitler named a three-man committee, consisting of Field Marshal Keitel, Martin Bormann and chief of the party chancery Hans Lammers, to mobilize all military, party and state agencies for the war effort. However, it was left to Goebbels publicly to grasp the nettle. On 18 February 1943, in an hour-long speech delivered at the Berlin Sportpalast, he ranged over the measures introduced in January to meet the demands of 'Total War'.

All men between the ages of sixteen and sixty-five, and women aged between seventeen and forty-five, were to be registered for compulsory war service. The Hitler Youth would be drafted to work on farms and collect scrap. The prison population was to be given war-related work. The net result was the registering of about three and a half million civilians, of whom about seven hundred thousand were put to work over the next seven months. Additionally, all non-war-related businesses were to be closed, including night clubs, luxury bars and restaurants, fashion and jewellery stores, and establishments dealing in postage stamps. The endemic corruption bred by warring petty fiefdoms within the Nazi Party hierarchy ensured that there were many exemptions and much wastage in the implementation of these measures.

While total war was Hitler's objective, Germany's allies were cautiously manoeuvring towards an exemption from their duties. Hitler's Fortress Europe contained within its boundaries a combination of cowed occupied peoples and increasingly sullen allies. The latter were reluctant to make any more sacrifices on the Eastern Front, where the Italian, Hungarian and Romanian Armies had been swept away by the Red Army counter-offensive during the battle for Stalingrad. Their headquarters were now out of the front line, attempting to pull together the remnants of their forces.

The Germans had openly regarded their allies as second class, and this did much to make them so. When Mussolini offered Hitler another seven hundred thousand men, the Führer observed that it would be pointless to equip them with German weapons, since these would only be surrendered at the first opportunity, adding, 'They can't even be assigned defensive combat duties.' Even the Finns, whose fighting qualities were undeniable, had asked to withdraw their five remaining battalions from the German Twentieth Mountain Army serving in the Murmansk sector on the Eastern Front.

Finland, Hungary and Romania lay directly in the path of the Red Army as it drove westward. If the Russian advance gathered momentum, they would find themselves in the front line. The Hungarian prime minister, Miklos von Kallay,[32] was already extending secret peace feelers to the British and Americans, using intermediaries in Turkey, Switzerland and the Vatican. In Madrid and Ankara, Romanian ministers were opening clandestine negotiations with the enemy. Hitler was aware of these rustlings in the diplomatic undergrowth; his intelligence services had given him hard evidence of this queasy manoeuvring. On 12 April, at the Berghof, the Romanian premier, Marshal Antonescu, who had authorized the approaches to the Allies, attempted to bluff it out with Hitler. So did the Hungarian leader, Admiral Horthy, when confronted a few days later by Hitler, who tartly reminded him, 'We are all in the same boat. If anybody goes overboard now, he drowns.'

—m—

The pressure of *sauve qui peut* bore down most heavily on the Italian dictator, Benito Mussolini. Never an equal partner with Germany, Italy was now a broken reed. At Stalingrad the Italian Eighth Army, originally two hundred thousand-strong, had been torn to shreds. In Tunisia, another two hundred thousand Italian troops faced the prospect of becoming prisoners of war. The clearing of North Africa by the Allies would provide them with a base from which to carry the war to Sicily and the Italian mainland.

Now that Il Duce's star was waning, many of his senior commanders conveniently discovered that they were royalists rather than Fascists and were reconsidering their position. Hitler was keenly aware of Mussolini's vulnerability. On 14 March he told his generals: 'In Italy we can rely on the Duce. There are strong fears that he may be got rid of or neutralized in some way.' This was inevitable for, as John Keegan has pointed out, 'There was a final and ultimately disabling impediment to Italy's effective commitment to war on Germany's side: the Italians harboured little or no hostility towards the enemies Hitler had chosen for them.'

In December 1942, Mussolini had sent his foreign minister, Count Galeazzo Ciano, to the Wolf's Lair with a proposal that a separate political settlement be made with the Soviet Union to free the Axis for the fight against Britain and the United States. On 7 April 1943, Mussolini met Hitler at Salzburg. A shadow of his former strutting self, hollow-cheeked and constantly in need of a supporting arm, he sat listlessly through a series of carefully staged briefings which said more about Hitler's lingering loyalty to his old ally than about the reality now pressing in on both of them. Before Mussolini's arrival, Hitler had unsuccessfully attempted to persuade the OKH chief of staff, General Kurt Zeitzler, to display wholly imaginary maps of the Eastern Front at the meetings as had been done on happier occasions in the past.

Once again Mussolini raised the question of seeking a separate peace with the Soviet Union. At this stage in the war Hitler had no illusions about the unlikelihood of dividing the grand alliance against him. Il Duce was sent on his way with variations on the no surrender theme, padded out with interminable lectures on

---

32 Kallay had been encouraged by Winston Churchill's proposal to the Turkish government that a Balkan League be formed, comprising Turkey, Hungary and Romania, as a future counterweight to Soviet power.

Frederick the Great and worthless promises of more oil for the Italian navy.

Yet Hitler was increasingly concerned about the Mediterranean theatre. Here, too, he was determined to hang on to every foot of occupied soil. After the fall of Tunis, his eyes ranged back and forth over the map as he pondered the most likely objectives for an Allied landing. OKW considered Sicily the obvious target, but Hitler thought it might be Sardinia. The approaches to the Balkans also occupied his attention, particularly the Peloponnese, and the Dodecanese islands lying off the south-western coast of Turkey. The Allies encouraged this guessing game with an ingenious deception plan, Operation Mincemeat.

On 30 April, a corpse with the false identity of a Royal Marines officer was floated ashore on the coast of Spain. A briefcase chained to his wrist contained equally false papers, which quickly reached German intelligence. They indicated that the Allies would make a feint attack on Sicily as a cover for the real target of Sardinia, the springboard for the invasion of northern Italy and the Balkans.

Through all this Hitler remained temperamentally incapable of settling on priorities. To keep the Allies away from the borders of the Reich, Italy would have to be defended, not least because of Hitler's well-founded doubts about the willingness of the Italians to stay in the war. As he wryly observed, 'The Italians never lose a war; no matter what happens, they always end up on the winning side.' Italy would need to be covered by garrisons in Corsica, Sardinia and Sicily. To secure the Balkans against Allied attack, strong forces were needed in Crete and Rhodes and dozens of smaller islands in the eastern Mediterranean. Hitler reasoned that the island garrisons would serve a double purpose, denying the British access to the Dardanelles and thus preventing the establishment of a direct sea-borne supply route to the Soviet Union. It also deterred Turkey from entering the war on the side of the Allies.

In the Mediterranean, as on the Eastern Front, Hitler's instinct was to defend everything along the perimeter. Although he liked to compare himself with Frederick the Great, he had forgotten one of the great Prussian king's most famous dicta, that he who defends everything defends nothing.

A DIVIDED HIGH COMMAND

If Hitler distrusted anyone more than his allies, it was his field commanders. After Stalingrad he had declared, 'There will be no more field marshals in this war. We'll only promote them after the end of the war. I won't count my chickens before they are hatched.' In his diary entry for 9 May, Goebbels reflected on Hitler's disenchantment with his commanders: 'He is absolutely sick of the generals. He can't imagine anything better than having nothing to do with them. His opinion of all the generals is devastating. Indeed, at times it is so caustic as to seem prejudiced or unjust, although on the whole it no doubt fits the case … All generals lie, he says. All generals are disloyal. All generals are reactionaries … he just can't stand them. They have disappointed him so often.'

The process of disillusionment had been gathering pace since February 1938 when Hitler had proclaimed himself the actual – as opposed to titular – commander-in-chief of the armed forces. In December 1941 he had dismissed the Army's C-in-C, the ailing Field Marshal von Brauchitsch, and had taken personal control of operations on the Eastern Front. Hitler had told General Franz Halder, the Army chief of staff and Zeitzler's predecessor, 'Anyone can do the little job of directing operations in war … I have therefore decided to take over command of the army myself.'

The immediate effect of Hitler's self-promotion was that OKH, the designated high command for operations on the Eastern Front, ceased to be a high command in all but name. Henceforth, operations in Russia, all the way down to battalion level, were executed according to the Führer's direction.

Hitler's chosen method of controlling the Nazi state had always been one of divide and rule, encouraging a chaos of competing empires and thus ensuring his personal supremacy. When the same principles were applied to the armed forces, it fatally fractured the unity of the German high command. OKH, its operations confined to the Eastern Front, was broken up and the Army General Staff retained as the instrument of Hitler's will. It was thus reduced to the status of OKW, which exercised responsibility for all other theatres. OKW had never fulfilled its envisaged role as a supreme joint services command, and in the hands of its chief of staff, General Alfred Jodl, merely duplicated the General Staff of OKH.[33]

Jodl's intermittent attempts to wrest operational control of the Army from OKH served only to increase tension within the high command. As he was only Hitler's executive, however, and had no active experience of command, his occasional spoiling forays were confined to matters of routine. Jodl's importance rested on the fact that he was the officer closest to Hitler, personally briefing him every day and discussing the plans and operational orders which he drafted in Hitler's name. His loyalty to Hitler, whom he regarded as a military genius, overrode the private misgivings he had about the conduct of the war from 1942. Content with such submissiveness, Hitler informed Göring that he considered Jodl 'a very good and solid worker, with an excellent staff training'.

While Jodl remained an irritant to OKH, unqualified contempt was reserved for his superior, Field Marshal Wilhelm Keitel, chief of OKW. Keitel exercised no influence over operations, acting merely as a functionary who faithfully executed Hitler's orders in a style which prompted the Führer to refer to him as *treu wie ein Hund*. (faithful as a dog). In less charitable mood, Hitler observed that Keitel had the brains of a cinema commissionaire. Mussolini's assessment of Keitel was that he was very pleased to be Keitel. Young staff officers referred to him as 'Lakaitel' (a pun on the German for servant) or 'nodding donkey' a reference to Keitel's constant readiness to agree with Hitler. General Walter Warlimont, deputy chief of operations at OKW, recalled Keitel's conduct at the

---

33 Nor did OKW have any control over the navy and Luftwaffe high commands OKM and OKL, whose chiefs reported directly to Hitler.

daily Führer briefings: 'He could hardly wait for some catchword or pause in Hitler's flow of speech to indicate by some word or gesture that, without further ado, he was in agreement.'

—ᴟ—

From the winter of 1941, Hitler had assumed the mantle of *Feldherr*, the warlord in control of Germany's destiny and in personal command of all naval, air and ground forces. He controlled the field formations in every theatre through two separate and squabbling staffs. And he exercised a direct control over every officer, from lieutenant to field marshal, through the Army personnel office which, in the autumn of 1942, was removed from OKW and placed under Hitler's military adjutant, General Rudolf Schmundt.

In a radio broadcast of 30 September 1942, shortly after the Sixth Army had occupied the greater part of Stalingrad, Hitler told the German people that victory had been secured, not over the enemy but over the 'old world' of hidebound military tradition represented by the red trouser-stripes and silver collar-tabs of the General Staff. In Hitler's classless society the future belonged to the brave and loyal Party man. Any attempts to merge OKW and OKH under a single C-in-C Eastern Front – someone like Manstein – were brushed aside by Hitler. As Warlimont observed: 'A combination of these two offices in the hands of one man would have been entirely opposed to Hitler's innermost conviction, for he always followed the principle of division of authority … Hitler did not want unity, he preferred diversity, such unity as there was being concentrated in his person alone.'

THE WOLF'S LAIR

It is significant that the two great dictators of World War II, Hitler and Stalin, both arrived at a system of command which suited their particular temperaments. However, while Hitler's solution to the problems of warfare left him in a permanent state of decidedly uncreative tension with his generals, Stalin was able, after the crushing setbacks of the first twenty months of hostilities, to make the best possible use of the outstanding military professionals who had emerged since the onset of Barbarossa.

In one respect the two dictators were very similar. During the war they both conformed to a secretive nocturnal routine which turned night into day. From the beginning of the Russian campaign, Hitler had fought the greater part of the war from the Wolf's Lair at Rastenburg. Freezing in winter and oppressively hot in summer, the personnel in the Wolf's Lair fed off the Führer's enervation and deepening gloom. Count Ciano, Mussolini's foreign minister and son-in-law, found the atmosphere there intensely depressing: 'One does not see a single colourful spot, not a single lively touch. The ante-rooms are full of people smoking, eating and chatting. Smell of kitchens, uniforms, heavy boots.'

Those who came and went, waited and smoked, or stood awkwardly silent as the Führer shuffled though the compound with his German Shepherd bitch Blondi at his side, were extras in a drama whose last act was being written by a man retreating step by step from reality. After Stalingrad, Hitler strove to conceal his mounting depression and deteriorating health behind a mask of rigid self-control. But the mask kept slipping, and his physical appearance shocked those who had not seen him for some time. Visiting Hitler at his headquarters in the Ukraine on 20 February 1943 to confirm his own appointment as Inspector-General of Armoured Troops, General Guderian found him greatly changed since their last meeting in December 1941. 'His left hand trembled, his back was bent, his gaze was fixed, his eyes protruded but lacked their former lustre, his cheeks were flecked with red. He was more excitable, easily lost his composure, and was prone to angry outbursts and ill-considered decisions.'

Lieutenant-General Count von Schwerin has also left a description of Hitler's physical appearance at the time: 'I reported in the prescribed manner and Hitler came over to me – a man stooping as though under a heavy burden, with slow, tired steps … Hitler was completely down, and in bewilderment I looked into his lustreless eyes with their unnaturally blue colour … There can be no doubt at all that those were a sick man's eyes. It may be that he rehearsed this scene.'

It was more likely that a significant contributory factor to Hitler's debilitated physical appearance was the treatment he was receiving at the hands of his personal physician, Dr Theodor Morell, a quack who was prescribing laxatives of increasing savagery for the severe constipation from which the Führer was suffering in the spring of 1943, the result of his wretched vegetarian diet and lack of exercise. This was a highly unsuitable regime for Hitler as he flitted back and forth between Berlin, Rastenburg and the Obersalzberg, gripped by growing tension over the deteriorating strategic situation in the Mediterranean and on the Eastern Front.

After Stalingrad, Hitler strove to conceal his mounting depression and deteriorating health behind a mask of rigid self-control.

Nevertheless, at Rastenburg Hitler, by a supreme effort of will, maintained his daily routine in all its stupefying monotony. He rose late in the morning and, accompanied by his *maison militaire*, attended a midday briefing conference lasting two or three hours. In the stuffy, crowded conference room Hitler was the only one who was seated, although an upholstered stool was usually provided for the corpulent Göring. Around the map table, illuminated by desk lamps with long, swinging arms, stood Hitler's adjutants, OKW staff officers, the Army General Staff and the Führer's liaison officers with the Luftwaffe, Kriegsmarine, Waffen-SS and Himmler's Ministry of the Interior. Albert Speer recalled that 'on the whole, they were rather young men with likeable faces, most of them holding the rank of colonel or major'. Keitel, Jodl and the Army chief of staff, General Zeitzler, stood casually among them. Throughout the conference there was a low background hum of conversation.

The Eastern Front was invariably the first item on the agenda. On the situation table Hitler would work his way from north to south on four large strategic maps, pasted together and each measuring about eight by five feet. They carried information on the previous day's events right down to the activities of patrols. The layman Speer was 'astonished at the way Hitler, in the course of hearing the reports, made deployments, pushed divisions back and forth or dealt with petty details'.

—⧓—

By this stage in the war, Hitler's compulsion to indulge in unrestrained monologues was running out of control and frequently frustrated the rational conduct of business. Warlimont recalled that:

> Urgent concrete questions and proposals under discussion would be drowned in this ceaseless, repetitive torrent of words in which matters old and new, important and unimportant, were jumbled up together. There would also frequently be long-winded telephone conversations with senior commanders at the front; sometimes the latter used the knowledge of the time at which the briefing conference took place to try to get urgent decisions out of Hitler; alternatively he would call them up in the vague hope that they would be able to supply him with more pleasant information than that presented by the chief of staff.

Technical experts, often from the traffic-control authorities, ministers, and secretaries of state were regularly summoned to these conferences to be questioned, lectured or threatened. Doubtless Hitler felt that their presence injected a sense of purpose and unity into the proceedings, but this was often dispelled by the savage delight he took in browbeating senior officers with barrages of the statistics he carried in his head. Manstein observed of this *rage de nombre*, 'He was amazingly familiar with the effects of the very latest enemy weapons and could reel off whole columns of figures on both our own and the enemy's war production. Indeed, this was his favourite way of sidetracking any topic that was not to his liking.' Warlimont, a superb military professional, and Speer, an amateur albeit highly intelligent onlooker, both agreed that the conferences were largely a waste of time.

Lunch was taken at a long, oblong table with the attentive Jodl on the Führer's left and a visitor such as Göring or Speer on his right. The liaison officers and adjutants ranged down the table were all ears as the Führer's table talk unreeled on an endless loop. After Stalingrad, however, he increasingly took to eating his meagre vegetarian meals alone. Lunch was followed by more meetings and conferences before Hitler took a break to guzzle cream cakes with his female secretaries. Late at night, after the last meeting, Hitler would reassemble this captive audience and continue talking until dawn, regaling them with crude invective about Churchill ('an alcoholic bullshit'), Roosevelt ('a cracked fool') and German commanders like Manstein ('a pisspot strategist'). The table talk would lurch randomly between subjects alternatively ludicrous and sinister: Ice Age catastrophes, the 'smears' of modern art, cannibalism among the defenders of Leningrad, the simplest way of dealing with a mutiny in Germany ('shoot a few thousand people') and the sound sense of the

Soviet regime which did not waste any time over 'all that humanitarian blather'.

A secretary who attended some of these marathon sessions in the high summer of 1941 wrote: 'I really must start writing down what the Chief says. It's just that these sessions go on for ages and afterwards you are just too limp and lifeless to write anything.' Struggling to stay awake in the company of the insomniac Führer must have become almost unendurable. Release finally came at dawn when, as Guderian recalled, Hitler would lie down for a brief sleep, from which the pushing brooms of the scrub-women at his bedroom door would awaken him by nine o' clock at the latest.

CITADEL

The Soviet offensive launched in January 1943 had been stopped in its tracks by a brilliantly weighted counterblow delivered by Field Marshal von Manstein in February–March. When the fighting died down in the mud of the spring thaw, it left a huge fist-shaped salient, centred on the city of Kursk in the heartland of the Ukraine and jutting westward into the German line.

The Kursk bulge exercised a horrible fascination on Hitler. He told Guderian that every time he thought of the impending attack on the salient his stomach turned over. The build-up to the launching of the operation, aimed at clawing back the initiative after the disaster at Stalingrad, took three months and was postponed several times by Hitler, who was fretting about the arrival in numbers of the new Mark V Panther medium tank. The plan envisaged a concentric attack of the type which had proved so effective in the summer of 1941, trapping the Red Army forces defending the salient in a massive pocket where they could be destroyed piecemeal. The operation, code-named Citadel (*Zitadelle*), was to be carried out by two army groups attacking the shoulders of the salient – Army Group Centre on the northern shoulder and Army Group South on the southern shoulder. Nearly a million men would be sent into action, supported by two thousand four hundred tanks, ten thousand artillery pieces and two and a half-thousand aircraft, many of them ruthlessly stripped from other sectors on the Eastern Front.

Alerted by the massive German preparations and well informed by the Lucy spy network in Switzerland and a mole inside Bletchley Park[34] in England, *Stavka*, the Soviet General Staff, had plenty of time to strengthen the defences of the salient, which was held by two Red Army Fronts (Army Groups),[35] Central and Voronezh.

---

34 The Soviet mole was John Cairncross, a British Army officer and Communist who, in 1943, briefly worked at Bletchley, where the German Enigma code and its successors had been broken. He collected raw decrypts and handed them over to his Soviet controller in London. During the long build-up to Kursk, which generated a huge volume of Enigma traffic, Cairncross played an important, albeit baleful, role in keeping Soviet intelligence abreast of the intelligence aspects of the coming battle. For this and other services he was given a medal by Stalin.

35 The Soviet high command used the term 'front' not only to designate a zone of deployment of troops and the line of battle but also a distinct operational organization of armed forces. Roughly equivalent to a German army group, a front consisted of some five to seven armies, with one or two tactical air armies, and special armoured and artillery formations in support. An entire front could total up to one million men and extend over a battle frontage of up to one hundred and fifty miles, with a depth – if one includes the rear zones of operations – of up to two hundred and fifty miles.

By the end of June, the salient was packed with one million three hundred thousand men, with a hundred guns per kilometre on the likely axes of advance. Some two thousand tanks and self-propelled guns deployed in the salient and the bulk of the remainder were held in reserve in Steppe Front's Fifth Guards Tank Army. In the north and south of the salient, a deeply echeloned eight-line defensive network, comprising dense minefields and trench systems linking anti-tank strongpoints had been constructed. Over three hundred thousand civilians had been employed on the construction of these killing grounds and in the repair and maintenance of the rail links from the salient to the Soviet interior.

It was in the killing grounds of the Kursk salient that Hitler's Panzers and his ambitions were dealt a blow from which they never recovered.

When Hitler launched his Panzers against the shoulders of the salient on 5 July 1943, they were caught in the killing grounds and mangled beyond repair. In the south on 12 July, at the northernmost point of the advance spearheaded by the Fourth Panzer Army, II SS Panzer Corps slammed headlong into Fifth Guards Tank Army, which was hastening up from the Steppe Front strategic reserve. In the ensuing armoured mêlée at Prokhorovka, the largest tank battle in World War II in which armoured vehicles clashed at point-blank range, II SS Panzer Corps was stopped dead in its tracks. It nevertheless inflicted heavy losses on the Red Army formation, knocking out or damaging at least four hundred out of a total of eight hundred vehicles at relatively small cost to itself.[36]

36 A 2007 study by the German Historical Institute in London has suggested that Soviet losses at Prokhorovka were not the result of an armoured battle but a catastrophic muddle. Most of Red Army's T-34s, according to the study, drove into a huge anti-tank ditch which had been dug several days earlier by its own infantry.

However, for the Fourth Panzer Army's elite units, Prokhorovka was the last straw. The terrible slog through the Red Army's defences in which, before the clash at Prokhorovka, it had lost three hundred and thirty tanks and assault guns, had already depressed morale to the point where the will to press home the attacks against the strong Soviet resistance was fast slipping away.

—◆—

Then a double blow descended on the German high command. On 10 July the Western Allies landed in Sicily. Two days later, from the Kursk salient, the Red Army launched a massive counter-offensive code-named Kutuzov, the first in a series planned to unroll along the Eastern Front. Hitler, now preoccupied with events in the Mediterranean and the Balkans, at first refused to sanction an organized withdrawal from the Kursk salient, leaving his commanders on the ground to improvise an escape from the Soviet whirlwind. The retreat continued all the way to the River Dnieper. The Germans could not hold the west bank, and on the night of 4 November, tanks of the Third Tank Army burst out of the Soviet bridgehead, headlights blazing and sirens howling. Two days later they had liberated Kiev.

Hitler had intended Citadel to be 'a beacon for the world', a rallying point for his disaffected allies. But by the time that *Stavka* was regrouping its forces for the battle of the Dnieper line, the war had been lost. Less than twelve months earlier, the Red Army had turned the tide at Stalingrad, where it seized the psychological intiative for the first time. But it was in the killing grounds of the Kursk salient that Hitler's Panzers, and his ambitions, were dealt a blow from which they never recovered. Victory was now a thing of the past. The premonition of defeat that had stirred at Stalingrad was now a daily spectre haunting the officers and men of the *Ostheer*, which was now facing the prospect of permanent retreat and an increasingly grave manpower crisis.

There were to be no more major German offensives in the East until the abortive attempt to relieve Budapest in January 1945. The story was now one of Russian advance and German retreat. After the war, Guderian reflected sadly on the fate of the Panzers – Hitler's pride and joy – committed to Citadel:

The armoured formations, re-formed and re-equipped with much effort, had lost heavily in both men and equipment and would now be unemployable for a long time to come. It was problematic whether they could be rehabilitated in time to defend the Eastern Front; as for being able to use them in the defence of the Western Front against the Allied landings that threatened next spring, this was even more questionable. Needless to say, the Russians exploited their victory to the full. There was to be no more quiet on the Eastern Front. From now on the enemy was in undisputed possession of the initiative.

Opposite: A Red Army T-34 medium tank in 1943. The mainstay of the Soviet Union's tank armies, the T-34 was a superb fighting machine whose basic excellence was underlined by the fact that it went through the war without major modification. Its broad tracks reduced ground pressure to a minimum and it was fast and agile, even in the roughest terrain. Its sloping armour increased resistance to shell penetration and, with an all-weather diesel engine, the T-34 had a range of 186 miles. Its long-barrelled, high-velocity 76.2mm gun completed a design which combined firepower, mobility and protection with the facility of rapid mass production and easy repair and maintenance in the field.

D-DAY

At the beginning of June 1944, Hitler was staying at the Berghof. To the Führer's Luftwaffe adjutant, Nicolaus von Below, it seemed as if the clock had been turned back to the days before the war. The familiar routine was maintained: afternoon walks to the Tea House across the valley from Berghof, where Hitler would preside over coffee and cakes; evenings spent by the fire as he talked on and on about the great men of history, architecture, his early political triumphs and the Jewish-Bolshevik threat. He seemed relaxed and looked relatively healthy. When on 3–4 June news began to break of the Allied entry into Rome, Hitler did not bat an eyelid. He was now waiting for the curtain to go up on the coast of north-east Europe when the long-awaited Allied invasion armies arrived. He would not have to wait much longer.

Anxious to deploy their massive manpower and materiel resources, the Americans had urged the launching of the invasion of north-west Europe as early as the spring of 1943. The British, fearful of heavy losses, sought to postpone a landing until Allied air power had fatally weakened the Third Reich. In the summer of 1942, the British headed off an American plan for a forty-eight-division invasion of northern Europe. Thereafter, the Allies focused their immediate attention on clearing North Africa and the invasion of Italy, which the British believed would draw German troops away from France before a cross-Channel invasion could be launched in sufficient strength to ensure its success.

The Russians, suffering terrible casualties on the Eastern Front, had long wanted an immediate invasion, a second front to take the heat off Stalin. Early in 1943 Churchill and Roosevelt agreed to increase the pace of the build-up in Britain but the Soviet supreme commander had nevertheless to wait until 6 June 1944 for the launching of Operation Overlord. After a month-long air offensive and the implementation of an Allied deception plan, code-named Fortitude, which convinced Hitler that the main attack would be made in the Pas de Calais where he held back a powerful armoured reserve, the largest amphibious operation in history got under way. The target was Normandy.

In the small hours of 6 June, Allied airborne troops landed to seize bridges and coastal batteries on the flanks of the invasion zone. The first Allied troops came ashore on Utah beach at 6.30 a.m. Hitler, who had gone to bed at around 3 a.m. on 6 June, was still sound asleep seven hours later. His adjutants had been afraid to wake him. Later, at the daily military conference, the Führer remained uncertain whether the Normandy landings were a diversion. Only after a fatal delay did he agree to deploy the armoured reserve against the Allied beachheads. Its movement, in daylight, was interdicted by Allied bombers, which enjoyed total air superiority.

The launching of Overlord galvanized Hitler. Goebbels noted in his diary that a great weight seemed to have been lifted from his shoulders. He was 'absolutely certain' that the Allied troops would be driven back into the sea. Goebbels went on,

'If we repel the invasion, then the scene in the war will be completely transformed. The Führer reckons for certain with this. He has few worries that this couldn't succeed.'

However, on only one of the five invasion beaches did the defenders of the Atlantic Wall mount fierce resistance. On Omaha Beach the US V Corps took heavy casualties from the battle-hardened and well dug-in German 352nd Infantry Division. When it broke out of 'Bloody Omaha', V Corps left two thousand four hundred American dead behind. By midnight on 6 June, fifty-seven-and-a-half thousand American, and seventy-five thousand British and Canadian troops had been landed in Normandy and the process of linking the beachheads had begun.

Mid-June 1944 was a time of desperate crisis for Hitler, the worst he had faced since the surrender at Stalingrad seventeen months earlier. Six days after the Normandy landings he launched his V-weapon campaign against Britain. The first of his revenge weapons (*Vergeltungswaffen*) was the FZG-76, the first operational guided missile, popularly known as the V-1. It was a ramp-launched mid-wing monoplane, propelled by a pulsating flow-duct motor and armed with a 1,874lb warhead. Hitler had long anticipated the devastating effect of the flying bombs launched en masse, drooling over images of a London reduced to a sea of rubble. However, the launch rate was much lower than he had anticipated, approximately eighty a day, of which only half reached the British capital or its suburbs. One rogue flying-bomb crashed directly on to Hitler's command bunker at Margival on 17 June during the course of the only visit he made to France throughout the Normandy battle.

V-2 AND BEYOND

The A-4 (*Aggregat 4*) rocket was a ballistic missile, also known as the V-2 (*Vergeltungswaffen 2*, or Vengeance Weapon 2) which was used to bombard English and Continental targets in 1944–45. The rocket had a range of some two hundred and fifteen miles and was a much more expensive weapon than the V-1 although, like its predecessor, it was highly inaccurate and could be expected to fall anywhere within a rectangle sixteen miles long and thirteen miles wide. The attack on England began on 8 September 1944, when the first V-2 fell on West London. Unlike the V-1, which chugged through the sky before its engine cut out and it plunged earthward, the arrival of the V-2 was preceded by no warning – if you didn't hear it, you bought it. The last V-2 landed in Orpington, Kent, on 27 March 1945. In all, one thousand and fifty V-2s were spotted by observers, five hundred and eighteen of which hit the London area, killing two thousand seven hundred and fifty-four people.

Long before the V-2 became operational, a complex of vast assembly and firing bases for Hitler's revenge weapons had been constructed by Polish and Russian slave labour in the Pas de Calais. They were ziggurats of reinforced concrete, and it was believed that they would prove impervious to Allied bombs. However, heavy air raids rendered these grim examples of Nazi architectural brutalism useless and they were overrun by the Allies after D-day. Two of the most chilling examples survive to this day. La Coupole, the colossal bomb-proof dome served by miles of underground tunnels near Wizernes, never fired a rocket in anger. The V-2 assembly factory in a forest near St Omer is, if anything, even more chilling. Looming from a wooded setting, which now rings with birdsong, it nevertheless makes the heart sink. The factory's ominously dank and dripping interior, truly the heart of darkness, is a metaphor for the emptiness and nihilism of the megalomaniac for whom this barbaric building was created, Adolf Hitler.

Hitler had arrived with his entourage in a convoy of armour-plated Mercedes limousines. The threat of Allied air attack forced the conference to be conducted in a nearby railway tunnel. Hitler, looking pale and listless, sat on a stool, fiddled with his spectacles, and played with his coloured pencils while his generals remained standing. Commander-in-Chief West, Field Marshal von Rundstedt, reporting on the first ten days of the battle for Normandy, concluded that the Allies could not be expelled from France. Hitler countered by arguing that the V-1s should be targeted against the Allied beachheads, only to be told that their guidance systems were insufficiently accurate. Undaunted, Hitler promised to commit fleets of new jet fighters to the battle, omitting to mention, as well he knew, that they had only just entered production.

After lunch Hitler talked with Erwin Rommel, now commander of Army Group B in Normandy and long an advocate that any Allied cross-Channel invasion would have to be met at the water's edge. Now the field marshal painted a pessimistic picture and urged the Führer to seek a political solution, only to receive the stinging reply, 'Pay attention to your invasion front, not to the continuation of the war.' Hitler flew to Germany shortly afterwards and remarked that evening that Rommel had clearly lost his nerve.

—⁂—

By the end of August 1944, the Allies had surged out of the Normandy bridgehead and were standing on the Seine from Troyes, a hundred miles south of Paris, to the sea. Paris had been liberated on 25 August and four days later the last German troops slipped across the Seine, leaving behind them in Normandy two thousand two hundred destroyed or abandoned armoured vehicles and two hundred and ten thousand prisoners. German casualties in the fighting had been two hundred and forty thousand men killed and wounded. Three months of fighting in Normandy had cost the German army in the West, the *Westheer*, twice as many men as had Stalingrad.

On 20 August, fifty thousand men had been trapped in the Falaise pocket, sealed off in the north by the Canadian First Army and the US Third Army. Two days after the Allied jaws had snapped shut, the Allied Supreme Commander, General Dwight D. Eisenhower, toured the battlefield, encountering 'scenes that could only be described by Dante'. It was literally possible to walk for hundreds of yards at a time stepping over nothing but dead and decayed flesh. Allied aircrew flying low over these scenes of carnage wrinkled their noses in disgust at the rising stench of corpses putrefying in the summer heat.

One casualty of the Falaise battle was Field Marshal Günther von Kluge, who had replaced Rundstedt as Commander-in-Chief West. On 15 July, while he was in the front line near Avranches, his wireless tender had been knocked out, cutting off communications with his headquarters for several hours. At Rastenburg, where Kluge was already a marked man, suspected of complicity in the July Bomb Plot against Hitler, it was assumed that the field marshal was trying to negotiate with the Allies. Kluge was relieved of his command and ordered to return to Germany. The field marshal preferred to commit suicide.

VALKYRIE

At the centre of a conspiracy which came within an ace of killing Hitler was Colonel Count Claus von Stauffenberg, chief of staff to General Friedrich Fromm, commander of the Home Army (*Ersatzheer*), who had served with distinction in Poland, in France, where he won the Iron Cross, First Class, and in North Africa. Stauffenberg had been severely wounded in a strafing attack in April 1943, losing his right eye, right arm and part of his left hand. On his release from hospital, he was asked by Major-General Henning von Tresckow to join the conspiracy to assassinate Hitler.

Stauffenberg[37] was a complex figure, an aristocrat and nationalist who had originally supported the Nazis and, like many of his caste, saw nothing wrong with the total subjugation of Poland. However, his resolve to remove Hitler, bring the war to an end and, in the process save millions of lives, had hardened into an iron determination. It was Stauffenberg's idea to subvert the Valkyrie plan, an official contingency measure to deal with an uprising of slave workers in Germany, and turn it into the mechanism by which the Nazi state would itself be overturned after the killing of the Führer. A man of action rather than a theoretician, he proposed that he should carry out the assassination. This was the July Bomb Plot, which Stauffenberg codenamed Valkyrie.

The Nazi state would itself be overturned after the killing of the Führer.

Gaining access to the Führer presented the conspirators with an immense problem. However, Stauffenberg's duties included attending briefings at Rastenburg. Since the nature of his injuries apparently placed him above suspicion, his briefcase was never examined by the guards at the Wolf's Lair. Thus, on 20 July 1944, Stauffenberg exploited this combination of circumstances to plant a bomb which he anticipated would kill Hitler. But fate took a hand. By the end of June 1944, the relatively airy aboveground huts and bunkers in which Hitler had held his daily conferences had been replaced by concrete blockhouses and bombproof underground steel-and-concrete shelters with sturdy walls. On 20 July, the bunker in which Hitler usually held his conferences was being repaired. The conference therefore was held in a flimsy hut above ground, and this saved the Führer's life.

When Hitler had taken his place and the midday conference had begun, Stauffenberg laid his briefcase against the leg at the far right end of the heavy table on which the situation maps were being examined, then slipped out of the room. This in itself was not unusual as there was always a great deal of coming and going during the Führer conferences. As he crossed the outer compound, Stauffenberg heard the bomb detonate. He boarded an aircraft bound for Berlin, ready to announce the death of Hitler and the formation of a new government.

---

37 Stauffenberg and his brother had been members of the circle around the poet Stefan George, who wished to restore German medieval greatness. George and his followers propagated the notion of a unique *Deutschtum*, or German-ness. On George's death in 1933, Stauffenberg and his brother were made George's heirs and organized candlelit readings of his poetry.

But Hitler was alive. During the conference, another officer inadvertently dislodged the briefcase, pushing the bomb away from its intended target behind a heavy wooden plinth supporting the table. When the bomb detonated, the force of the explosion blew out the top at the end of the table. Of the seven men standing at that end, four died and two more were gravely injured. One of the dead was General Schmundt, Hitler's adjutant. The flash set light to Hitler's hair and clothing, shredding his trousers and burning his right leg. The ceiling collapsed, bringing with it part of a roof beam that skinned Hitler's buttocks 'like a baboon's', as he later put it.

The shock of the assassination attempt and his seemingly miraculous survival gave Hitler an immense adrenalin boost. Bathed, and with his burns dressed and his right arm in a sling, he donned a new uniform and drove to meet the arriving Mussolini. Film footage of the event shows Hitler in manic high spirits on the platform of Rastenburg's secret railway station, code-named Görlitz, greeting his subdued visitor.

Hitler took Mussolini back to the ruined hut, gleefully giving a blow-by-blow account of his recent good fortune: the windows had been open at the time of the explosion, lessening the effects of the blast. Had Hitler held the conference in the deep shelter, he would not have survived. He told Mussolini that he had been saved by the hand of Providence and that he believed 'the great destiny which I serve will transcend its present perils and that all will be brought to a triumphant conclusion'.

The plot had failed. Even had it succeeded, it is difficult to see how the mainly conservative conspirators, a mixture of civilians and the military, would in the immediate aftermath of the assassination have been able to mobilize the people of Germany against the regime. Moreover, failure at Rastenburg had been matched by a failure of nerve in Berlin. Vital hours were lost through vacillation, poor organization and sheer bad luck. At 6.45 p.m. the news of Hitler's survival was broadcast throughout the Reich and the conspiracy collapsed. Only in Paris was there an all-too-brief measure of success. General Karl-Heinrich von Stülpnagel,[38] the military governor of Occupied France, succeeded in rounding up the SS and Gestapo, but without the backing of his commander, Field Marshal von Kluge, he could do nothing.

Stauffenberg was shot that night in Berlin, the first in a grisly series of executions. The conspirators, as well as those suspected of being sympathetic to them, were either given the dubious privilege of committing suicide or were executed after show trials. One of the suicides was General Ludwig Beck. At least two hundred and fifty men, including two field marshals and sixteen generals are known to have met their ends in this way: the death agonies of some were filmed for the entertainment of the Führer and his entourage. In the fall-out of the failed Bomb Plot, an estimated ten thousand people were sent to concentration camps, gassed, shot or hung. Rommel, under suspicion, was forced to commit suicide. Tresckow, serving on the Eastern Front, deliberately walked into Red Army fire.

This bloodletting – a brutal echo of the Night of the Long Knives – reanimated Hitler. His patience with the Army was now exhausted. His first recourse was to the spirit of National Socialism. General Fromm, executed after the Bomb Plot, was succeeded by Heinrich Himmler as head of the Home Army. The appointment of the hated *Reichsführer*-SS was greeted by the officer corps, who universally loathed him – without a murmur of protest. Field Marshal von Brauchitsch, inactive since his dismissal in December 1941, was wheeled out, willingly or otherwise, to condemn the July traitors and laud Himmler's appointment as a sign of closer co-operation between the Army and the SS.

Opposite: Hitler and Mussolini inspect the wrecked conference hut at Rastenburg, scene of the July 1944 attempt on Hitler's life. Mussolini was by now a back number, deposed in July 1943 and imprisoned in the Gran Sasso, from which he was rescued by a German commando unit led by Otto Skorzeny. A broken man, he was then installed as the puppet ruler of the 'Italian Social Republic' in northern Italy.

---

38 Stülpnagel had long been an opponent of the Nazi regime. In 1939 he had planned a coup which had to be abandoned for lack of support, but he continued to recruit like-minded officers. In May 1944 he was planning to conclude an armistice with the Western Allies but Rundstedt, the C-in-C West, refused to participate. Kluge, Rundstedt's successor, later offered his support but only if Hitler was killed. When Hitler survived Stauffenberg's bomb Stülpnagel was doomed, and got no help from Kluge. He failed in a suicide attempt, was tried with fellow conspirators and hanged.

OPERATION BAGRATION

Normandy was not the only front to demand Hitler's attention in June 1944.

Between December 1943 and June 1944, a series of Soviet offensives had driven the Germans out of the Crimea and the Ukraine and back into eastern Poland. While the fighting in Normandy boiled up, the Red Army was gathering itself for a renewed attack.

Operation Bagration, named after Napoleon's Russian adversary, opened on 22 June, the third annniversary of the launching of Operation Barbarossa, and tore great holes in the front held by Germany's Army Group Centre. When Bagration finally ran down in August as it approached the River Vistula, it had punched a two-hundred-and-fifty-mile gap in the German line, advanced four hundred and fifty miles to the Gulf of Riga and the borders of East Prussia, and destroyed the equivalent of twenty-five enemy divisions. Army Group Centre had been smashed beyond repair and Army Group North isolated on the Baltic coast where it was to remain, cut off, for the rest of the war.

Bagration had brought the Red Army to the gates of Warsaw where, on 1 August, the Polish Home Army, whose members were loyal to the government-in-exile in London, rose up against the Germans. However, in July the Soviet Union had established its own Communist government-in-waiting in the liberated Polish city of Lublin. The Russians did not come to the aid of the Home Army but stood by while in Warsaw the SS did their work for them. The uprising was crushed with utter ruthlessness. Captured Polish fighters were summarily executed by squads of released convicts, as were doctors and nurses attending the wounded. Civilians were marched in front of tanks as human shields. Gas was used to flush out those who attempted to flee through the sewers. In the uprising some fifteen thousand members of the Home Army and approximately two hundred and twenty-five thousand civilians lost their lives. The survivors were deported to German camps while the SS garrison set about the total destruction of the ancient city.

On both fronts, East and West, Germany was staring defeat in the face. A majority of the experienced commanders knew full well that the game was up. Many would have agreed with Rundstedt's outburst at a staff conference early in July when, asked what should be done, he barked, 'Make peace, you fools!' This insight was rewarded with dismissal; his successor, Kluge, did not last long. Rundstedt, at least, survived and was soon to return to high command.

THE BATTLE OF THE BULGE

On 15 August 1944, the Allies landed in the South of France, capturing Toulon and Marseilles two weeks later. In north-east Europe they raced into the Low Countries, liberating Brussels on 3 September. On 11 September American patrols crossed the German border near Aachen. However, hopes that the war would be over by Christmas were soon dashed. A bold airborne attempt to turn the northern end of the West Wall, the German defensive line running along the Dutch and French borders, came to grief at Arnhem. The British failed to clear the Scheldt estuary, which denied Allied shipping the use of the vital port of Antwerp until November 1944. In the great forests on the German frontier, the Reichswald and the Hürtgen, there was fighting reminiscent of the slogging matches of World War I.

Hitler now planned to deal the Allies a stinging blow in the West. He could see that the Allied logistical chain was badly over-stretched and he had a low opinion of the morale and fighting qualities of American troops. Now he sought to split them from their British allies. Poring over his maps in the Wolf's Lair, his gambler's eye had spotted an opportunity for a counterstroke. On 16 September, he told Jodl: 'I have made a momentous decision. I shall go over to the offensive … Out of the Ardennes, with the objective Antwerp.'

Here, where in May 1940 he had settled the fate of France in a single afternoon, Hitler planned another all-or-nothing gamble. A quick victory was necessary, he argued, before the French began to conscript their manpower. It was as if, in Hitler's mind, the war would last for ever and that after five years he had merely returned to square one – like a Monopoly player passing 'Go' – and was readying himself for the second round of the game. Once again, German armies would drive through the forests of the Ardennes to the Meuse, then sweep north to seize Antwerp. Cut off from their American allies, the British Second and Canadian First Armies would be encircled and destroyed. The coalition against the Axis would fall apart and Germany would then turn to deal with the looming threat in the East.

Hitler planned another all-or-nothing gamble. A quick victory was necessary.

This was the last occasion on which the Führer still held enough chips to double the stakes. His was a bold plan, sweeping in concept, and all but impossible to execute. When it was unveiled to a recalled but still sceptical Field Marshal von Rundstedt on 24 October, the old soldier was 'staggered … It was obvious to me that the available forces were far too small – in fact no soldier really believed that the aim of reaching Antwerp was really practicable. But I knew by now it was useless to protest to Hitler about the possibility of anything.'

Even the fanatically loyal General Sepp Dietrich, in the late 1920s the leader of Hitler's bodyguard and now commander of Sixth SS Panzer Army, one of the two armies earmarked for the operation, was uneasy. He complained: 'All Hitler wants me to do is to cross a river, capture Brussels and then go on and take Antwerp. And all this in the worst time of the year through the Ardennes, when the snow is waist deep and there isn't room to deploy four tanks abreast let alone armoured divisions. When it doesn't get light till eight o'clock and it's dark again at four and with re-formed divisions made up chiefly of kids and sick old men – and at Christmas.'

Rundstedt, and Field Marshal Walther Model, commander of Army Group B, tried and failed to persuade Hitler to scale down the offensive to a more modest attempt to excise the American forces which had pushed beyond Aachen to the River Roer. They failed – Hitler was seeking what the General Staff called a 'total decision' (*ganzer Entschluss*). The plans for the operation were drawn up in conditions of the greatest secrecy, with Hitler controlling every detail, right down to the daily decisions as to the supply of vehicles and horses to individual divisions. The Führer beavered happily away, lost in a scheme which promised renewed strategic success. For him, the dreamers were Eisenhower and his subordinates. He was later to muse, 'Perhaps they also believed that I might already be dead, or at least suffering from cancer somewhere – unable to drink or live on much longer, which would rule me out as a danger.'

The Führer wandered in a fog of detail, dictating orders for the initial artillery bombardment and inspecting plans adapted to spread grit on icy roads. When Rundstedt received his final orders, 'Not To Be Altered' was scrawled across them in Hitler's spidery hand. Thoroughly dispirited, Rundstedt relinquished overall control of the operation to Model, and spent the greater part of the offensive reading novels and drinking cognac.

—⁓—

Hidden by bad weather from Allied air surveillance, a formidable force assembled in the narrow, mist-bound valleys and thick forests of the Eifel, on the German side of the Ardennes. It consisted of two Panzer armies, Sixth SS commanded by Sepp Dietrich in the north; and Fifth in the south, led by the diminutive, hard-driving General Hasso von Manteuffel, one of the best of Hitler's younger armoured commanders. Between them they deployed twenty-eight divisions, including eight Panzer and two Panzergrenadier[39] divisions in which were concentrated twelve hundred and fifty of the two thousand six hundred tanks and assault guns amassed for the Ardennes operation, now code-named Watch on the Rhine (*Wacht am Rhein*).

Most of the armoured divisions had been brought up to strength and included two hundred and ninety-four Mark V Panthers and forty-five Mark VI Tigers. However, the Volksgrenadier divisions which were to support their armoured spearheads, were less impressive formations, their ranks made up with 'ethnic' Germans – those who owed their nationality to frontier changes. The Sixty-second Volksgrenadier Division, for example, contained many Czech and Polish conscripts, whose sympathies were more likely to lie with the Allies than the army in which they had been impressed.

These underlying manpower deficiencies were accompanied by a shortage of fuel. Only a quarter of the minimum requirement was available when the operation began, the greater part held east of the Rhine. The leading German attack elements were expected to exploit their breakthrough with captured fuel supplies. Nevertheless, Hitler refused to contemplate defeat.

---

39 The Panzergrenadier divisions had evolved within the German Army as a motorized infantry formation to augment the true Panzer division. As the war progressed, however, the distinction between the two became increasingly blurred, particularly within the SS as their allocation of armoured fighting vehicles grew larger. The Leibstandarte Adolf Hitler, which achieved divisional status in 1942, fielded two tank battalions, one of Tigers and one of Mark IVs, two Panzergrenadier regiments, and mobile anti-tank and assault-gun detachments

On 12 December at Rundstedt's headquarters, he took his generals on an extravagant *tour d'horizon* in which he dismissed the Allies as 'heterogeneous elements with divergent aims, ultra-capitalist states on the one hand, an ultra-Marxist state on the other'. Britain, he declared, was a 'dying empire'; the United States, its former colony, was a nation bent on inheriting the British imperial mantle. Hitler continued, 'The Soviet Union is anxious to lay hands on the Balkans, the Dardanelles, Persia and the Persian Gulf. Britain is anxious to keep her ill-gotten gains and to make herself strong in the Mediterranean. These states are already at loggerheads and their antagonisms are growing visibly from hour to hour. If Germany can deal a few heavy blows, the artificially united front will collapse at any moment with a tremendous thunderclap.'

And then, with exquisite irony, he pronounced, 'In the last resort wars end when one side or the other realizes that victory is impossible.'

The speech represents a distillation of Hitler's grand strategy as it had evolved from the summer of 1944. In the East the distances were too great and the Red Army too strong. In the West, however, there was no such tyranny of distance, and the enemy coalition could still be fatally fractured, just as it had been in 1940. In spite of Rundstedt's scepticism and the logistical shortcomings in the

Above: A German armoured vehicle runs past a knocked-out US M4 Sherman during the Battle of the Bulge. By the end of the battle, on 16 January 1945, the roles had been reversed. Both the Allies and the Germans had lost some eight hundred tanks, but for the German Western Army the losses could not be made good. In the last two months of 1944, some two thousand three hundred German tanks and assault guns and eighteen new divisions had been committed to the West but only nine hundred and twenty tanks and five divisions to the East, where the Eastern Army faced two hundred and twenty-five Red Army rifle divisions, twenty two tank corps and twenty-nine other armoured formations with only one hundred and thirty-three divisions, thirty of which were threatened with encirclement in the Baltic.

planning of Watch on the Rhine, Hitler had shrewdly chosen the place to cause the Western Allies the maximum embarrassment, as he had done in 1940. In contrast, the Americans deemed the Ardennes a 'quiet sector', and its eighty-mile front was held by only six divisions, two of which had been badly mauled in the Hürtgen.

—ɯ—

Hitler's last offensive in the West opened on 16 December 1944 and achieved total surprise, knocking the Allies badly off balance. Initially, something like blind panic erupted behind the American lines as Eisenhower strove to regain a tight grip on the battle. On the northern shoulder of the salient driven into the Allied line, the so-called bulge, the US V Corps blocked the Sixth SS Panzer Army. The vital transport hub of Bastogne, lying athwart the centre line of the German advance, possession of which was vital to both sides, was denied to the Germans by the US 101st Airborne Division and elements of the Tenth Armoured Division. After some extremely hard fighting, these formations were relieved by the arrival of the US Fourth Armoured Division on 26 December – General Patton's US Third Army had come to the rescue. Within seventy-two hours, Patton had swung seven divisions of the Third Army to exert inexorable pressure on the southern flank of the bulge. In the north the Germans were blocked by the Americans and the British; to the south they were steadily channelled into an attenuating sack, at the tip of which, just three miles short of the Meuse, they ran out of fuel and were subjected to a merciless pounding by American armour and artillery.

> **Hitler's offensive in the Ardennes had merely caused a hiccup in the Allied preparations to break into Germany.**

By 25 December, the mists which had masked the German concentration and initial assault had lifted, allowing Allied ground-attack aircraft to range over the battlefield. Hitler ignored pleas to call off the offensive and on 1 January launched a second, abortive attack southwards from the Saar. By now the Allies had regained their balance and were counter-attacking. On 29 December, Major-General F.W. von Mellenthin, on his way to take up a new appointment with Ninth Panzer Division, was making his way through the wooded hills north-east of Houffalize, in the centre of the salient: 'The icebound roads glittered in the sunshine and I witnessed the uninterrupted air attacks on our traffic routes and supply dumps. Not a single German plane was in the air, innumerable vehicles were shot up and their blackened wrecks littered the roads.'

By 16 January, the Bulge had been eliminated. In the month-long offensive the Fifth and Sixth SS Panzer Armies had inflicted some nineteen thousand fatal casualties on the US Twelfth Army Group and had taken fifteen thousand prisoners. The cost to the *Westheer* was a hundred thousand killed and wounded and eight hundred tanks destroyed. These losses could not be made good. In contrast, the Americans shipped over seven new divisions, three of them armoured and fully equipped, while the Battle of the Bulge was raging. The Luftwaffe lost about a thousand aircraft in the battle and was now entering its death throes.

Hitler had given the Allies a nasty shock, prompting Eisenhower to surround himself with bodyguards and forcing him briefly to contemplate sending black American troops, previously segregated, into action alongside whites in fully integrated units. Even after the salient had been pinched out, Hitler believed that there had been, 'a tremendous easing of the situation … the enemy has had to abandon all his plans for attack. He has been obliged to regroup his forces. He has had to throw in again units which were fatigued. He is severely criticized at home … Already he has had to admit that there is no chance of the war being ended before August, perhaps not before the end of next year.'

—␣␣␣—

The war had just four months to run. Hitler's offensive in the Ardennes had merely caused a hiccup in the Allied preparations to break into Germany. For the Germans, the battle had been waged at the expense of transferring from, or denying to, the *Ostheer* the men and materiel desperately needed on the Eastern Front. In the last two months of 1944, only nine hundred and twenty tanks and five divisions were committed to the East, where the *Ostheer* faced two hundred and twenty-five Red Army rifle divisions, twenty-two tank corps, and twenty-nine other armoured formations, with only one hundred and thirty-three divisions, thirty of which were already threatened with encirclement in the Baltic states. Hitler had borrowed from Peter to pay Paul, and was soon to pay the full price.

ALL FALL DOWN

By late 1944, the war had strangely transformed areas seemingly untouched by the conflict. Whole forests sparkled with the 'Window' anti-radar tinsel, thousands of tons of which had been dropped over Germany by Allied bombers, festooning trees with an eerie Christmas glitter. By the turn of the year, the trains from Berlin were no longer carrying weekend holidaymakers into the countryside.

Hans-George von Studnitz, an official in the information and press section of the German Foreign Ministry, noted with alarm in his diary:

> At the main Berlin railway stations scenes occur such as have not been experienced since the days of the mass air raids in the late autumn and winter of 1943–44. When I took Mariette [his wife] to the station yesterday about midnight to catch the train to Hanover, we saw people fighting their way into the compartments and trampling over anyone who got in their way … Thousands of men on leave are squatting in the railway stations. What they are doing here, when the situation at the front is so desperate, no one knows.

By a supreme effort of will Hitler kept going. His nerve did not falter but his judgement had long since run off the rails. In the past his powers to decide on a course of action had often become jellified when a major decision confronted him. This lay behind the failure in 1943 to extricate the Afrika Korps from Tunisia before it was too late, and the long, agonizing delay in launching Citadel in the spring and early summer of the same year. He was always at his best when defying disaster, as before Moscow in December 1941. The Führer never fully recovered from the shock of Stalingrad, but with the approach of the New Year, he drew on his dwindling reserves of willpower. On 28 December 1944, in his snowbound headquarters in Bad Nauheim, the Eagle's Nest, he addressed the commanding generals of the divisions preparing to launch the abortive thrust in northern Alsace, Operation North Wind. He admitted that the Ardennes offensive had broken down and that Germany was now fighting for survival. Hitler continued:

> Never in my life have I accepted the idea of surrender, and I am one of those men who have worked their way up from nothing. Our present situation, therefore, is nothing new to me. Once upon a time my own situation was entirely different, and far worse. I say this only that you can grasp why I pursue my goal with such fanaticism and why nothing can wear me down. No matter how much I might be tormented by worries, even if my health were shaken by them – that would still not have the slightest effect on my decision to fight on …

He went on to cite the 'miracle of the House of Brandenburg', when Frederick the Great, defeated in the Seven Years War, regained by the Peace of Hubertusburg all the territory he had lost after the coalition against him fell apart. Hundreds of thousands of soldiers and civilians were to die while the Führer waited for another miracle.

Since the failure at Kursk in July 1943, Hitler had become the prisoner of events rather than their master. As his strategic horizons shrank ever smaller, his will alone was all that mattered. Armies and battles did not figure in this crackpot equation. Military and economic weakness was irrelevant so long as the Führer did not weaken. But although Hitler's psychological powers to galvanize those around him still burned with fitful brilliance, his physical powers were fading fast. His face was drawn, his hair grey and his moustache flecked with white. His hands trembled uncontrollably over the maps at his midday situation conferences (which now rarely began before five in the afternoon), setting up a terrible rustling which those in his company did their best to ignore. He was no longer able to write, and his signature on official documents had to be forged by a trusted civil servant. Admiral Assmann, a regular participant in the war conferences, noted that the Führer's 'handclasp was weak and soft, all his movements were those of a senile man'.

On 1 January 1945, the British writer and politician Harold Nicolson wrote in his diary: 'Viti [his wife Vita Sackville West] and I hear the New Year in crouching over the fire in the dining room. I turn on Berlin, the Deutschlander, and then Hamburg – and we get Hitler's horrible but unmistakeable voice. The reception is not so good

and he gabbles off his piece so fast that I may have missed something. But it seemed to consist entirely about reflections upon Germany's fate if she loses her moral staunchness.'

The broadcast to which Harold and Vita were listening in mild discomfort was the first that Hitler had made since the unsuccessful attempt to assassinate him at the Wolf's Lair on 20 July 1944. He told the German people:

> … This nation, this state and its leading men are unshakeable in their will and unswerving in their fanatical determination to fight this war to a successful conclusion in all circumstances – if it means taking in our stride all the reverses which fickle fate may impose on us … we are resolved to go to the extreme … whatever our enemies destroyed was rebuilt with superhuman industry and unparalleled heroism and this will continue until one day our enemies' undertaking comes to an end.

Hitler stubbornly clung to the conviction that Germany would emerge victorious in spite of the terrible pounding the Reich and its armed forces had received at the hands of the Allies. But the candle was stuttering. Three days earlier he had confided in General Thomale, Chief of Staff of the Inspectorate of Panzer Troops, 'The war will not last as long again as it has lasted. That is absolutely certain. Nobody can endure it. We cannot, and the others cannot. The only question is who will endure it longer? It must be he who has everything at stake.'

Time, however, was running out faster than Hitler either imagined or was prepared to admit. On 13 January, he held his last military conference at the Eagle's Nest. He instructed his commanders in the West, Field Marshals Rundstedt

Hitler stubbornly clung to the conviction that Germany would emerge victorious.

and Model, to hold off the Western Allies for as long as possible. At 6 p.m. he was driven to the station to board his special train, where he held another conference. It had barely begun when General Guderian telephoned, requesting that 'everything be thrown into the Eastern Front'. When business was concluded, the Führer's train moved off to Berlin.

Berlin had never been a centre of Nazi strength. Before Hitler came to power in 1933 it had been a Communist stronghold, and throughout the war Hitler had spent little time in the capital. Like a medieval king he had moved from one purpose-built headquarters to another. Their crumbling concrete ruins still litter Europe, from Soissons in France to Rastenburg in East Prussia, now part of Poland. Much of his time had been spent at Rastenburg, the Wolf's Lair. Now that his 'skirmishing in the Vosges', as Guderian acidly put it, was over, the Reich Chancellery and then the bunker in its garden were to be the last of the Führer headquarters.

The day Hitler returned to Berlin, Guderian attended a military conference held in the Führer's study, overlooking the desolate, rubble-strewn courtyard of the Chancellery. After an encouraging start, when Hitler announced his decision to go on to the defensive on the Western Front to allow the transfer of forces to the East, the meeting quickly ran into trouble. Anticipating Hitler's belated recognition of reality, Guderian had prepared a plan for the eventual deployment of these reinforcements in an attack on the flanks of the Russian advance. To his astonishment, however, he was informed by Jodl that the most important strategic element in the formations awaiting transfer to the East, Sixth SS Panzer Army, was to go to Hungary to relieve Budapest and safeguard the Hungarian oilfields and refineries.

In vain Guderian protested that the Sixth SS Panzer Army had to be brought to bear in the battle for the Oder, where two army groups faced destruction, rather than in the secondary theatre in Hungary. Hitler stood fast, declaring, 'I'm going to attack the Russians where they least expect it! Sixth Panzer Army is off to Budapest!

'If we start an offensive in Hungary, the Russians will have to go too.'

ADOLF HITLER

If we start an offensive in Hungary, the Russians will have to go too.' Oil remained uppermost in his mind as he chided Guderian, 'If you don't get any more fuel, your tanks won't be able to move and the aeroplanes won't be able to fly. You must see that. But my generals know nothing about the economics of war.'

The meeting went from bad to worse. When Hitler began to rave about the idiotic setting of the major defence line on the Vistula, the stenographic record was produced to demonstrate that the decision had been his own. Next came the location of the reserves; according to Guderian, Hitler thought that they had been held 'too far back from the front, while the generals held exactly contrary views and blamed Hitler for having insisted that they be too far forward'. Casting around for a scapegoat to take the blame for the debacle, Hitler lit on the hapless General Josef Harpe, who was now to be replaced by General Ferdinand Schörner as the commander of Army Group A. The diehard Nazi Schörner was then in command of Army Group North which, on Hitler's orders, was bottled up in the Courland peninsula where, as Guderian scathingly observed, 'there were no more laurels to be won'.

—m—

The main Soviet assault across the Vistula was launched on 12 January 1945. It swiftly gathered momentum, cutting off further German forces in East Prussia, and reached the Oder at the end of the month. Warsaw had been liberated on 17 January. The first Red Army men into the city picked their way through a scene of total devastation. After the suppression of the Warsaw uprising in October 1944, the Germans had laid waste to what remained of the city. Driven solely by the terrible nihilism which had characterized Nazi rule in Poland, they piled destruction on destruction with no military aim. Thus, Russians troops entered a silent city whose pre-war population of one million three hundred thousand had been reduced to about a hundred and sixty thousand famished survivors.

HITLER'S LAST OFFENSIVE

In Berlin, successive convulsions had followed the fall of Warsaw, which had been evacuated against Hitler's orders, and the collapse of the front in Poland. Hitler's contempt for the German officer corps knew no bounds. In a towering rage, he shrieked at Guderian, 'I'm out for the General Staff's blood! The General Staff clique has got to be stamped out!' Convinced that his field commanders were withdrawing because of cowardice or failure of nerve, Hitler issued an order that no commander of any formation, from divisional level upward, was to attack, counter-attack, or withdraw, without first notifying his intentions through the normal military channels to the high command in sufficient time to enable the Führer to intervene. Hitler was now ready to conduct his war games from Berlin. Like a chess grand master facing opponents on a dozen or more boards, in his own mind at least he was still the master of every move.

Hitler's daily conferences were now taking ever more surreal turns. On 20 January he demanded that work begin on a long-range jet bomber, indicating that, for the moment at least, he was casting himself as a twentieth-century Frederick the Great, planning for a Seven Years War while the enemy was at the gates. Worse was to follow the next day when, at a conference with Guderian and Jodl, Hitler announced that the *Reichsführer* SS, Heinrich Himmler, was to take command of the new Army Group Vistula to plug the huge gap which had opened up between Army Group Centre, fighting in East Prussia, and Army Group A in Poland. The *Reichsführer* SS was also to assume responsibility for organizing the 'national defence on German soil behind the entire Eastern Front.'[40]

Guderian suggested that such a task would be more appropriately undertaken by Field Marshal Maximilian von Weichs, who had conducted the withdrawal of Army Group F from the southern Balkans, not an operation likely to set Hitler's pulse racing. Weichs was brushed aside after Jodl had pointedly made a sneering reference to the field marshal's religious faith, a quality calculated to set the Führer's teeth on edge. Hitler brought the argument to an end by telling Guderian that Himmler had given 'a good account of himself' on the upper Rhine. Moreover, as commander of the Home Army, Himmler had a ready source of reinforcements to hand when strengthening his front. Only Himmler, Hitler declared, would provide the necessary ruthlessness which was so singularly lacking in worn-out generals like Weichs.

The eruption of the Red Army's Second Belorussian Front into East Prussia triggered a torrent of German refugees pouring westward in search of safety. By the end of January, an estimated three and a half million German civilians were on the move, all of them under no illusion about the treatment they could expect at the hands of Soviet troops.

---

40 Himmler's command of Army Group Vistula lasted until mid-March 1945. He was in no way fitted for military command and, thanks to his insatiable appetite for empire-building, was already overburdened with multifarious responsibilities. He was not dismissed by Hitler but was finally persuaded to step down by Guderian. Himmler was replaced by the experienced General Gotthard Heinrici, the German Army's leading expert on defensive warfare.

—◊◊◊—

At the beginning of January 1945, four German divisions had been trapped in Budapest. A rescue attempt made by IV SS Panzer Corps, called down from Army Group Centre, fought its way to within twelve miles of the city but was forced to withdraw by the end of the month. The fall of Budapest on 13 February had served only to stoke Hitler's obsession with the Hungarian oilfields at Nagykanisza, fifty miles south west of Lake Balaton, which produced well over half the oil remaining to Germany. A plan was drawn up, code-named Spring Awakening (*Frühlingserwachen*), in which Army Group South was to trap and destroy the Red Army's Third Ukrainian Front between Lake Balaton and the Danube.

The major thrust was to be launched by Sixth SS Panzer Army, attacking southeast from the northern end of Lake Balaton to a line on the Danube between Budapest and Baja, around ninety miles south of the Hungarian capital. South of Balaton, the Second Panzer Army was to drive east while a supporting attack was launched northward from the Yugoslavian border by Army Group E in the direction of Mohacs. Budapest would be retaken, the oilfields retained and an entire Red Army front struck off Stalin's order of battle. Such, at any rate, was the plan.

Preparations for the operation were made in great secrecy, and the approach to the start lines conducted in driving rain and deep mud. The attack went in on 5 March. In the vanguard was the Sixth SS Panzer Army, desperate to redeem itself after its failure in the Ardennes. Among the six hundred tanks scraped together for the formation were Mark VI 'King' Tiger heavy battle tanks, armoured on a massive scale and armed with an 88mm gun.

At the limit of the German advance – a salient driven twenty miles into Third Ukrainian Front's line – more than six hundred tanks and self-propelled guns tried to batter their way through the Soviet positions north-east of Lake Balaton. By 15 March it was all over. Hundreds of tanks were left stranded on the waterlogged Hungarian plains, their fuel tanks dry, to be pounded by Soviet artillery and attack aircraft. The Red Army counter-offensive swept past their gutted hulks, smashed through the Hungarian Third Army covering Sixth Panzer Army's left flank, and rolled on to Vienna, scene of Adolf Hitler's unhappy youth.[41]

THE DEATH FACTORIES

In January and February 1945, as the Red Army drove through western Poland into the Reich and struck south into the industrial heartland of Silesia, the soldiers of the First Belorussian and First Ukrainian Fronts uncovered another form of Nazi industry as they overran the labour and extermination camps established by the SS.

---

41 The Waffen-SS was now added to the long list of those who had disappointed the Führer. Hitler ordered the officers of Sixth SS Panzer Army to be stripped of their decorations and their men to hand over their prized divisional armbands. Himmler was sent to the front to ensure that the orders were carried out, but even he bridled at this, telling Hitler, 'I would have to drive to Lake Balaton to take the crosses off the dead. A German SS man cannot give more than his life to you, my Führer.'

THE HOLOCAUST

On 30 January 1939, Hitler gave a speech in which he threatened that 'if the international Jewish financiers in and outside Europe should succeed in plunging the nations once more into world war, then the result will not be the Bolshevization of the Earth, and thus the victory of Jewry, but the annihilation of the Jewish race in Europe'. On the face of it, these words seem an unequivocal promise of the Holocaust, but the path to the physical destruction of the Jews in Europe took many twists and turns before Himmler stated in 1943, 'We had the moral right, we had the duty to our people, to destroy a people which wanted to destroy us.'

No systematic plan of extermination existed before 1941. A scheme in 1940 envisaged transporting European Jews to a kind of penal colony in the Vichy French island of Madagascar. Naturally they would have to pay for the privilege of their own incarceration. The plan was shelved, but the tide of German conquest brought matters to a head. Between September 1939 and December 1941, the defeat of Poland and the overrunning of European Russia had delivered millions of Jews into Hitler's hands. The massive territorial gains made in the Soviet Union in the first phase of Barbarossa produced the so-called Final Solution, a euphemism for the extermination of European Jewry.

In January 1942, at a secret conference in the Berlin suburb of Wannsee chaired by Reinhard Heydrich, the Final Solution was systematized. In the East the killing had initially been undertaken by *Einsatzgruppen* (task groups), often with the help of local auxiliaries. Heydrich programmed the killing, establishing extermination camps based on the already existing network of concentration camps. Clusters of camps were built in Poland – Treblinka, Belzec, Majdanek, Sobibor and Auschwitz-Birkenau the most notorious among them. Adolf Eichmann and his subordinates organized the transportation to these and other camps (in all, the Nazi regime ran twenty five major concentration camps and eight extermination camps) of Jews, Slavs, Red Army prisoners-of-war, gypsies, political prisoners and homosexuals. They came from every part of occupied Europe, and meticulously logged railway movements have provided postwar historians with the harrowing details of the Final Solution. The camps were sometimes linked to industrial complexes run by the SS, and those deemed capable of work on arrival were given a stay of execution. The rest – the old and infirm, the children – were gassed. At Treblinka, a camp some fifty miles north-west of Warsaw, nearly a million people were gassed between July 1942 and August 1943 by just two hundred SS and Ukrainian guards and about a thousand Jewish auxiliaries. The site of Treblinka occupies ground measuring six hundred by four hundred metres. In a facility whose sole business was death there was no great need for space.

The Final Solution caused the death of some 5.7 million Jews – 40 per cent of world Jewry – and at least a million more people who were either non-Aryan or otherwise deemed undesirable by the Nazis. No written order for the killing of the Jews from Hitler has been found. However, in January 1944, Himmler publicly stated that Hitler had given him a Führer Order to give absolute priority to the 'Jewish question'. Hitler's authority was such that it encouraged initiatives from below, provided that they coincided with his overall thinking. History is witness to the fact that Himmler, Heydrich, the SS men at Treblinka, and all the other functionaries in their empire of death, were faithfully 'working towards the Führer'(see p. 91).

As the Red Army drew near, the SS began evacuating the areas which remained under their control and to step up the killing. Chelmno in western Poland had been evacuated in 1944, but a special *kommando* of inmates remained to dismantle the camp's crematoria. Now it was their turn to die. There had originally been about a hundred men in the *kommando*, but a reign of casual terror had reduced their number to about forty. To amuse themselves, the SS guards had lined the men up, placed bottles on their heads and then enjoyed target practice, whooping with delight when the bullets missed their original mark and another man slumped out of the line. On 17 January the shooting became more systematic, in batches of five. Only two men survived, one of them shot through the neck and rescued by the arrival of the Russians.

In the Auschwitz-Birkenau complex in southern Poland, an area which contained numerous camps and factories, about sixty thousand inmates, Jews and non-Jews, remained, many of them barely alive. On 18 January the order was given to evacuate the survivors by foot to railheads from which they could be dispersed into camps all over Germany. Thousands who were too enfeebled to march were shot on the spot; those who stumbled or fell out of line on the march suffered the same fate. No one was allowed to turn his head while the ragged columns trudged on through the snow, the terrible sound of shuffling feet punctuated by single gunshots as another straggler was executed.

It was not until April that the British and Americans were confronted with similar horrors after crossing the Rhine. In this theatre, the Germans were marching the concentration camp prisoners eastwards, their progress marked by a trail of battered emaciated corpses. The SS could not contain their mania for killing, even when the Americans were on the point of overtaking them. As a column from Buchenwald, near Weimar, was intercepted near Posing by men of the US Ninetieth Infantry Division, the guards began shooting hundreds of prisoners at the rear to form a human roadblock.

On 15 April, in Lower Saxony, the British Eleventh Armoured Division liberated the concentration camp at Belsen. The camp, which hitherto had been run with a semblance of brutal efficiency by its commandant, Josef Kramer, had collapsed under the weight of some thirty thousand new arrivals. In Block Three, the so-called maternity block, women of all nations lay in cages along the walls, two to a cage, their stomachs hideously distended by a combination of pregnancy and hunger, their moaning and crying filling the building with a terrible cacophony. Typhus raged through the camp, and when the British arrived they found some thirteen thousand corpses littering the ground in obscene piles. Anne Frank had died of typhus in Belsen a month before.

Two days later a Jewish Army chaplain, Leslie Hardman, drove to Belsen. He recalled, 'Towards me came what seemed to be the remnants of a holocaust – a staggering mass of blackened skin and bones, held together somehow with filthy rags. "My God, the dead walk", I cried aloud, but I did not recognize my voice.' The survivors crowded around Hardman '[peering] at the double star, the emblem of Jewry on my tunic … one poor creature touched and then stroked the badge of my faith, and finding that it was real, murmured "Rabbiner, Rabbiner" [Rabbi]'. Later, a survivor made a few quavering attempts to sing a few lines of a Hebrew song: 'The pathos of this attempt was so poignant that I put my head on the table and wept; and then they comforted me.' Years later Hardman told an interviewer: 'If all the trees in the world turned into pens, all the waters in the oceans turned into ink and the heavens turned into paper, it would still be insufficient material to describe the horrors these people suffered under the SS.'

—◊◊◊—

By early April, the east bank of the Rhine had been cleared by the Western Allies, but the starting pistol for the race to Berlin had yet to be fired. It remained silent. Eisenhower had decided to advance as far as the Elbe and to halt there. He was reluctant to sustain heavy casualties in racing the Red Army to a city which would shortly be placed in the Soviet occupation zone as agreed at the Yalta conference, the last great Allied summit of the war, in February 1945.

On 28 March Eisenhower cabled Stalin, on his own initiative and without informing the Joint Chiefs of Staff or the British and American governments, or even his deputy, Air Chief Marshal Sir Arthur Tedder: 'My immediate operations are designed to encircle and destroy the enemy defending the Ruhr ... I estimate this phase ... will end in late April or even earlier, and my task will be to divide the remaining [German] forces by joining with your forces [on the Elbe].' Stalin was delighted with the cable, informing Eisenhower on 1 April – April Fool's Day – that it conformed entirely with his own plans and that 'Berlin has lost its former strategic significance'. Stalin then sat down to plan the Battle for Berlin.

THE BUNKER

Hitler waited for the last battle in the bunker in the Chancellery gardens. As the round-the-clock Allied bombing of Berlin increased in intensity, he spent ever longer periods of time in the concrete shelter. Eventually he moved underground permanently, into what was to become the thirteenth and last Führer headquarters, part tinny echo of the caves of the Nibelungen, part throwback to the World War I dugouts in which Corporal Hitler had sheltered during his days as a company runner.

The *Führerbunker* was contained within a complex of shelters, one of which housed the staff of the ever-present Martin Bormann, another contained a field hospital and, during the Battle for Berlin, the headquarters of SS General Wilhelm Mohnke, the Chancellery's commandant. Buried fifty-five feet below the garden, the main Führer shelter was built in two storeys, with exterior walls six feet thick and an eight-foot-thick concrete canopy on top of which was piled thirty feet of earth. The kitchen and the staff living quarters were on the upper level of the bunker and, as the end approached, provided rooms for Goebbels and his family.

Connected to the upper bunker by a short spiral staircase was the *Führerbunker* proper, divided into a series of cramped, low-ceilinged rooms grouped on either side

of a central passage decorated with paintings from the Chancellery, which was partitioned off for daily conferences. To the right of the passage, next to the machine
room, was Bormann's office, with the main telephone switchboard and teleprinter
units from which Hitler had snatched, page by page, the Yalta communiqué. The walls
of Bormann's office were covered with maps of Germany and Berlin, each masked
with a celluloid sheet on which the progress of enemy bomber formations was marked
with chinagraph pencil, a routine which exerted a morbid hold on Hitler.

Further down the passage were rooms occupied by Goebbels and the SS physician Dr Stumpfegger. To the left of the passage was a suite of six sparsely furnished
rooms occupied by Hitler. The small living room – ten feet by fifteen – was dominated by Anton Graff's oil painting of Frederick the Great, the one constant item
of decor in all of the Führer's headquarters. In the bunker, Hitler would spend long,
lonely hours brooding over the image of the soldier-king. On one occasion his
orderly, Sergeant Roschus Misch, accidentally broke into one of these reveries: 'It
was very late, and I thought that the Führer had already retired. … There was Der
Chef, gazing at the picture by candlelight. He was sitting there, motionless, his chin
buried in his hand, as if he were in a trance. The king seemed to be staring right
back. I had barged in, but Hitler took no notice of me. So I tiptoed out. It was like
stumbling on someone at prayer.'

The other feature of the underground complex from which Hitler drew strange
comfort was a large-scale model of the city of Linz as it was to be rebuilt. The model
had been designed and installed by the architect Professor Hermann Giesler. In this
vision, Linz, where Hitler had first heard Wagner's *Rienzi*,[42] would rise from the ruins
caused by Allied bombing to replace Budapest as the most majestic city on the Danube.

Here there would be a concert hall capable of holding thirty-five thousand people
and a five-hundred-and-fifty-foot bell tower at whose base Hitler's parents would be
re-buried. The Führer himself would be the principal patron of the vast art gallery
which Giesler had designed. When Hitler took Ernst Kaltenbrunner, his security chief
and a native of Linz, to view the model, he told him, 'My dear Kaltenbrunner, do you
imagine I could talk to you like this about my plans for the future if I did not believe
deep down that we are really going to win the war in the end?'

The airless claustrophobia of the bunker was the final bleak expression of the
artificiality and isolation of Hitler's own existence. In the baleful glare of its electric
lights, night merged into day. The last military conferences often ended at six in the
morning, after which Hitler would slump exhausted on his sofa, seeking solace in
plate after plate of cream cakes. In the hours of darkness he would occasionally
emerge from the bunker to take his German Shepherd, Blondi, for a short walk
through the rubbish-strewn paths of the Chancellery garden, his SS guards hovering
discreetly at a distance.

---

42 Wagner's early work *Rienzi* or, to give it its full title, *Rienzi, the Last of the Tribunes*, was a monumentally long 'grand
opera'. The original manuscript score remains missing and is reputed by musicologists to have been in Hitler's
possession at the end of the war. The work's doomed hero is a charismatic revolutionary and idealist who overthrows
the nobility in fourteenth-century Rome, only to suffer betrayal, and death by fire.

DISINTEGRATION

Keitel and Jodl had pressed Hitler to move his headquarters to Zossen, fifteen miles south of Berlin, but Hitler expressed his doubts about the soundness of 'army concrete'. In the bunker, surrounded by SS guards, he remained safe to draft the script for the last act of the Third Reich, with Josef Goebbels as his chief collaborator in the operatic orchestration of the strategy of doom. As the bombs rained down on Berlin, Goebbels threw himself into the task in a state of manic exultation: 'The bomb terror spares the dwellings of neither rich nor poor; before the labour offices of total war the last class barriers go down.' Chaos had to be embraced as the necessary preliminary to the establishment of a New Order: 'Now the bombs, instead of killing all Europeans only smash the prison walls which held them captive … In trying to destroy Europe's future, the enemy has only succeeded in smashing its past; and with that, everything old and worn-out has gone.'

Hitler presented a dreadful physical spectacle, like a man risen from the grave.

Those who made the trip to the bunker were left with an indelible impression of its suffocating atmosphere, pregnant with fear and suppressed hysteria. It was a journey inside the mind of the Führer himself. Captain Beermann, one of the SS guards, recalled the enervating effect of long spells spent underground:

> It was like being stranded in a cement submarine, or buried down in some charnel house. People who work in diving bells probably feel less cramped. It was both dark and dusty, for some of the cement was old, some new. In the long hours of the night it would be deathly silent, except for the hum of the generator. When you came upon flesh-and-blood people their faces seemed blanched in the artificial light. The ventilation could now be warm and sultry, now cold and clammy. The walls were sometimes grey, sometimes bleached orange; some were moist and even mouldy … Then there was the fetid odour of boots, sweaty woollen uniforms, acrid coal-tar disinfectant. Towards the end, when the drainage packed up, it was as pleasant as working in a public urinal.

To all those who saw him, Hitler presented a dreadful physical spectacle, like a man risen from the grave. Awash with drugs provided by the 'Reich Injection Master' Professor Morell; hunched and shaking, with faltering voice, foul breath, and glaucous eyes; a crust of spittle and cake crumbs flecking his lips; his jacket blotched with food stains.

Major Gerhardt Boldt, Guderian's orderly, saw Hitler for the first time when he attended a briefing in the bunker early in February: 'His head was slightly wobbling. His left arm hung slackly and his hand trembled a good deal. There was an indescribable flickering light in his eye, creating a fearsome and wholly unnatural effect. His face and the parts around his eyes gave the impression of total exhaustion. All his movements were those of a senile man.'

Only one man had the courage and detachment to contemplate killing Hitler and, at a stroke, bring the whole grisly charade to an end. Albert Speer, the most ambivalent of Hitler's inner circle, was in an intriguing position. He had prolonged the life of the Third Reich; now he wished to bring it to an end. As Armaments Minister from 1942, Speer had applied his considerable abilities as a technocrat to sustaining the Third Reich's war industry. By employing a policy of dispersal, he ensured that only a fraction of German industrial capacity was located in the major manufacturing centres regularly attacked by the RAF and the USAAF. As a result, production rose by over three times between January 1942 and July 1944. Thereafter, Speer's efforts were thwarted by the Allies' destruction of Germany's transport infrastructure and synthetic oil plants, and Hitler's 'scorched earth' orders to destroy all industrial plant which lay in the path of the Allied advance. Speer had spent most of his time trying as best he could to prevent these orders from being carried out. In February 1945 he had toyed with the idea of flooding the bunker with tabun poison gas, but the coincidental covering of the air intake with a tall metal chimney meant that his scheme was stillborn.

On 12 April, hope of a deliverance of some kind flickered briefly in the bunker. President Roosevelt had died of a massive brain haemorrhage. In London, at 10 Downing Street, Winston Churchill had sat hunched in his black leather armchair for five long minutes

Below: End of the road – Hitler pats the cheeks of the boy defenders of Berlin in the Chancellery garden on 20 April 1945, his fifty-sixth birthday. That day the Nazi paladins gathered for the last time in the Court of Honour, in front of the old Chancellery, which remained relatively unscathed by Allied bombing and Red Army shell fire.

before reaching for the telephone and asking for Buckingham Palace. In Moscow Stalin felt moved to grasp the hand of the US ambassador Averell Harriman and hold it wordlessly.

In Berlin there was a mood of wild exultation in the bunker. Now, surely, the alliance against Germany would collapse, saving Hitler just as Frederick the Great had been saved by the death of the Tsarina Elizabeth. Goebbels, who had been reading aloud to Hitler extracts from Thomas Carlyle's *History of Frederick II of Prussia*, telephoned Hitler in a frenzy of excitement: 'My Führer, I congratulate you. It is written in the stars that the second half of April will be the turning point for us.' An exhilarated Hitler told his orderly Misch that soon the Russians and the Americans would be exchanging artillery fire over the bunker's concrete canopy. The mood soon passed. Later, Speer recalled, 'Hitler sat exhausted, looking both liberated and dazed, as he slumped in his chair. But I sensed that he was still without hope.'

THE BATTLE FOR BERLIN

On Saturday 15 April, Hitler's mistress Eva Braun arrived in the bunker. Since the middle of March she had been living in her private apartments in the Chancellery. One of Hitler's SS guards mordantly observed, 'The angel of death has arrived.'

The day after Eva Braun's arrival, the Red Army erupted from the Küstrin bridgehead on the Oder, fifty miles from Berlin. In the Vistula-Oder operation, three Red Army Fronts had sliced like a giant snowplough into the heart of Germany. At its tip was Marshal Zhukov's First Belorussian Front. For the Berlin operation, First Belorussian Front had received seven million shells by rail and road for nine thousand guns massed at a density of three hundred to each attack kilometre, a figure which Zhukov intended to increase to four hundred and fifty as the ring closed around the capital of the Third Reich. Sixteenth Air Army had assembled three thousand two hundred aircraft to support Zhukov.

The Russian Marshal was under no illusion about the complex nature of the Berlin operation: 'In the experience of war we had not yet had the occasion to take such a strongly fortified city as Berlin. Its total area was almost three hundred and fifty square miles. The city's subway and well-developed underground engineering structures gave the enemy manoeuvring capability. The city and its suburbs were carefully prepared for a stubborn defence. Every street, square, alley, house, canal and bridge constituted a part of the overall defence of the city.'

> 'In the experience of war we had not yet had the occasion to take such a strongly fortified city as Berlin.'
> **MARSHAL ZHUKOV**

A modern city can devour an army committed to a house-to-house battle. Stalingrad had shown as much, and *Stavka* had no desire to repeat the experience on a vastly greater scale in Berlin. The city was to be taken in an all-out power drive. Specially chosen assault groups drawn from veteran infantry units would be supported by armour, massed artillery laying down a red-hot path of destruction all the way to the Reichstag, the 'Lair of the Fascist Beast'.

Between the Baltic coast and Görlitz, a hundred miles south-east of Berlin, were some fifty field divisions of the German Army, five of them armoured, supplemented by a patchwork of makeshift battle groups and about a hundred *Volkssturm* battalions.[43] They faced a total of nearly two hundred Red Army divisions, the fighting strength of which was heavily reduced, averaging between two and a half and five and a half thousand men. For the assault on Berlin, the Red Army was relying on its massive superiority in artillery, aircraft and armour.

—ɯɯ—

It was not until March that any serious thought was given to the defence of Berlin, when a makeshift 'obstacle belt' was thrown up in a ring some thirty miles outside the city. A second ring was improvised around the city's railway system, whose cuttings, culverts and overhead lines provided, as Zhukov feared, a formidable barrier to Soviet armour. The last-ditch defence ring, ominously named Citadel, contained eight wedge-shaped command sectors lying at the heart of the city. Within the command sectors were six huge flak towers, massive concrete ziggurats virtually impervious to bombs and artillery.

The largest tower, at the Berlin Zoo, was a hundred and thirty feet high, with five storeys above ground. Its walls were six feet thick and heavy steel doors covered all the apertures. The top floor housed a one-hundred-strong garrison, the floor below a well-equipped hospital for VIPs, and the third had been turned into a warehouse for many of Berlin's art treasures. The lower floors were big enough to hold fifteen thousand sheltering civilians and a radio studio. With its own water and electricity supply, a bulging magazine, and well-stocked food stores, the tower was self-sufficient, although almost unbearably noisy when its eight 128mm guns were in action.

Initially, the defence of the German capital lay in the hands of some sixty thousand *Volkssturm*; the only unit of any operational value was the Berlin Guard Battalion. In Berlin's streets the erection of flimsy barricades prompted the sour joke that it would take the Red Army two hours and fifteen minutes to break them down – two hours laughing their heads off and fifteen minutes smashing them up.

Meanwhile, the terrain facing Zhukov's bridgehead at Kustrin was unsuitable for armoured operations – a ten-mile-wide valley, heavily mined and slashed with streams, ditches and canals and overlooked by the heavily defended Seelow heights. Zhukov decided to commit his armour only when the heights had been seized.

The initial attack went in on 16 April, but it met with unexpectedly fierce resistance, and at noon Zhukov sent in his armour – thirteen hundred tanks and self-propelled guns – a full twenty-four hours before he had thought it would be necessary. The heights were taken on 17 April after ferocious fighting, and on the following day the second German defensive line was breached. By the evening of 19 April sheer weight of metal had told, and Zhukov had prised open the Oder Line

---

43 The German equivalent of the British Home Guard, established in September 1944 under the direct control of the Nazi Party. All males between the ages of sixteen and sixty who were not in the armed services but capable of bearing arms were liable for service. Although organized and trained on military lines, the political nature of its leadership and the severe shortage of arms severely limited its military effectiveness. At the end of January 1945, Hitler ordered that, whenever it was possible, *Volkssturm* units were to be combined with regular troops into mixed battle groups under a unified command.

on a forty-mile frontage, two days behind schedule. On 20 April, Berlin's outer north-east perimeter was breached. Shortly before 2 p.m. the heavy guns of the Third Shock Army opened fire on the city, their shells plummeting into the fires started by the last great Allied bombing raid of the European war.

It was Hitler's fifty-sixth birthday and the occasion was marked by a special stamp issue and, rather more practical, an extra allocation of food rations to Berlin's civilian population. The recipients gave them a sardonic nickname, *Himmelsfahrtrationen* (Ascension Day rations). That afternoon there was a birthday reception at the Chancellery, where the Nazi paladins – Speer, Ribbentrop, Bormann, Goebbels and Göring – gathered for the last time.

After inspecting a line of troops drawn up for him in the Chancellery garden, Hitler and his party descended into the bunker, where he received Grand Admiral Karl Dönitz, Field Marshal Keitel and General Jodl in his conference room before emerging for the daily meeting, at which Dönitz's adjutant saw an old man, 'broken, washed up, feeble and irritable'.

Hitler resisted urgings that he leave Berlin for the south, agreeing only to the establishment of both a northern and southern command in case Germany was split in two. Then his confederates took their leave. Hermann Göring, his face glistening with sweat, announced that he had 'extremely urgent tasks in the south'. Hitler stared vacantly beyond him. This was also Hitler's last meeting with Heinrich Himmler. The *Reichsführer* SS drove back to his headquarters, at Ziethen Castle in Schleswig-Holstein, to continue his secret negotiations with a representative of the World Jewish Congress, Norbert Masur, to whom he promised the release of the Jewish women held in the concentration camp at Ravensbrück.[44]

After the leave-taking, Hitler retired to his room with Eva Braun. Shortly afterwards she emerged, seemingly vivacious and wearing a magnificent dress of silver-blue brocade. She was determined to celebrate. One of Hitler's secretaries, Traudl Junge, recalled:

… she took everyone she met with her up into the old living room on the first floor of the Führer's apartment, which was still standing. The beautiful furniture was all down in the bunker, but the large round table was there and it had been laid out in festive manner once more. Even the Reichsleiter Bormann had left Hitler's side and abandoned his command post. Fat Theodor Morell, Hitler's personal physician, had come out of the safety of his bunker, despite the continual rumble of artillery. Someone had brought a gramophone, but only one record, a popular pre-war hit called 'Red Roses Bring You Happiness'. It is a very catchy tune and everyone started dancing. We drank champagne and laughed loudly, but it was a very hollow kind of

44 A concentration camp in Mecklenburg, Ravensbruck was established in 1934 and used for the imprisonment of female political prisoners. Medical experiments on gas gangrene were carried out there on Polish women, and it was also the place of execution for Allied female secret agents

laughter. I joined in but there was a big lump in my throat. Suddenly a sharp explosion shook the building, making the windows tremble; the telephone rang and someone hurried to take the call and write down the message; someone else received some important reports … The muffled roar of the artillery seemed to become louder than the laughter and the music.

ARMY OF GHOSTS

From the *Führerbunker* came a ceaseless stream of irrational, contradictory orders, none of which was capable of being fulfilled. General Manteuffel, whose Third Panzer Army was now all that was left of Army Group Vistula, dryly observed: 'I have no doubt that on Hitler's maps there is a little flag saying Seventh Panzer Division, even though it got there without a single tank, truck, piece of artillery or even a machine gun. We have an army of ghosts.'

One of the flags with a phantom existence on Hitler's map was Operational Group Steiner, which had been ordered to sweep down from Eberswalde, north of Berlin, on to Zhukov's right flank. Operational Group Steiner did not exist. In the confusion which followed Hitler's orders, units of Zhukov's Second Guards Tank, Third Shock and Forty-Seventh Armies broke through to the northern outskirts of Berlin.

On 22 April, crisis point was reached in the bunker. Berlin was now cut off on three sides and Soviet tanks had been reported probing around to the west of the city. At the midday briefing, Hitler suddenly lost his self-control, turning blue in the face and fulminating against the cowardice, incompetence and treachery of the assembled military. Finally he blurted out that the war was lost – the unmentionable had at last been admitted. Keitel and Jodl were free to leave and conduct operations as best they could. Hitler declared that he would never leave Berlin. As he was in no physical condition to fight, and could never contemplate capture and exhibition in a 'Moscow zoo', he would commit suicide. Any negotiating with the enemy that remained to be done was to be left to Göring.

As Hitler struggled to get a grip on himself, Goebbels assured him that he, too, would remain in the bunker with his family. When, on the following day, two of Hitler's secretaries pleaded to be allowed to stay with him, his eyes misted over and he said with a sigh, 'Ah, if only my generals were as brave as my women.' Then he rose to kiss Eva Braun on the lips, something he had never before been seen to do in public. With the help of the drugs administered by his valet, he achieved a kind of serenity. Later that day he received Albert Speer, who had flown in from Hamburg to bid farewell to the Führer. When Speer confessed that for weeks he had been striving to thwart Hitler's scorched earth orders, the Führer showed not a flicker of emotion.

—〰—

Meanwhile, the exodus continued. Keitel and Jodl, who had attended every one of Hitler's command conferences throughout the war, left the bunker on 22 April for the comparative safety of Fürstenburg, thirty miles north of Berlin, where they were close to Ravensbrück concentration camp which housed the so-called *Prominenten*, a group of well-connected foreign prisoners who were being held as hostages. Grand Admiral Dönitz had already removed himself to Plon, near Kiel on the Baltic, which had been his naval headquarters since March. Others came and went, the most spectacular arrival being that of General Robert Ritter von Greim, the commander of Luftflotte Six, based in Munich. Summoned to the bunker, he had arrived in Berlin on 26 April, flying a Fieseler Storch light aircraft and accompanied by the female test pilot, Hanna Reitsch, a fanatical Nazi. Greim, who had been at the controls, had been badly wounded in the foot just before touching down, leaving Reitsch to seize the stick and make a perfect landing on Berlin's east–west axis.

As soon as Greim arrived in the bunker, he was appointed field marshal, a promotion which could equally well have been made by telephone. Now the new commander of the Luftwaffe was stranded, badly wounded, in the *Führerbunker*. His predecessor, Göring, had secured his own dismissal on 23 April when he sent a telegram to Hitler from Berchtesgaden:

> My Führer, in view of your decision to remain in the fortress of Berlin, are you agreed that I immediately assume overall leadership of the Reich as your Deputy, in accordance with your decree of 29 June 1941 with complete freedom of action at home and abroad? Unless an answer is given by 10 p.m. I will assume that you have been deprived of your freedom of action. I shall then regard the conditions laid down by your decree as being met, and shall act in the best interests of the people and the Fatherland. You know my feelings for you in these hardest hours of my life. I cannot express them adequately. May God protect you and allow you to come here soon in spite of everything. Your loyal Hermann Göring.

Göring was planning to fly to meet Eisenhower to ask for peace terms. What worried him most, however, was which of his many splendid uniforms he should wear for this momentous meeting. Hitler issued orders for Göring to be placed under house arrest. He then telegraphed his erstwhile colleague: 'Your actions are punishable by the death sentence, but because of your valuable services in the past I will refrain from instituting proceedings if you voluntarily relinquish your offices and titles. Otherwise steps will have to be taken.' This prompt rap on the knuckles forced the *Reichsmarschall* to drop his baton.

In the *Führerbunker* hopes now rested on General Walther Wenck's Twelfth Army, south-west of Berlin. In the early hours of 23 April Keitel arrived at Wenck's headquarters in the Weisenberg Forest. With much pointed waving of his field marshal's baton, Keitel ordered Wenck to turn east and dive through Potsdam to Berlin, declaring portentously: 'The Battle for Berlin has begun.' In truth it was already over, as Wenck well knew. He heard Keitel out, but he made his own plans. Twelfth Army was to play it by the book, shifting towards Berlin but not abandoning its position on the Elbe. In this way a corridor could be kept open to the west. Wenck's army was surrounded by half a million refugees, and appeals to save Hitler's life from

Keitel, the ultimate desk general, no longer had any meaning to a weary professional soldier like Wenck.

In the *Führerbunker* the unanswered cry of '*Wo ist Wenck?*' was to bounce off the mouldering walls of Hitler's last headquarters as the Third Reich slid towards oblivion.

—⁓—

At the same time that Keitel was haranguing Wenck, Stalin issued the order that decided which of his commanders would win the race to take the prize of Berlin. *Stavka* directive No. 11074 set a boundary between the First Belorussian and First Ukrainian Fronts, which ran along a line from Lübben to the Anhalter Station in the centre of Berlin, placing Marshal Ivan Konev's front a crucial one hundred and fifty yards to the west of the Reichstag, the pre-eminent symbolic objective in the Battle of Berlin. The Reichstag lay within the command sector controlled by the victor of Kursk, Marshal Zhukov. He was to be the conqueror of Berlin.

Now the Soviet armies which had encircled Berlin – four hundred and sixty-four thousand men, supported by twelve thousand seven hundred guns, twenty-one thousand rocket launchers and fifteen hundred tanks – closed on Berlin's S-Bahn ring, which was breached on 26 April. By nightfall of the next day, Fortress Berlin had been squeezed down to an east-west belt ten miles long and three miles wide. On the night of the 26th, the first Russian shells struck the Chancellery, sending vibrations through the *Führerbunker* as tons of masonry toppled to earth, while the bunker's ventilation system sucked in sulphurous fumes from the shell blasts, further poisoning an atmosphere rank with unwashed bodies, sweat and fear.

On the night of 28 April, with the Red Army less than a mile away, Hitler was dealt the final blow. At about 10 p.m. a Propaganda Ministry official handed him a copy of a Reuter's report that Heinrich Himmler had contacted the Swedish diplomat Count Bernadotte in order to negotiate a surrender in the West. Hitler was consumed by a terrible fury. Göring's treachery could be dismissed as the aberration of a corpulent drug addict. But the defection of Himmler, '*der treue Heinrich*' (the faithful Heinrich) the one subordinate on whose loyalty Hitler could depend absolutely, was the bitterest stroke of all. It had been a week since the Führer had admitted to his commanders that the war was lost and that he intended to commit suicide. Now, after a characteristic period of hesitation and wavering, he made up his mind.

The first victim of Himmler's treachery was Eva Braun's brother-in-law, SS General Hermann Fegelein, an illiterate former jockey who had become the SS *Reichsführer*'s personal liaison officer with Hitler. On the night of the 27th, Fegelein was arrested in his foreign mistress's apartment, his pockets stuffed with Swiss francs and diamonds. He had been missing from the bunker complex for two days and, it seemed, had every intention of taking flight. Fegelein was frogmarched to the command post in the bunker complex and then hauled, roaring drunk, before a court martial, his breeches sticky with excrement. Deemed unfit to plead his case, Fegelein was handed over to General Johannes Rattenhuber, the Chancellery's security chief, and shot.

LAST ORDERS

After the departure of Hanna Reitsch and the new commander of the Luftwaffe, Ritter von Greim, who had been ordered to fly out of Berlin to arrest Himmler, Hitler married his recently deceased liaison officer's sister-in-law. The ceremony, conducted in the small hours of 29 April by a minor official in the Propaganda Ministry, Walter Wagner, was a model of petit-bourgeois respectability. Adolf Hitler and Eva Braun affirmed that they were of pure Aryan descent and were free of hereditary diseases, and were declared man and wife. In her excitement Eva Braun began to sign her maiden name on the wedding certificate, then crossed out the letter B and wrote 'Eva Hitler, née Braun'. With prim bureaucratic efficiency, Wagner altered the incorrectly entered date on the certificate from 28 to 29 April. Within an hour, back on duty with the *Volkssturm*, he was dead, shot through the head,

> **'Above all I charge the leaders of the nation ... to merciless opposition to the universal poisoners of all peoples, international Jewry.'**
> ADOLF HITLER

After the wedding there was a melancholy little reception in Hitler's suite. Amid the clink of champagne glasses the conversation ranged, for the last time, over the triumphs of past years. One of the guests, Professor Schenck, a surgeon who had been assisting in the complex's hospital, later recalled of Hitler that, 'His eyes, although he was looking directly at me, did not seem to be focusing. They were like wet, pale-blue porcelain, glazed, actually more grey than blue. They were filmy, like the skin of a soft grape. The whites were bloodshot. I could detect no expression on his vapid, immobile face.'

Observing Hitler's uncontrollably shuddering left arm and left leg with a clinical eye, Schenck concluded that he had the classic symptoms of Parkinson's disease and, had he lived, would soon have become a hopeless cripple.

At about 2 a.m. on 29 April, Hitler retired with a secretary to dictate his personal testament. Like the Bourbons, he had learned nothing and forgotten nothing. The testament concluded: 'Above all I charge the leaders of the nation and those under them to scrupulous observation of the laws of race and to merciless opposition to the universal poisoners of all peoples, international Jewry.' Other provisions stated that Speer, Göring and Himmler were expelled from the Party and deprived of their now meaningless offices of state. Grand Admiral Dönitz was named as Hitler's successor in the posts of President, Minister of War and Supreme Commander of the Armed Forces. Goebbels and Bormann, whose sinister, insinuating influence hisses through the document, received their own empty rewards, the offices of Chancellor and Party Minister respectively.

Three men were selected to deliver copies of the testament to Dönitz's headquarters and to the last wartime commander-in-chief of the Army, Field Marshal Schörner, who was now in Munich. An additional message was despatched to Field Marshal Keitel, a stinging dismissal of the General Staff from their Supreme Commander:

The people and the Wehrmacht have given their all in this long and hard struggle. The sacrifice has been enormous. But my trust has been misused by many people. Disloyalty and betrayal have undermined resistance throughout the war. It was therefore not granted to me to lead the people to victory. The Army General Staff cannot be compared with the General Staff of the First World War. Its achievements were far behind those of the fighting front.

During the course of the day news arrived of the death of Mussolini and his mistress Clara Petacci – summarily executed by partisans near Lake Como and then suspended by their heels from the roof of a Milan garage, before being mutilated by a jeering crowd. On the same day, German forces in Italy capitulated. Hitler set about preparing his own death. The effects of the poison capsule he intended to use were tested on his beloved German Shepherd bitch, Blondi.

Late that night there was one more conference, the last of Hitler's life. General Weidling, the commander of LVI Panzer Corps, reported that ammunition was now all but exhausted. Communications with the outside were now cut off as the balloon which supported the bunker's radio transmitting aerial had been shot down that morning and the switchboard had shut down. Still there was no sign of Wenck. Weidling informed the Führer that resistance in Berlin would end within twenty-four hours. After an interminable silence, Hitler turned to SS General Mohnke and asked for his assessment of the situation. Mohnke replied that he could only agree with Weidling, who now raised the question of a breakout. Hitler merely indicated a map on which the dispositions had been marked by means of listening in to enemy radio stations – since his own formations were no longer listening to or obeying his orders.

Hitler then gave Weidling permission to order his troops to break out in small groups but insisted that there was to be no surrender in Berlin. Shortly after the meeting broke up, Keitel delivered the news that Wenck could no longer move on Berlin. The Ninth Army, south-east of the city, was surrounded.

The Red Army was now only a few blocks away from the Chancellery. On 30 April Hitler took lunch with two secretaries and his vegetarian cook, Fraülein Manzialey. The Führer toyed with pasta and tossed salad while he rambled on about the proper breeding of dogs and ventured the suggestion that French lipstick was made from grease collected in the sewers of Paris.

At 1 p.m. three Red Army assault battalions blasted their way into the Reichstag and a Red banner was hoisted at the entrance. Two hundred yards away, Hitler was saying farewell to Goebbels and Bormann. His secretary Traudl Junge watched the scene: 'The Führer looked more stooped than ever as he came out of his room and moved slowly towards us. He offered his hand to each of us, and as he shook hands he looked straight at me, but I knew he didn't see me. His right hand was warm. He seemed to be a thousand miles away. He whispered some words that I couldn't make out. I've never known what his last words were.'

At about 3.20 in the afternoon, Hitler withdrew into his suite with Eva Braun, who was wearing her and the Führer's favourite dress, black with pink roses at either side of a low square neckline. Her hair was perfectly coiffed. The heavy iron door shut behind them. Outside, those who remained in the bunker waited. One of them was Major Otto Gunsche, Hitler's senior SS adjutant:

> Hitler had stood back to let Eva go through first. I was busy giving instructions to the men and officers who were to carry the bodies outside. Hitler had told me to wait ten minutes before entering the apartment. They were the longest minutes of my life. I stood by the door like a sentry. Suddenly Magda Goebbels [Goebbels's wife] came rushing towards me, as if to force her way through. I couldn't push her back, so I opened the door to ask what I should do. She practically knocked me over in her desire to get into the room, but she came out immediately. Hitler hadn't wanted to listen to her and she left sobbing … Ten minutes later, after hearing the shot, I went into the room. Hitler's body was crumpled up, his head hanging towards the floor. Blood was running from his right temple on to the carpet. The pistol had fallen to the ground. Eva, who was sitting in the other corner of the sofa, her legs curled under her, had stayed in the same position. She showed no trace of any wound. Her pistol was beside her. A vase of flowers had fallen to the floor …

Hitler had shot himself with his Walther 7.65mm pistol, which he had been carrying for some weeks, in all probability also biting into a cyanide capsule. Eva Braun took poison. Gunsche had the table and chairs cleared out of the way and blankets spread on the floor. Three guards took Hitler's body, wrapped it in a blanket and carried it away. Martin Bormann lifted Eva's body before Gunsche took it from him and handed it over to the guards. While they were climbing the stairs to the Chancellery garden, Erich Kempka, Hitler's chauffeur, arrived with a detail of men carrying about forty gallons of petrol in jerrycans.

The bodies of Adolf Hitler and Eva Braun were placed in a trench, doused with petrol and set alight with pieces of flaming paper. Gunsche recalled that, as the flames shot up, all the men present raised their arms in the Nazi salute. Once the flames had died down, the bodies were buried in a deeper trench dug out of a shell crater, where they were later found by the Russians.[45]

Inside the bunker, those who remained lit cigarettes.

---

45 Hitler's death was verified by Marshal Vasiliy Sokolovsky, Zhukov's deputy, who compared the charred body with the Führer's dental records.

AFTERMATH

Two of the principal members of the 'Hitler gang' left the stage long before the end of World War II. Rudolf Hess had been Deputy Führer until 3 September 1939, when he was succeeded by Hermann Göring. Thereafter Hess became a back number until 10 May 1941, when he flew an Me 110 on a lone and unauthorized mission to Scotland. Hess's aim was to make contact with the Duke of Hamilton, whom he had met before the war, and, using him as an intermediary, persuade the British government to come to terms with Germany. To his great surprise, he was treated simply as a prisoner of war and his proposals were ignored. At the end of the war Hess was arraigned with the other surviving Nazis at Nuremberg and sentenced to life imprisonment in Spandau Prison, Berlin, where he remained until his suicide in 1987.

SS General Reinhard Heydrich, the evil genius behind the formulation of the 'Final Solution' at the Wannsee Conference of 20 January 1942, had been rewarded for his work with a new appointment as Reich Protector of Bohemia and Moravia, which made him to all intents and purposes the ruler of Czechoslovakia. On 4 June 1942, he died of wounds sustained when his car was ambushed by a party of British-trained Czech Resistance fighters. In the German reprisals one thousand three hundred Czech civilians died, some three hundred and forty of them men, women and children from the village of Lidice, which was also destroyed.

Josef Goebbels died by his own hand in the Berlin bunker. After Hitler's death, while the rest of the bunker's occupants planned to break out, he came and went, gaunt, chain-smoking and looking like a bankrupt restaurateur waiting for the last guests to leave. At about 8.30 p.m. on 1 May, his wife Magda administered poison to their six children, who were also in the bunker, and then joined her husband in the Chancellery garden where they both took poison. Like Hitler, Goebbles shot himself in the head as he bit on the capsule. A perfunctory effort was made to burn their bodies but although the corpses were horribly charred, they remained recognizable.

Martin Bormann joined the third escape party to leave the bunker. With the death of Hitler, his authority had evaporated. Before he left the bunker, he had been told to 'get lost' by an SS man, to the delight of all who heard this belated reproof. Shortly thereafter, while trying to thread his way past Red Army patrols in the company of Dr Stumpfegger, he and his companion committed suicide on the railway tracks leading out of the Lehrter railway station. Their bodies were noticed by another escapee from the bunker, Artur Axmann, whose account was subsequently confirmed in 1972. Workers constructing an exhibition park on the site of the station had uncovered two skeletons in a shallow grave, one of a tall man, the other short and burly. Lodged in their jawbones were splinters from glass cyanide ampoules. Forensic examination confirmed that here was the last resting place of Martin Bormann.

Heinrich Himmler was captured by the British Army on 21 May 1945 when, disguised as a private soldier, he was arrested at a British control point halfway between Hamburg and Bremen. The *Reichsführer* SS went unrecognized for two days before he revealed his identity to an interrogating officer. When he was shown photographs of the victims of the death camps, Himmler remained unmoved, declaring, 'Am I responsible for the excesses of my subordinates?' He was then taken to an interrogation centre at Lüneberg, where he was stripped and searched. However, his captors could not prevent Himmler from biting on a cyanide capsule concealed in his mouth. On 26 May, Himmler's body, wrapped in a camouflage net, was secretly buried on Lüneberg Heath.

Robert Ley, head of the German Labour Front, was captured by US troops on 16 May 1945. Due to stand trial for war crimes, he committed suicide in his prison cell on 26 October 1945, hanging himself with strips of cloth cut from a tea towel. The surviving Nazi leaders were duly tried for war crimes at Nuremberg, the spiritual home of the Nazi Party and the scene of the spectacular annual rallies of the 1930s. Hermann Göring, who had been captured by the Americans, deprived of his spectacularly tasteless uniforms and weaned off the drugs which had sustained him during the war years, gave a robust account of himself, but was nevertheless condemned to death. He cheated the hangman on 15 October 1946, the eve of his execution, by taking poison, possibly with the connivance of one of his guards. In death Göring still cut a dash of sorts – his corpse turned bright green.

Of Göring's co-defendants at Nuremberg – Hans Frank, General Jodl, Field Marshal Keitel, Joachim von Ribbentrop, Wilhelm Frick, Alfred Rosenberg, Fritz Sauckel, Artur von Seyss-Inquart, Julius Streicher and Ernst Kaltenbrunner, the last the highest-ranking survivor of the SS apparat – were sentenced to death. Admiral Raeder and Walther Funk received life imprisonment. Baldur von Schirach and Albert Speer were both sentenced to twenty years' imprisonment while Admiral

Above: The spoils of war – captured Nazi standards are tossed on a pile outside Lenin's tomb on Red Square in Moscow. It is estimated that some sixty-four million people died as a result of World War II, twenty-four million servicemen and forty million civilians. The Soviet Union suffered 8.6 million soldiers dead or missing and some eight million civilians killed, although the figure is constantly being revised upwards. Germany lost 3.5 million military personnel dead or missing and two million civilians. In Yugoslavia civil and guerrilla war killed at least a million people. The civilian and military casualties in Eastern Europe were swollen by the savagery of the war in this theatre and the German racial oppression of Jews and Slavs. Before June 1940 and after November 1942 France lost two hundred thousand military dead, while four hundred thousand French died in air raids or concentration camps. The British lost two hundred and forty-four thousand servicemen and some sixty thousand civilians. In the United States there were no civilian casualties while US military losses, in the West, Far East and Pacific, were two hundred and ninety-two thousand dead or missing. The Japanese lost 1.2 million men in battle and nearly a million civilians.

Dönitz, Raeder's successor as commander-in-chief of the Kriegsmarine, received a sentence of ten years. Von Neurath, Ribbentrop's predecessor as foreign minister, was given a sentence of fifteen years. The wily Hjalmar Schacht was acquitted, as was Hans Fritzsche, the head of the news division in the Nazi Propaganda Ministry, who was tried in the absence of his boss, Josef Goebbels. Franz von Papen was also acquitted, but in 1947 was reclassified as a war criminal by a German de-Nazification court and sentenced to eight years' hard labour. He appealed successfully and was released after serving two years.

The war crimes trials at Nuremberg were accompanied and followed by many related trials marking the de-Nazification of Germany after World War II. One of the most significant was that of Adolf Eichmann, which took place in Israel in the spring and summer of 1961. Eichmann was found guilty and sentenced to death in December 1961. After an unsuccessful appeal, he was hanged on 31 May 1962 and his ashes were scattered in international waters in the Mediterranean.

FURTHER READING

Recent years have seen a mushrooming growth in books devoted to Hitler and the Nazis. For an exhaustive biographical analysis of Hitler, the reader should consult Ian Kershaw's two-volume biography, *Hitler 1889–1936: Hubris* (1998) and *Hitler 1936–1945: Nemesis* (2000). Of greater vintage but still invaluable are Joachim Fest's *Hitler* (1976) and Allan Bullock's groundbreaking *Hitler: A Study in Tyranny* (1952). The story of the Stauffenberg assassination plot in July 1944 has been ably told by one of the plotters, Philipp von Boeselager, in *Valkyrie: The Plot to Kill Hitler* (2009). The collapse of Nazi Germany and the death of Hitler were stylishly chronicled by Hugh Trevor-Roper in *Hitler's Last Days* (2002) and Joachim Fest in *Inside Hitler's Bunker* (2004). Hitler's grisly end has also been recorded by an unblinking eyewitness, his secretary Traudl Junge, in *Until the Final Hour: Hitler's Last Secretary* (2004).

Equally invaluable but encompassing a massively broader canvas is *The Third Reich* trilogy by Richard J. Evans (2004–2008). Other authoritative sources on aspects of Nazi Germany are Michael Burleigh's *The Third Reich* (2000), Laurence Rees's *The Nazis: A Warning from History* (1997), Richard Grunberger's *The Social History of the Third Reich* (1971), Joachim Fest's *The Face of the Third Reich* (1970), an incisive study of the Nazi leadership, and Ian Kershaw's *Hitler, the Germans and the Final Solution* (2008), a rigorous examination of the Holocaust and Hitler's determining role in it. *The Goebbels Diaries* (1977) provides a nightmarish picture of the madhouse that was the Third Reich. Another Nazi paladin, Albert Speer, gave his own nuanced account of the regime in *Inside the Third Reich* (1979). Richard Overy has provided a masterly analysis of Nazi psychology with *Interrogations: Inside the Minds of the Nazi Elite* (2001), and an overview of the Nazi war economy in *War and the Economy in the Third Reich* (1994). A highly original biographical approach to Hitler was taken by Timothy W. Ryback in *Hitler's Private Library: The Books That Shaped His Life* (2009), an analysis of the surviving volumes from the Führer's private libraries which fell into Allied hands at the end of World War II and are now housed in the Library of Congress. Frederic Spotts's *Hitler and the Power of Aesthetics* (2003) throws fascinating light on the Führer's artistic and architectural obsessions.

Robert O'Neil's *The German Army and the Nazi Party* (1966) is an essential portrait of both these pillars of the Nazi state. Matthew Cooper's *The German Army, 1933–1945* (1978) is a thoroughgoing account of Hitler's initially fruitful and then increasingly unproductive relationship with his generals. The ordinary German soldier's point of view is vividly conveyed in Omer Bartov's *Hitler's Army* (1992). For an overall view of World War II and Hitler's role in precipitating and prosecuting it, an excellent starting point is John Keegan's *The Second World War* (1989). A penetrating insight into Hitler's strategic thinking in 1940–41, the moment on which the fate of Third Reich hinged, is provided by Martin van Creveld's *Hitler's Strategy: the Balkan Clue* (1973). In spite of the odium which he has attracted in recent years, David Irving's *Hitler's War* (1977) remains one of the most interesting books on the conflict and Hitler's strategic thinking. Hugh Trevor-Roper's *Hitler's War Directives* (1964) remains a vital guide to understanding Hitler's thought processes as the war progressed and, inexorably, the tide turned against the Third Reich. Walter Warlimont's *Inside Hitler's Headquarters* (1964) is an authoritative account of the Führer in wartime written by an immensely able military professional who observed his commander-in-chief at close quarters.

Killing Hitler (2006) by Roger Moorhouse is a brisk canter through the many failed attempts to assassinate the Führer. *Hitler's Empire* (2008) by Mark Mazower is a superbly researched picture of Nazi rule in Occupied Europe and its countless confusions, contradictions and barbarities. *The Order of the Death's Head: The Story of Hitler's SS* (2000) by Heinz Hohne tells the sobering history of that sinister organization, while *The Architecture of Oppression: The SS, Forced Labour and the Nazi Monumental Building Economy* (1999) by Paul B. Jaskot outlines many of the inherent absurdities and fatal inefficiencies of the Third Reich, all of which had their baleful origins in the singular mind and methods of Adolf Hitler.

INDEX

First published in Great Britain in 2009 by
Quercus
21 Bloomsbury Square
London
WC1A 2NS

A CIP catalogue record for this book is available from the British Library

UK ISBN 978 1 84724 999 9
US ISBN 978 1 84866 020 5
PACK ISBN 978 1 84866 032 8

10 9 8 7 6 5 4 3 2 1

Picture acknowledgements

Getty Images Heinrich Hoffmann/Hulton Archive 10. Keystone 49, Popperfoto 206.
AKG Images 13, 27, 32, 37, 39, 58-59, 62-63, 75, 104, 125, 127, 166-167, 172, 193, 218.
Topfoto 31, 103, 138, 188 / The Granger Collection 99, 103, 128, 161 / Ullsteinbild 136-137, 182, 201 / HIP 149 / Roger-Viollet 152.
Interfoto / Lebrecht Music & Arts 65.
Press Association / Associated Press 107.

All other pictures private collection.